BEST of the BEST
from

Nevada

COOKBOOK

Selected Recipes from Nevada's
FAVORITE COOKBOOKS

In Nevada, cowboys still hold a place in modern culture, working on ranches, herding cattle, and riding the trails as they've always done. They even sing the same old cowboy songs. Lamoille Canyon, Ruby Mountains near Elko.

BEST of the BEST
from
Nevada
COOKBOOK

Selected Recipes from Nevada's
FAVORITE COOKBOOKS

Edited by
Gwen McKee
and
Barbara Moseley

Illustrated by Tupper England

QUAIL RIDGE PRESS
Preserving America's Food Heritage

Recipe Collection ©2004 Quail Ridge Press, Inc.

Reprinted with permission and all rights reserved under the name
of the cookbooks, organizations or individuals listed below.

All American Meals Cookbook ©2004 JB Publications; *Authentic Cowboy Cookery Then & Now* ©2004 JB Publications; *Best Bets* ©1993 Nathan Adelson Hospice; *The Best of Down-Home Cooking* ©2003 Holy Trinity AME Church; *Chorizos in an Iron Skillet* ©2002 by Mary Ancho Davis; *A Cowboy Cookin' Every Night* ©2004 JB Publications; *Easy Cookin' in Nevada & Tales of the Sagebrush State* ©1984 by June Broili; *Easy Gourmet for Diabetics* ©2004 JB Publications; *From Sunrise to Sunset* ©1997 Sunrise Children's Foundation; *The Great Nevada Cookbook* ©1993 *Nevada Magazine; The Great Nevada Food Festival Cookbook* ©1997 *Nevada Magazine; The Hooked Cook* ©2004 JB Publications; *Hoover Dam Cooks, 1933* ©2003 Toothpick Productions; *Lake Tahoe Cooks!* ©2002 Parents' Clubs of Zephyr Cove Elementary School, Kingsbury Middle School, and George Whittell High School; *Las Vegas Glitter to Gourmet* ©2001 Junior League of Las Vegas; *The Melting Pot* ©2003 Moms in Business Network; *Never Trust a Skinny Chef...II* ©1999 by Les Kincaid; *Our Daily Bread* ©2003 Old St. Paul's Episcopal Church; *Partyline Cook Book* ©1995 Jackson Mountain Homemakers; *The Protein Edge* ©2004 JB Publications; *Use Your Noodle! Three Italians Cook* ©2004 JB Publications; *Wild Man Gourmet* ©2004 JB Publications.

Library of Congress Cataloging-in-Publication Data

Best of the best from Nevada cookbook : selected recipes from Nevada's favorite cookbooks /
    edited by Gwen McKee and Barbara Moseley ; illustrations by Tupper England.
    p. cm.
    Includes index.
    ISBN 1-893062-64-3
    1. Cookery, American 2. Cookery—Nevada. I. McKee, Gwen. II. Moseley, Barbara.

TX715.B48564132 2004
641.59793—dc22   2004012291

Front cover photo courtesy of Lake Tahoe Visitors Bureau.
Back cover photo by Greg Campbell • Design by Cynthia Clark
Printed in Canada.

QUAIL RIDGE PRESS
P. O. Box 123 • Brandon, MS 39043 • 1-800-343-1583
email: info@quailridge.com • www.quailridge.com

Contents

PHOTO BY JUDY TYLER

Editor Gwen McKee enjoyed examining petroglyphs in the beautiful Valley of Fire State Park. These fascinating drawings of symbols, animals, and birds . . . could there be a very early cookbook here? (Just kidding.)

Preface

A beautiful and fascinating state, Nevada practically defies description. . . rugged and wild, adventurous and fun, scenic, historic, amusing . . . amazing!

Named by early Spanish explorers, Nevada means "snow-capped," and there are many mountains that almost always appear that way. The warm colors of the rocks and sand, the deep azure of the lakes, the greens of the trees, and blue, blue skies can be so vivid as to set the standard for camera-perfect brilliance.

The Old West is center stage in the Silver State. Dude ranches, cattle drives, and real cowboys keep Western traditions alive. There's Indian history here, too. The Anasazi, Washo, Paiute, Goshute, and Shoshone lived there long before the settlers arrived.

Did you know that Nevada is the largest producer of gold in the United States? The mining boom began around 1859 and many of the mines still operate today. Besides silver and gold, the semi-precious gemstone, Nevada Turquoise, and the Virgin Valley fire opals—among the most treasured gems in the world—are also found in many parts of the state.

Then there's Las Vegas—a city that glitters like a diamond in the desert—and never closes. Besides gaming, Las Vegas is a lively mecca of art, entertainment, and history—and just plain fascinating.

Nevada's cuisine stems from the 1870s, when Basque sheep-herders from the Pyrenees Mountains of northwestern Spain and southwestern France migrated to Nevada, bringing with them much of their food culture. The Basque hotels—a dozen or so of which still exist—provided a home-away-from-home setting where the food fare mostly consisted of beef, lamb, chorizo, soup, beans, potatoes, bread, and flan. Many recipes will surprise you, like the use of chocolate in game recipes—like Chicken with Chocolate (page 180). Influences of American Indian, Chinese, Greek, Mexican, Italian, and African American cultures all lend an important influence.

Chuck wagon food consisted of sourdough biscuits, beef stews, and Dutch oven fare, and yes, mountain oysters, too. A Cowboy's "Real Chili Got No Beans in It, Ma'am" Chili (page 62) sort of

expresses their macho/spicy recipes, while Doc's Secret Remedy (page 65) is supposed to cure just about anything that ails you. Miners brought Cornish pasties made from lamb or rabbit or beef with vegetables for their meals in the mines (page 139). There's fancy food, too, like Perfect Hostess Beef Medallions with Cognac Sauce (page 133) and things that lean toward a healthier diet such as Baked Tomatoes and Zucchini Provençal (page 103). Home cookin' in Nevada is where the real food culture comes to the family table in the form of Darned Good Skillet Supper (page 155), American Southwest Corn Salad (page 80), and Strawberry Long-Cake Roll (page 205)—you won't believe how fantastic this is!

We've included lots of state history and facts and photos. Did you know that the oldest living things on earth—the Bristlecone Pines—still grow in Nevada? Or that you will drive west to get to Reno, Nevada, from Los Angeles, California?

We have to thank a lot of people for helping us to make this book come together. All the contributing cookbooks are each special in their own way—the people so lovely to chat with—and we are delighted to present these cookbooks in the contributor's section on page 263. Don't miss looking through this comprehensive list. We are grateful to so many food editors, tourist agents, store managers, and people we met in Nevada who helped us with our research. Thanks especially to our illustrator, Tupper England, who brought a taste of the West to us with her drawings. And thanks to our in-house editor, Terresa Ray, for her diligent efforts throughout the process of gathering and editing.

Though it wasn't specifically planned that way, Nevada happens to be the last state to be published in the BEST OF THE BEST STATE COOKBOOK SERIES (see listing on page 288). Once you have tried these unique and delicious Silver State recipes, perhaps you will conclude . . . we have saved the best for last.

Gwen McKee and Barbara Moseley

Contributing Cookbooks

All American Meals Cookbook
Authentic Cowboy Cookery Then & Now
Best Bets
The Best of Down-Home Cooking
Bless This Food
CASA Cooks
Chorizos in an Iron Skillet
Church Family Recipes
A Cowboy Cookin' Every Night
Easy Cookin' in Nevada
Easy Gourmet for Diabetics
Elko Ariñak Dancers Cookbook
Family and Friends Favorites
Feeding the Flock
The Food You Always Wanted to Eat
From Sunrise to Sunset
The Fruit of the Spirit
A Gathering of Recipes
God, That's Good!
The Great Nevada Cookbook
The Great Nevada Food Festival Cookbook
Historical Boulder City Cookbook
Home Cooking
The Hooked Cook
Hoover Dam Cooks, 1933
Kitchen Chatter
Lake Tahoe Cooks!
Las Vegas Glitter to Gourmet

Contributing Cookbooks

Let Freedom Ring
The Melting Pot
Never Trust a Skinny Chef...II
NSHSRA High School Rodeo Cookbook
Our Daily Bread
Partyline Cook Book
The Protein Edge
Recipes from Sunset Garden Club
Recipes from the Heart
The Ruby Valley Friendship Club Cookbook I
The Ruby Valley Friendship Club Cookbook II
Sharing Our Diabetics Best Recipes
Soup for Our Souls
Still Cookin' After 70 Years
Tasteful Treasures
Timbreline's Cookbook
Traditional Treasures
Twentieth Century Club Cook Book
Use Your Noodle!
Virginia City Alumni Association Cookbook
Wild Man Gourmet

Beverages & Appetizers

Lake Tahoe, located in both California and Nevada, is nestled in the Sierra Nevada Mountains. At 22 miles long, 11 miles wide, and an average depth of 989 feet, it is the largest alpine lake in North America. Nevada lays claim to 30 percent of Lake Tahoe, some 31,700 acres.

Methodist Tea Punch

3 cups sugar
3 cups hot tea
1 cup lemon juice
2¼ cups orange juice

3 pints soda water
3 pints ginger ale
Sliced oranges

Mix sugar and hot tea to dissolve sugar. Add lemon juice and orange juice. At this point you can store in refrigerator several days—this is your base. Before serving, add soda water and ginger ale. Add sliced oranges and ice. Makes 1 large punch bowl. I often triple recipe for large gatherings. Also, I often cut back on the sugar, but nobody notices.

Helpful Hint: You can make the tea and sugar solution ahead, and add lemon juice and orange juice at the time you are ready to serve, and figure out your proportions accordingly. That way you don't waste lemon or orange juice.

Tasteful Treasures

Bruno's Lazy Day Margaritas

3 ounces sour mix
1¼ ounces tequila
½ ounce brandy

½ ounce Cointreau
1 teaspoon lime juice

Serve over crushed ice in chilled salt-rimmed glass. Serves one.

The Hooked Cook

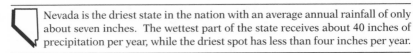

Nevada is the driest state in the nation with an average annual rainfall of only about seven inches. The wettest part of the state receives about 40 inches of precipitation per year, while the driest spot has less than four inches per year.

White House After Dinner Mocha

3 tablespoons sugar
¼ cup instant coffee
1½ cups water
1 (1-ounce) square
   unsweetened chocolate

Salt
3 cups milk
Whipped cream

In saucepan, combine sugar, coffee, water, chocolate, and a dash of salt; stir over low heat until chocolate melts. Simmer 4–5 minutes, stirring constantly. Gradually add milk; heat and stir till hot. Remove from heat and beat with rotary beater until frothy. Pour into cups; spoon dollop of whipped cream on each. Makes 3 or 4 servings.

Recipes from Sunset Garden Club

Irish Coffee

According to the Irish, this drink will "keepeth and preserveth the head from whirling, the eyes from dazeling, the toong from lisping, the mouth from maffling, the teeth from chattering, and the throte from rattling."

8 warm coffee cups (or Irish
   coffee glasses)
16 teaspoons superfine sugar
8 cups freshly brewed strong
   stiff coffee

6–8 ounces Irish whiskey
1 cup heavy cream, whipped

Heat cups or glasses by rinsing with very hot water, or let them sit near or on a warm stove. Fill each glass with 2 teaspoons superfine sugar. Fill each glass ¾ full with strong, hot coffee. Stir until sugar is dissolved. Add ¾–1 ounce of Irish whiskey to each glass and stir well. Top each serving with a dollop of whipped cream. Serve immediately. Do not mix the cream through the coffee. The hot, whiskey-laced coffee is to be sipped through the velvety cream. Serves 8.

Traditional Treasures

Tom and Jerry Hot Holiday Beverage

BATTER:

6 egg yolks
3 egg whites

1 pound powdered sugar

Combine ingredients and beat with electric mixer until moderately thick. This can take up to half an hour, depending on the size and speed of your mixer. Refrigerate until ready to use. This keeps for about one week. It may separate—if so, beat it again.

HOT HOLIDAY BEVERAGE:

Boiling water or hot milk
Rum, brandy for flavoring

Freshly grated nutmeg

To make Tom and Jerrys, put a large tablespoon of the batter in a mug. Stirring constantly, slowly add boiling water or hot milk to fill the mug about ¾ full. Then stir in rum and brandy mix, just brandy, or other liquor of your choice, or leave out the alcohol and flavor with a flavoring of your choice: vanilla, rum, brandy, etc. Top each mug with nutmeg and serve. Serves 12–15.

God, That's Good!

Shrimp in Jackets

1 pound frozen, medium,   1 teaspoon garlic salt
  shelled shrimp, thawed   1 pound bacon (about 15 slices)

Sprinkle shrimp with garlic salt; wrap each in ⅓ slice of bacon. Arrange on broiler rack. Broil 3–4 inches from heat just until bacon is crisp and browned, 8–10 minutes, turning occasionally. Makes about 40 servings.

The Best of Down-Home Cooking

Hot and Healthy Buffalo Chicken Wings

1 pound chicken wings, skin   1 teaspoon onion powder
  removed   ½ teaspoon cayenne pepper
½ cup skim milk   1 tablespoon chili powder
½ cup unseasoned bread   1 teaspoon garlic powder
  crumbs

Soak chicken wings in milk 15 minutes. Combine bread crumbs and spices in a plastic bag. Drain excess milk from chicken and dip wings in bread crumb mixture until coated. Spray a 9x13-inch baking pan with nonfat cooking spray. Line chicken in pan and bake 25 minutes or until juices run clear.

DIP:
1 cup nonfat sour cream   4 ounces nonfat cream cheese
1 tablespoon chopped chives

Combine sour cream, chives, and cream cheese. Serve with chicken and celery sticks. Serves 4.

Nutritional analysis per serving: Calories 226; Protein 32g; Fat 5g; Carbohydrates 14g.

The Protein Edge

Broiled Mustard Chicken Wings

2 tablespoons plain yogurt
2 tablespoons plus 1½
  teaspoons Dijon mustard,
  divided
1 large garlic clove, minced
  and smashed to a paste with
  ½ teaspoon kosher salt

1½ pounds chicken wings
  (about 8)
2 tablespoons fine dry bread
  crumbs
1 teaspoon mustard seeds
Salt and pepper to taste
4 teaspoons olive oil

Preheat broiler. In a large bowl, stir together yogurt, 1½ teaspoons mustard, and garlic paste. Cut off chicken wing tips, reserving them for another use (such as making chicken stock). Add wings to yogurt mixture, stirring to coat well, and marinate 10 minutes.

In a small ramekin, stir together bread crumbs, mustard seeds, and salt and pepper to taste. Arrange wings, skin-side-down, on oiled rack of broiler pan, and season with salt and pepper. Broil wings 3–4 inches from heat until golden brown, about 10 minutes. Turn wings skin-side-up and season with salt and pepper. Broil wings 5 minutes more. Spread skin side with remaining 2 tablespoons mustard, and sprinkle with bread crumb mixture. Drizzle olive oil over each wing, and broil wings until crisp and golden, 3–5 minutes. Serve wings hot or room temperature. Yields 2 servings.

Never Trust a Skinny Chef...II

The National Championship Air Races and Air Show in Reno is the only place in the world where you can see real air racing by multiple classes of aircraft up close and personal. This event, the world's fastest motorsport, has been held annually each September since 1964. Only once has it been interrupted—in September 2001 when all aircraft in the U.S. were grounded following the terrorist attacks in New York and Washington.

All American Buffalo Chicken Wings

BLUE CHEESE DRESSING:

4 tablespoons minced yellow onion

2 garlic cloves, minced

¼ cup minced parsley

2 cups mayonnaise

1 cup sour cream

2 tablespoons fresh lemon juice

2 tablespoons white vinegar

¾ cup crumbled blue cheese

½ teaspoon black pepper

¼ teaspoon cayenne pepper

Combine all ingredients in bowl; cover and chill.

CHICKEN WINGS:

40 chicken wings

2–4 cups vegetable oil for deep-frying

1 stick butter

1 small bottle hot sauce

40 celery sticks

Disjoint wings at elbow and discard tips. Heat oil in deep-fryer to 375°. Fry wings until crisp and golden, about 8–10 minutes. Drain on paper towels. Melt butter in a saucepan and blend in the bottle of hot sauce. Place chicken wings in large bowl and pour hot butter sauce over wings. Toss well to coat. Arrange wings on platter and serve with celery sticks and the bowl of Blue Cheese Dressing for dipping. Serves 8–12.

All American Meals Cookbook

Cocktail Meatballs with Madeira Sauce

6 tablespoons finely chopped onion
4 tablespoons butter
2/3 cup fine bread crumbs
2 cups half-and-half
2 pounds lean ground beef
2 eggs
3 teaspoons salt
1/2 teaspoon pepper
1/4 teaspoon nutmeg
1 chicken bouillon cube
1 cup water
1/4 cup Madeira wine
Parsley

Sauté onion in butter until brown. Soak crumbs in half-and-half. Combine beef, eggs, salt, pepper, and nutmeg; mix until smooth. Chill for 2 hours.

Shape into balls. Fry in butter to brown evenly. Place in glass chafing dish. Combine bouillon cube, water, and wine. Heat and dissolve cube completely. Pour over meatballs and warm before serving. Garnish with parsley.

Kitchen Chatter

Crab Dip in Sourdough Bread

1 (7-ounce) can crabmeat
1 (8-ounce) can water chestnuts, chopped
1 (8-ounce) package cream cheese, softened
4 ounces grated Swiss cheese
1/2 cup mayonnaise
1 teaspoon lemon juice
1 teaspoon chopped green onion
1 round loaf sourdough bread

Preheat oven to 350°. In a large bowl, combine all ingredients, except bread, mixing well. Cut the top off the sourdough bread. Scoop out the inside of the bread and cube into bite-size pieces. Place crab mixture inside the sourdough bread and replace top. Wrap bread in foil. Bake 40 minutes. Use cubed bread for scoopers.

Lake Tahoe Cooks!

Hot Artichoke Dip

½ cup chopped frozen spinach
½ cup mayonnaise
½ cup sour cream
½ cup grated Parmesan cheese
¾ cup grated Cheddar cheese
1 (8-ounce) can diced green
   chiles
1 (14-ounce) can chopped
   artichoke hearts, drained
1 teaspoon minced garlic

Thaw and drain spinach and mix together with all ingredients. Pour into glass 9x13-inch casserole dish and bake at 350° until hot and bubbly. Serve hot with bread or crackers.

The Fruit of the Spirit

Artichoke Dill Dip

2 (14-ounce) cans artichoke
  hearts, drained and chopped
1 cup grated Parmesan cheese
1 cup mayonnaise
2 teaspoons garlic powder
¼ teaspoon Worcestershire
  sauce
1 teaspoon dill weed

Combine all ingredients in a 1-quart casserole dish sprayed with cooking spray. Bake at 350° for 20–25 minutes or until heated through. Serve with toast rounds and/or vegetables.

Elko Ariñak Dancers Cookbook

Nevada is said to be the gambling and entertainment capital of the United States.

Sheepherder Dip

1 round loaf of bread
2 bunches green onions,
  chopped, including tops
1 quart mayonnaise

6 or 7 hard-boiled eggs,
  chopped
2 cans crabmeat, rinsed
2 cans tiny shrimp, rinsed

Cut top off bread. Remove all the insides of the loaf. Combine mayonnaise, green onions, and some of the interior parts of the bread torn into pieces. Let set in refrigerator overnight.

Next day, add eggs, crabmeat, and shrimp to mayonnaise mixture. Mix well. Place in hollowed-out loaf and serve with extra bread pieces and crackers.

Church Family Recipes

7 Layer Mexican Dip

2 pounds ground beef
2 packages taco seasoning mix
1 pound Jack cheese, grated
1 pound Cheddar cheese,
  grated
1 (30-ounce) can refried beans

1 (16-ounce) container salsa
1 (14-ounce) container
  guacamole dip
1 (16-ounce) container sour
  cream

Cook the ground beef with taco seasoning mixes. Blend the cheeses together. Layer as follows, bottom to top: refried beans, salsa, 1/3 cheese blend, seasoned taco meat, guacamole, sour cream, and remaining cheese on top. Refrigerate before serving.

Church Family Recipes

Nevada Ranchers' Cactus Salsa

2 cups chopped ripe tomatoes
1 cup chopped red onion
1 cup nopalitos (cactus meat)*,
    drained and rinsed

½ cup chopped fresh cilantro
¼ cup diced serrano chiles
½ teaspoon coarse salt
⅓ cup fresh lime juice

Combine all ingredients. Chill at least one hour before serving.
Serves 4 rough-riding cowgirls or 6 city gals with sports cars.

*If you can't find nopalitos, substitute mild green chiles.

Authentic Cowboy Cookery Then & Now

Mango Salsa

Great served over grilled fish.

1 red pepper, diced
1 small red onion, diced
1 mango (firm, not overripe),
    diced
½ cup chopped cilantro
2 tablespoons fresh lime juice

1 tablespoon olive oil
1 tablespoon seasoned rice
    vinegar
1 garlic clove, minced
¼ teaspoon cayenne pepper

Mix together red pepper, red onion, diced mango, and cilantro.
Whisk together lime juice, olive oil, rice vinegar, garlic, and
cayenne. Toss ingredients with dressing. Chill until ready to
serve. Best if prepared a few hours ahead of serving time.

Lake Tahoe Cooks!

Carson City, one of the least populated state capitals in the United States, was
named for frontiersman and scout, Kit Carson, who guided John C.
Fremont's mapping expedition across the Nevada Territory in 1843.
Fremont's skills as a map maker earned him the title, "The Pathmaker of the West."

Fun Girls Wonton

WONTON:

2 cups sifted all-purpose flour	**⅔ cup lukewarm water**
1 teaspoon salt	**Cornstarch**

Sift flour and salt into a bowl and make a well in the center. Pour water into well. With a wooden spoon, stir until the dough forms a ball. Turn onto a floured surface and knead until stiff. Cover with a damp cloth and let the dough stand for 30 minutes.

Sprinkle the board with cornstarch and roll the dough into a long strip, 6 inches wide and less than ⅛ inch thick. Cut into 3-inch squares.

FILLING:

¼ pound ground beef or chicken	**1 teaspoon soy sauce**
1 green onion, minced	**½ teaspoon dry sherry**
1¼ teaspoons salt	**1 tablespoon broth or water**
⅛ teaspoon freshly ground black pepper	**1 egg, beaten**
	Oil for deep-frying

In a bowl, mix together meat, onion, salt, pepper, soy sauce, sherry, and broth. Place 1 teaspoon of the mixture in the middle of each square. Moisten edges of squares with beaten egg and press opposite corners together to form a triangle. Fry in hot oil until golden brown. Makes about 36 wontons.

Let Freedom Ring

Nevada is home to 17 of the 20 largest hotels in the world. The MGM Grand in Las Vegas, which boasts a whopping 5,034 rooms is THE largest hotel in the world. Amenities include a sports arena, entertainment dome, and a wedding chapel, not to mention numerous bars and restaurants.

Hot Mushroom Turnovers

FILLING:

3 tablespoons butter or
  margarine
½ pound mushrooms, minced
1 large onion, minced
¼ cup sour cream

1 teaspoon salt
¼ teaspoon chopped thyme
  leaves
2 tablespoons flour

In 10-inch skillet over medium heat in 3 tablespoons hot butter or margarine, cook mushrooms and onion until tender, stirring occasionally. Stir in sour cream, salt, thyme, and flour; set aside.

DOUGH:

1 (8-ounce) package cream
  cheese, softened
1½ cups all-purpose flour

½ cup butter or margarine,
  softened
1 egg, beaten

In large bowl with mixer at medium speed, beat cream cheese, flour, and butter or margarine until smooth; shape into ball. Wrap and refrigerate for 1 hour.

On floured surface with floured rolling pin, roll ½ of dough ⅛ inch thick. With floured 2½-inch-round cookie cutter, cut out as many circles as possible. Repeat.

Preheat oven to 450°. Onto ½ of each Dough circle, place a teaspoon of mushroom mixture. Brush edges of circle with egg; fold Dough over Filling. With fork, firmly press edges together to seal. Prick top. Place turnovers on ungreased cookie sheet; brush with remaining egg. Bake for 12–14 minutes until golden.

Virginia City Alumni Association Cookbook

Here's to the USA Crostini

12 slices Italian crusty bread
2½ tablespoons olive oil,
  divided
2 (6-ounce) jars marinated
  artichoke hearts, rinsed and
  drained
2 tablespoons heavy cream
Salt and black pepper to taste
½ cup sliced greek olives
¼ cup chopped red onion

Preheat broiler. Arrange bread slices on a baking sheet and brush tops with 2 tablespoons olive oil. Broil 5 inches from heat until golden, about 30 seconds. Turn toasts over and broil until golden. Transfer to a rack to cool.

Combine artichokes and cream in a food processor. Transfer to a bowl and season with salt and pepper to taste. Combine olives, onion, and remaining oil in a bowl. Spread toasts evenly with artichoke cream and top with olive mixture. Drizzle with a little more olive oil before serving. Makes 12 hors d'oeuvres.

All American Meals Cookbook

Chiles Rellenos

1½ teaspoons butter
1 can whole green chiles,
  drained, split, and seeded
½ pound Tillamook or
  Monterey Jack cheese, sliced
5 eggs
¼ teaspoon salt

Melt butter in a 9x9-inch baking pan. Place chiles in pan and cover with cheese slices, leaving about ½ inch between slices. Beat eggs with salt and pour over cheese. Bake in preheated 325° oven until cheese is melted and eggs have set, about 25 minutes. Remove from oven. Let set for 20 minutes, then cut into squares.

The Fruit of the Spirit

Shrimp Cocktail "Martini Style"

10 cups chopped, very ripe
  seedless watermelon,
  divided
4 cups superfine sugar
¼ cup light corn syrup
Juice of 1 lemon
2 cups peeled, seeded, finely
  chopped red tomatoes
1 tablespoon finely chopped
  seeded fresh jalapeño chiles
3 scallions
1 tablespoon chopped fresh
  cilantro

1 tablespoon each Tabasco
  sauce and fresh lime juice
2 tablespoons olive oil blend
  (do not use extra virgin olive
  oil)
Salt and pepper to taste
2 heads frisée lettuce or
  chicory
16 large cooked shrimp,
  peeled, deveined, chilled
8 each red and yellow teardrop
  tomatoes, halved
Sprigs of fresh cilantro

Purée 8 cups watermelon in batches in a food processor. Pour into a bowl. Add sugar, corn syrup, and lemon juice. Stir until sugar dissolves. Pour mixture into a freezer container. Freeze overnight. Process frozen mixture in a food processor until slushy. Return to freezer container and freeze for 2 hours.

Mix chopped tomatoes, remaining 2 cups watermelon and jalapeño chiles in a bowl. Cut the green part off the scallions and reserve for garnish. Chop remaining white part finely; add to the tomato mixture. Add chopped cilantro, Tabasco sauce, lime juice, and olive oil. Season with salt and pepper and toss to mix well. Cover and chill until serving time.

Rinse lettuce in cold water. Separate leaves and pat dry. Place lettuce leaves in bottom of 4 frozen martini glasses. Top with 1 tablespoon scoop of tomato mixture and 1 tablespoon scoop of watermelon sorbet. Place 4 shrimp around the rim of each glass. Garnish each with tomato halves, green part of scallions, and cilantro sprigs. Yields 4 servings.

Recipe by James Perillo, Executive Chef,
Caesar's Palace Hotel and Casino

Las Vegas Glitter to Gourmet

Miniature Reubens

2 (8-ounce) packages cocktail
  rye bread
Mustard
½ pound thinly sliced corned
  beef
1 (8-ounce) can sauerkraut,
  drained

1 (8-ounce) package thinly
  sliced Swiss cheese
½ pound (2 sticks) margarine,
  divided

Spread half the bread slices with mustard. Top with a folded piece of corned beef, covering the bread completely but not extending over the edge. Spread about 1 teaspoon sauerkraut oven the meat. Place 2 thin slices of Swiss cheese over sauerkraut; trim edges even with bread. Top with remaining bread.

In large skillet, melt 4 tablespoons margarine. Sauté sandwiches over moderate heat a batch at a time; do not crowd. When underside is golden, turn and brown other side. Add additional margarine as needed; serve warm.

If not serving immediately, place on baking sheet and freeze. When almost frozen, remove from freezer and cut each sandwich in half. Sandwiches are easier to cut when partially frozen. May be frozen for up to 3 months. Reheat frozen. Before serving, bake at 400° for 10–15 minutes until heated through and bubbling.

Recipes from Sunset Garden Club

Bread & Breakfast

PHOTO © NEVADA COMMISSION ON TOURISM

The desert bighorn (or Nelson) sheep is smaller than its Rocky Mountain cousin, but has a wider spread of horns. The bighorn is well-suited for Nevada's mountainous desert country because it can survive for long periods without water.

Let Freedom Ring Buttermilk Drop Biscuits

3 cups all-purpose flour
2 tablespoons sugar
4 teaspoons baking powder
1 teaspoon salt

1 teaspoon baking soda
1½ sticks chilled unsalted
   butter, cut into ¼-inch pats
1 cup buttermilk

Preheat oven to 425°. Whisk together flour, sugar, baking powder, salt, and baking soda. Using fingers or dough cutter, cut butter into dry ingredients until mixture resembles coarse meal. Add buttermilk and stir until moistened. Drop biscuits (about ¼ cup dough per biscuit) onto baking sheet about 2 inches apart. Bake until biscuits are golden, about 15 minutes. Serve warm. Serves 12.

All American Meals Cookbook

Sara's Angel Biscuits

4½ teaspoons active dry yeast
¼ cup warm water
2 cups warm milk
5 cups flour
⅓ cup sugar

1 tablespoon baking powder
1 teaspoon baking soda
2 teaspoons salt
1 cup shortening

Heat oven to 350°. Mix dry yeast and warm water together and let it sit. It will come out gooey looking. After it gets gooey, put the warm milk in the yeast mixture and let it sit. Mix flour and everything else. Mix yeast mixture into flour mixture. You may need to add flour, a little at a time, so it's not sticky. When the dough doesn't stick to your hands, you can roll-up golf ball-sized biscuits and then slightly flatten it, so that it's not a little ball. Bake until golden brown.

Bless This Food

Back at the Ranch
Spicy Cheese Biscuits

7 cups all-purpose flour
4 tablespoons baking powder
2 tablespoons sugar
4 teaspoons cayenne pepper
1 teaspoon salt
2 cups grated sharp Cheddar
   cheese

1 cup grated sharp Romano
   cheese
1 cup cold shortening, cut into
   pieces
2½ cups cold buttermilk

Preheat oven to 450°. Grease a large baking sheet. Sift first 5 ingredients into a bowl. Mix in cheeses. Add shortening and mix with your fingers until mixture resembles coarse meal. Add buttermilk, stirring until dough begins to form. Turn dough onto floured surface and knead gently until smooth, about 8 turns. Roll out dough to about 1 inch thick. Use a biscuit cutter to cut out biscuits. Gather dough scraps and repeat roll out. Cut out biscuits. Put biscuits on baking sheet and bake until golden, about 15 minutes. Serve hot with butter and honey. Serves 4 cowboys on a Friday night or 10 ranch guests on Monday morning.

Authentic Cowboy Cookery Then & Now

Freezer Biscuits

5¼ cups flour
4 teaspoons baking powder
1 teaspoon baking soda
4 tablespoons sugar
1 teaspoon salt

1 cup vegetable shortening
2 packages yeast
¼ cup warm water
2 cups buttermilk

Sift dry ingredients together. Cut in shortening with a pastry blender. Dissolve yeast in warm water; stir until smooth and add to buttermilk. Combine flour and buttermilk mixture and blend. Turn out on floured bread board; knead quickly 20 times. Roll out and cut into biscuits (regular size or miniature size). Freeze biscuits on baking sheet until frozen; transfer to tightly sealed freezer bags.

At baking time: Place biscuits on buttered baking sheet and let biscuits thaw about 15–20 minutes. Preheat oven to 400° and bake for 10 minutes or until biscuits are brown. Yields about 36 biscuits.

Easy Cookin' in Nevada

Popovers

1 cup flour, sifted
¼ teaspoon salt
1 teaspoon sugar

1 tablespoon oil
1 cup skim milk
2 eggs

Preheat oven to 400°. In a small bowl, mix flour with salt and sugar. Combine oil, milk, and eggs in blender; process until very smooth. Add to the blender the flour mixture. Process at high speed for about 1 minute. Fill greased muffin pans half full with the batter. Bake for about 40 minutes or until brown. Keep oven door closed while baking to prevent popovers from collapsing. Serves 12. Serve immediately.

Nutritional analysis: Calories 72; Carbohydrates 10g; Fat 2g; Sodium 720mg; 1 starch exchange per serving.

Sharing Our Diabetics Best Recipes

Delicate Rolls

2 cups milk
4 tablespoons shortening
6 cups flour, divided
1 package yeast

2 tablespoons sugar
2 teaspoons salt
1 egg, beaten

Scald milk, then add shortening; cool. Put 5 cups flour, dry yeast, sugar, and salt in large mixing bowl. Add milk and shortening; stir. Then add egg. Stir until well mixed.

Sprinkle board with remaining flour and turn dough out on board and knead until flour is used. Put into greased bowl to rise for 1–1½ hours. Shape into rolls; let rise 35–40 minutes. Bake at 400°–425° for 15 minutes. Makes 2 dozen rolls.

The Ruby Valley Friendship Club Cookbook II

No Knead Hot Rolls

1 package dry yeast
1 tablespoon sugar
1 teaspoon salt
1 cup warm water

2½ cups flour, divided
1 egg
2 tablespoons soft butter

Dissolve yeast, sugar, and salt in warm water. Add 1¼ cups flour and stir. Add egg, butter, and remaining 1¼ cups flour and stir. Cover and let rise for 45 minutes. Turn out on floured board and work just until dough will roll out. Butter dough and shape into rolls. Place into greased pans and let rise for 45 minutes. Bake for 20 minutes in 400° oven.

The Best of Down-Home Cooking

Corn Cake

½ cup butter, softened
¾–1 cup white sugar
2 eggs
1 cup yellow cornmeal

1½ cups all-purpose flour
2 teaspoons baking powder
½ teaspoon salt
1½ cups milk

In mixing bowl, cream butter and sugar together. Add eggs; beat well. Add cornmeal. Sift flour with baking powder and salt. Stir in alternately with milk. Pour in greased 8-inch-square pan. Bake at 350°, 30–35 minutes. May also use batter for muffins.

Recipes from the Heart

American Indian-Style Chipotle Corn Bread

1 cup yellow cornmeal
1 cup all-purpose flour
¼ cup sugar
2 teaspoons baking powder
1 teaspoon baking soda
1 teaspoon salt
1 cup grated sharp Cheddar cheese

1 cup buttermilk
3 large eggs
6 tablespoons (¾ stick) unsalted butter, melted, cooled
2 tablespoons canned chipotle chiles, seeded and minced

Preheat oven to 375°. Grease a 9x5x2-inch metal loaf pan. Combine first 6 ingredients. Fold in cheese. Whisk together buttermilk, eggs, melted butter, and chiles. Add buttermilk mixture to dry ingredients and stir until blended. Pour batter into loaf pan. Bake until tester inserted into center comes out clean, about 35 minutes. Cool in pan 15 minutes. Turn bread out. Let cool completely before slicing. Makes 1 loaf.

All American Meals Cookbook

Drop Scones

2 cups all-purpose flour
1 tablespoon baking powder
¼ cup granulated sugar
Pinch of salt
½ cup cold butter, cut into
   small pieces

2 eggs, beaten
½ cup whipping cream
½ cup raisins or dried
   cranberries or other dried
   fruit and nuts

Preheat oven to 400°. Mix flour, baking powder, sugar, salt, and butter together. Using pastry blender or 2 knives, cut in flour mixture, then mix briefly with a fork until dough resembles coarse meal.

In separate bowl, combine eggs and cream, and beat together. Pour egg mixture into flour mixture and blend until dry ingredients are just moistened. Add dried fruit and nuts, and mix briefly. Drop batter in 3-ounce rounds (about half the size of a tennis ball) onto well-greased cookie pan. Bake until tops are golden brown, about 18–20 minutes. Makes 10–12 scones.

Note: With cranberries I add ½ cup walnuts and 2 teaspoons orange zest; with apricots I add ½ cup slivered almonds and 1 teaspoon almond extract. You can use chocolate chunks with roasted hazelnuts, also.

Soup for Our Souls

Potato Cheese Muffins

2 cups all-purpose flour
8 packets sugar substitute
4 teaspoons baking powder
1 teaspoon salt
2 eggs
1½ cups 2% milk

½ cup cooked mashed
  potatoes
¾ cup grated light Cheddar
  cheese
⅓ cup margarine, melted

Preheat oven to 400°. Line muffin tins with paper cups or spray with vegetable oil spray. In a large mixing bowl, combine flour, sugar substitute, baking powder, and salt. In a medium-size mixing bowl, beat eggs well with an electric mixer or a wooden spoon. Stir in milk, mashed potatoes, grated cheese, and melted margarine. Mix well. Add egg mixture to flour mixture and stir just until mixed. Spoon batter into paper lined cups and bake 25 minutes or until firm and lightly browned. Makes 10 servings.

Exchanges: 1½ starch and 2 fat exchanges per muffin.

Sharing Our Diabetics Best Recipes

Peanut-Cornflake Muffins

1¾ cups cornflakes
1 cup milk
½ cup peanut butter
½ cup firmly packed brown
  sugar
1 egg

2 tablespoons vegetable oil
1¼ cups flour
1 tablespoon baking powder
½ teaspoon salt
¼ cup berry preserves (your
  choice)

Combine cereal and milk in large bowl. Let stand to soften cereal. Add peanut butter, sugar, egg, and oil. Beat until smooth. Combine flour, baking powder, and salt. Add to cereal mixture, stirring just until dry ingredients are moist. Fill oiled muffin cups ½ full; top each with 1 teaspoon preserves. Top with remaining batter to fill cup ¾ full. Bake 20 minutes at 400°. Makes 12 muffins.

Timbreline's Cookbook

Cranberry Bread

2 cups cranberries
2 cups flour
½ teaspoon baking soda
1 cup sugar
1½ teaspoons baking powder
½ teaspoon salt

1 egg
2 tablespoons butter or salad
  oil
Juice and rind of 1 orange with
  enough water to make ¾ cup

Cut or chop cranberries in food processor. Transfer berries to mixing bowl; add flour, baking soda, sugar, baking powder, and salt, and mix well. Add remaining ingredients and mix well. Pour into greased and floured loaf pan; bake at 325° for 1 hour.

Our Daily Bread

Dill Bread

While I was working in a doctor's office in Carson City in the '80s, a patient came in with a basket of dill bread still warm from the oven, along with some nice, soft butter. We sat down and had a feast on what seemed like the most delicious bread I had ever eaten. It remains a real treat at our family gatherings.

2 tablespoons dill seed
  (ground up)
1 tablespoon dried onion
4 tablespoons sugar or honey
½ teaspoon baking soda
2 teaspoons salt

2 eggs
2 tablespoons butter
1 pint cottage cheese
2 packages yeast, dissolved in
  1 cup very warm water
5 cups flour, maybe 6

Mix dill seed, dried onion, sugar, baking soda, and salt. Add eggs, butter, cottage cheese, and yeast; mix thoroughly. Add flour, 1 cup at a time; knead at least 8 minutes, adding flour until stiff. Put in a greased bowl in a warm place and let rise until double in size, about 1 hour. Remove; knead again. Place in greased loaf pan(s); let rise until double, about 20 minutes. Bake at 350° for 30–45 minutes, depending on the size of the pan.

God, That's Good!

Orange Walnut Bread

1½ cups all-purpose flour
½ cup granulated sugar
2 teaspoons baking powder
½ teaspoon baking soda
½ teaspoon salt
2 eggs, beaten

¼ cup butter, melted
½ cup orange juice
2 tablespoons grated orange peel
2 tablespoons water
1 cup chopped walnuts

Mix flour, sugar, baking powder, baking soda, and salt into a large bowl. Set aside. Blend eggs, butter, orange juice, orange peel, and water in a small bowl. Stir into flour mixture just until blended. Stir in the walnuts. Spoon into a greased and floured 8½x4½x2-inch loaf pan. Bake at 350° for 50 minutes. Cool on wire rack.

The Fruit of the Spirit

Mom's Cinnamon Coffee Cake

5 cups flour
1½ cups sugar
2 cups brown sugar
1 tablespoon cinnamon
1 teaspoon salt

1½ cups oil
2 teaspoons baking soda
2 teaspoons baking powder
2 eggs
2 cups buttermilk

Mix flour, sugars, cinnamon, salt, and oil with a fork; save 1½ cups for topping. Add remainder to baking soda, baking powder, eggs, and buttermilk. Mix together and pour into 4 greased 9-inch pie or cake pans. Sprinkle with reserved topping. Bake 30 minutes at 350°. Makes 4 cakes.

Feeding the Flock

Potato Lefsa

2 cups mashed potatoes
½ teaspoon salt

1 tablespoon shortening
¾ cup flour

Boil potatoes; cool, peel and rice (with potato ricer). Mix ingredients together. Heat lefsa griddle (or iron skillet) on high. Prepare lefsa board with lefsa cloth and flour board. Use a lefsa roller (or rolling pin) with cloth sleeve to roll out flat. Transfer to the hot lefsa griddle (or iron skillet) until brown spots occur, then flip and brown other side. Use butter or other spread. Serve hot or cold. Store in refrigerator.

Home Cooking

Mashed Potato Doughnuts

2 cups hot mashed potatoes
2 cups sugar
1 cup milk
3 eggs, separated
Salt

Nutmeg or vanilla
3 tablespoons melted Crisco or
Snowdrift
Flour (about 5 cups)
5 teaspoons baking powder

Mix potatoes and sugar. Add milk, beaten egg yolks and beaten egg whites (beaten separately), pinch of salt, and flavoring. Add shortening and then flour mixed with baking powder to make a stiff dough. Roll and cut out as doughnuts. Fry in deep fat, turning each doughnut as it rises.

Hoover Dam Cooks, 1933

 Native American tribes are still an important part of Nevada life. The Anasazi, Washo, Paiute, Goshute, and Shoshone lived there long before the settlers arrived. In fact, powwows (festivals) are still held throughout the state.

Soft Pretzels

2 packages yeast
2 cups warm water
½ cup sugar
2 teaspoons salt
¼ cup butter, softened

1 egg
6½–7½ cups flour
1 egg yolk
2 tablespoons water
Coarse salt (optional)

In a large bowl, dissolve yeast in warm water. Add sugar, salt, butter, and egg. Stir in 3 cups flour; mix until smooth. Add enough additional flour to make a stiff dough. Cover bowl tightly with foil; refrigerate for 2–24 hours. Punch dough down and divide in half.

On a slightly floured surface, cut each half into 16 equal pieces. Roll each piece into a 20-inch rope. Shape into the traditional pretzel shape and place on a greased baking sheet.

In a small bowl, combine egg yolk and water; brush over the pretzels. Sprinkle with salt, if desired. Cover and let rise in a warm place until doubled, about 25 minutes. Bake at 400° for 15 minutes or until browned. Yields 32 pretzels.

Partyline Cook Book

The largest silver strike in the world was discovered while miners were searching for gold in 1859. Since that time, the Comstock Lode has yielded more than $400 million in gold and silver and remains the richest known silver deposit ever discovered in the U.S. The excavations descended more than 3,200 feet until the inflow of hot water, plus the halt in silver dollar coinage, brought operations to an end in 1898.

Bob's Sweet Rolls

4 cups warm water
½ cup sugar
4 tablespoons powdered milk
  (or 1 cup milk and subtract
  1 cup water)

10 cups flour, unsifted, divided
1 tablespoon salt
½ cup shortening, soft, or oil
3 packages yeast

Mix water, sugar, milk, 6 cups flour, salt, shortening, and yeast on low speed of mixer, or by hand for 5 minutes; gradually add 2 more cups flour. Mix well and add 2 more cups flour, if needed. Mix well. Let proof or rise for about 1 hour. Work down; let rise for 10 minutes, then roll out and cut into doughnuts, rolls, or sweet rolls. Bake sweet rolls at 350° for 20–25 minutes.

GLAZE:
2 tablespoons milk
1½ cups powdered sugar

1 teaspoon vanilla
Pinch of salt

Mix together and spread on baked sweet rolls.

Variation: For cinnamon rolls, combine 1 cup sugar and 1 tablespoon cinnamon. Roll out dough and spread with melted butter. Sprinkle with cinnamon mixture. Roll up and slice. Let rise for about 45 minutes and bake as before.

NSHSRA High School Rodeo Cookbook

Orange Rolls
(Bow Ties)

1 cup milk, scalded
⅓ cup sugar
1 teaspoon salt
½ cup shortening
1 package yeast
¼ cup warm water

2 eggs, beaten
¼ cup orange juice
2 tablespoons grated orange
  peel
5 cups sifted flour

Mix together milk, sugar, salt, and shortening; cool to warm. Soften yeast in warm water. Add to above lukewarm mixture. Then add eggs, orange juice, and orange peel; beat well. Add sifted flour. Mix to a soft dough.

Let rise 1 hour; knead down. Let rise again; knead down. Roll into a 10x16-inch rectangle. Cut in strips 10 inches long by ¾ inch wide. Roll each strip lightly in your fingers and tie in knot. Tuck ends under and arrange on a greased baking sheet. Let rise until double. Bake in a 400° oven for 10–12 minutes. Frost while hot with Orange Icing.

ORANGE ICING FOR ORANGE ROLLS:
2 tablespoons orange juice   1 cup powdered sugar
1 teaspoon grated orange peel

Mix well and brush on hot rolls with pastry brush.

The Ruby Valley Friendship Club Cookbook I

Orange Rolls

3 tablespoons dry yeast
²/₃ cup lukewarm water
1 cup butter, chopped
½ cup sugar
2 teaspoons salt

2 cups milk, scalded
2 eggs, beaten
6 cups flour

Dissolve yeast in water in a small bowl. Combine chopped butter, sugar, and salt in a large bowl. Add hot milk and mix to dissolve butter. Let stand until lukewarm. Add yeast, eggs, and flour, and mix well to form a sticky dough. Let rise, covered, in refrigerator for 8 hours or longer.

Remove from refrigerator 2–2½ hours before baking. Divide dough into halves and roll each on a floured surface.

FILLING:
14 tablespoons butter, softened   Grated peel of 2 oranges
1½ cups sugar, divided

Mix softened butter, sugar, and orange peel in a bowl.

Spread Filling on the dough. Roll up to enclose the Filling. Cut into 1-inch pieces with dental floss. Place in greased muffin cups. Let rise until doubled in bulk. Bake at 400° for 10–15 minutes or until golden brown. Yields 4 dozen.

From Sunrise to Sunset

Baked French Toast

1 large loaf French bread
8 eggs
3 cups milk
3/4 cup sugar, divided
2 teaspoons vanilla extract

4–5 baking apples, peeled,
  sliced
1 1/2–2 teaspoons cinnamon
2 tablespoons butter

Butter the bottom and sides of a 9x13-inch baking pan. Cut bread into 1 1/2-inch slices. Arrange closely in single layer in buttered pan. Combine eggs, milk, 1/4 cup sugar, and vanilla in a bowl and beat until smooth. Layer half the egg mixture, apple slices, and remaining egg mixture in the prepared pan. Sprinkle with a mixture of 1/2 cup sugar and cinnamon; dot with butter. Bake at 400° for 35 minutes. Let stand for 5–10 minutes before serving. Serve with maple syrup. Yields 8–10 servings.

From Sunrise to Sunset

Fabulous French Toast

5 eggs
2/3 cup half-and-half
2 tablespoons orange juice
  concentrate
2 tablespoons sugar
Grated zest of orange

2 teaspoons cinnamon
6 stale plain croissants, cut
6 tablespoons butter
Confectioners' sugar or orange
  marmalade

Beat eggs and cream together. Add orange juice, sugar, zest, and cinnamon, and whisk until blended. Pour into shallow pan. Dip each croissant half in egg mixture. Melt a few tablespoons butter in skillet over medium heat. Fry croissants until golden. Sprinkle sugar or marmalade over croissants and serve. Serves 6.

Recipes from Sunset Garden Club

Club Soda Waffles

2 cups Bisquick
3 tablespoons oil

1½ cups club soda
1 egg

Mix all ingredients well and bake in hot waffle iron as usual. Crisp and delicious.

Twentieth Century Club Cook Book

Breakfast Casserole

8 slices bread, cubed
2 cups (½ pound) shredded
    Cheddar cheese
20 (1½ to 2 pounds) pork
    sausage links

4 eggs
2¾ cups milk, divided
¾ teaspoon dry mustard
1 (10¾-ounce) can cream of
    mushroom soup

Arrange bread cubes in bottom of greased 9x13-inch baking dish. Sprinkle with shredded cheese. Brown pork sausage links; drain and cut into fourths; arrange on top of cheese. Beat eggs with 2¼ cups milk and dry mustard. Dilute soup with remaining milk; pour over casserole. Bake in 350° oven for 1½ hours.

The Ruby Valley Friendship Club Cookbook II

In order for gold and silver mines to have access to processing mills, railroads had to be built. Chinese contract workers were brought in to build the railroads in the mid-1800s. These railroads helped spur growth and create wagon trails for newcomers. You can still ride the old-time trains in Virginia City and Ely, and enjoy underground tours of pioneer Comstock mines.

Breakfast Brunch

6 eggs
1 cup Bisquick
½ cup butter, melted
3 cups milk
Seasoned salt to taste

Lemon pepper to taste
1 teaspoon minced onion
Dash of Worcestershire sauce
1 cup chopped ham
2 cups grated cheese

Mix well the eggs, Bisquick, butter, milk, salt, pepper, minced onion, and Worcestershire sauce in a blender. Pour into greased 9x13-inch baking dish. Add ham; top with cheese. Bake at 350° for 45–60 minutes. Let stand 5–10 minutes before cutting.

Our Daily Bread

Brunch Casserole

This is wonderful to serve to guests for a mid-morning brunch.

6 slices white bread
2 cups shredded Jack cheese
2 cups shredded Cheddar
  cheese
1 pound link sausage, cooked
1 (4-ounce) can mild diced
  chiles
6 eggs

2 cups milk
1 teaspoon salt
½ teaspoon pepper
1 tablespoon oregano
¼ teaspoon dried mustard
¼ teaspoon garlic powder
½ teaspoon paprika

Cut crust from bread. Butter one side and place buttered-side-down in 9x13-inch pan. Layer ½ cheeses, chopped sausage, remaining ½ cheeses, then chiles. Beat together eggs, milk, and spices. Pour over ingredients in pan. Cover and chill overnight.

Bake uncovered at 325° for 50 minutes. Serves 6–8. Serve with fresh fruit.

Home Cooking

Italian Omelet

8 eggs, beaten
1 cup ricotta cheese
1/2 cup milk
1/2 teaspoon dried basil
1/4 teaspoon salt
1/4 teaspoon crushed fennel
  seed
1/4 teaspoon pepper

1 (10-ounce) package frozen
  chopped spinach, thawed and
  drained
1 cup chopped tomatoes
1 cup shredded mozzarella
1/2 cup thinly sliced green
  onions
1/2 cup diced salami (optional)

In large mixing bowl, combine eggs and ricotta. Beat till just combined. Stir in milk, basil, salt, fennel, and pepper. Fold in spinach, tomatoes, mozzarella, green onions, and salami. Spread evenly in a greased 9x13-inch casserole. Bake at 325° for 30–35 minutes or till knife inserted near center comes out clean. Let stand 10 minutes. Makes 6–8 main dish servings.

Traditional Treasures

Roughcut Cactus and Egg Omelet

2 tablespoons butter
1 (8-ounce) can nopalitos
  (cactus), drained and rinsed
1/8 cup chopped yellow onion

8 large eggs
1/3 cup milk
1/4 teaspoon salt
1/4 teaspoon black pepper

Melt butter in a skillet and sauté nopalitos and onion until tender. In a bowl, beat together eggs, milk, salt, and pepper. Pour egg mixture over nopalitos and onions and cook over low heat until eggs set. Fold eggs over with a spatula. Continue cooking about 3–5 minutes to desired doneness. Serve hot. Serves 1 hungry cowboy or 2 ranch guests.

Authentic Cowboy Cookery Then & Now

Healthy Nevada-Style Western Omelet

2 teaspoons olive oil
8 egg whites
1 whole egg
¼ cup diced extra lean ham
2 tablespoons diced green bell
  pepper

2 tablespoons diced red onion
⅛ teaspoon salt
⅛ teaspoon ground black
  pepper
No-oil salsa for garnish

In nonstick skillet, heat oil. Beat egg whites and egg in a bowl and stir in remaining ingredients, except salsa. Pour egg mixture into skillet. When omelet begins to set, gently lift with spatula and turn over. Cook until eggs are firm. Serve hot with salsa.

Nutritional analysis per serving: Calories 195; Protein 22g; Fat 4g; Carbohydrates 3g.

The Protein Edge

Soups, Chilies & Stews

Skiing is a popular winter sport in Incline Village. Located near Lake Tahoe, it boasts more than 30 feet of snow and 300 days of sunshine annually.

Basque Vegetable Soup

1 pound white pea beans
½ pound dried peas
Meaty ham knuckle
3 bay leaves, divided
1 onion, stuck with 2 whole
   cloves
3 quarts water
6 potatoes, cut small
4 carrots, sliced

4 turnips, diced
5 leeks, cut up
6 garlic cloves, chopped
1 teaspoon thyme
1 small cabbage, shredded
12 sausages
Grated cheese
French bread

Soak pea beans and dried peas overnight in water (unless they are the quick-cooking type).

   Next day, drain and put them into a deep kettle with a meaty ham knuckle, 2 bay leaves, onion with cloves, and 3 quarts water. Cook 1 hour and taste for salt (if ham is salty, salt will not need to be added.) Cook until beans are tender, and drain, reserving liquid. In bean liquid, cook potatoes, carrots, turnips, leeks, garlic, thyme, and remaining 1 bay leaf. When tender, add shredded cabbage, the beans and peas, meat from ham bone, and sausages. Cook until cabbage is just tender and soup very thick. Serve with grated cheese on top and French bread. Serves 6–8.

The Great Nevada Cookbook

Onion Soup Basquaise

Using cooked bread as a basic ingredient makes this soup very Basque.

2 small French bread rolls,
   thinly sliced
⅓ cup cooking oil or olive oil
4 medium onions, cut in
   ½-inch-thick slices

½ pound Swiss cheese, grated
   (4 cups)
3 (10¾-ounce) cans beef
   consommé
3 cans water

Place bread slices on a cookie sheet and bake at 250° for about 40 minutes. While the bread is baking, heat oil in a frying pan and sauté onions until they are limp. Remove bread slices from oven; increase temperature to 350°.

In a 3- to 4-quart casserole, layer half the toasted bread slices; top with half the onions, then half the Swiss cheese. Repeat layers.

In a separate pan, mix consommé and water and heat to boiling on the stove. Gently pour hot consommé over layers in casserole. Bake casserole, uncovered, at 350° for 30 minutes. Yields 8–10 servings.

Note: The soup puffs up as it bakes, so do not fill casserole too full. Leave at least 2 inches between soup and top of casserole.

Chorizos in an Iron Skillet

The silver rush of the 1850s brought Basque people from their European mountain homeland to Nevada. After the boom went bust, they went back to their heritage as sheep ranchers. Their strength, endurance, and appreciation of good food are celebrated in Basque festivals in northern Nevada.

Spanish Evenings Gazpacho

4 ripe tomatoes, peeled and
  chopped
1 cup seeded and chopped
  cucumber
½ cup chopped red bell
  pepper
¼ cup chopped green bell
  pepper
⅓ cup diced scallions

2 garlic cloves, minced
1 (12-ounce) can vegetable
  juice cocktail
2 tablespoons balsamic vinegar
1 tablespoon olive oil
¼ teaspoon salt
¼ teaspoon black pepper
Cucumber slices for garnish
Hot pepper sauce (optional)

Combine tomatoes, cucumber, peppers, scallions, garlic, vegetable juice cocktail, vinegar, oil, salt, and pepper in a large
bowl. Cover and chill. Serve garnished with cucumber slices.
If desired, sprinkle with hot pepper sauce. Makes 4 servings.

Nutritional values: Serving equals ¾ cup: Calories 94; Protein 2g; Fat 4g; Carbohydrates 15g; Sodium 458mg; Cholesterol 1mg

Easy Gourmet for Diabetics

White Bean Soup with Tortellini

There's nothing like a good soup that's easy to prepare as well.

2 (15-ounce) cans white beans
3 (15-ounce) cans broth,
  vegetable or chicken
1 (14½-ounce) can diced
  tomatoes

½ (10-ounce) package frozen
  spinach
1 (9-ounce) package frozen
  cheese tortellini

Combine beans, broth, tomatoes, and spinach in large saucepot;
bring to a boil over medium heat. Five minutes before you're
ready to serve, add the tortellini. Serve with French bread.

Soup for Our Souls

Baked Tortellini Soup

1½ pounds sausage links
1 cup chopped onion
1 teaspoon minced garlic
¼ teaspoon black pepper
2 tablespoons olive oil
4 cups beef broth
2 cups water
1½ teaspoons Italian
   seasoning
1½ cups peeled and thinly
   sliced carrots

1 (16-ounce) can whole
   tomatoes
1 (16-ounce) can kidney beans,
   drained and rinsed
1 (6-ounce) can pitted, sliced
   black olives, drained
2 cups diced zucchini
16 ounces cheese tortellini
Freshly grated Parmesan
   cheese for garnish

Preheat oven to 400°. In roasting pan, combine sausage, onion, garlic, and pepper. Add olive oil and toss to coat. Roast, uncovered, stirring occasionally, 20–30 minutes, until sausage is brown. Remove from oven. Reduce oven temperature to 325°. Drain any grease from sausage and cut into ¼-inch slices. Return to roasting pan. Add broth, water, seasoning, and carrots. Bake 30 minutes, until sausage is tender. Remove from oven. Squeeze tomatoes by hand to break up, then stir tomatoes with juice, beans, olives, and zucchini into roasting pan with sausage. Bake 15–20 minutes. Add tortellini and bake 5 minutes longer. Ladle into bowls and garnish with Parmesan cheese. Great served with garlic bread.

Note: This soup may be cooked on the stovetop, also.

CASA Cooks

The U.S. government owns 87 percent—about 60 million of approximately 70 million acres—of the state of Nevada. Much of this land is set aside for the protection of its natural resources by the Federal Bureau of Land Management, such as the the Humboldt-Toiyabe National Forest. Vast tracts are also used for the Nellis Air Force Base, and the Nevada Test Site, which is itself the size of Rhode Island.

Cream of Broccoli Soup

1 large carrot, sliced	⅛ teaspoon pepper
2 small onions, chopped	4 medium potatoes, quartered
1½ tablespoons butter	1 pound broccoli
1 quart chicken broth	1 egg yolk
1 teaspoon salt	3 tablespoons heavy cream

Sauté carrot and onions in butter until translucent. Add chicken broth, salt, pepper, and quartered potatoes. Boil until potatoes are tender, about 40 minutes. Cook broccoli separately in boiling water for about 15 minutes or until almost tender. Drain and set aside. When potatoes are tender, lift out all vegetables from chicken broth and place in a food processor. Add broccoli and process until very smooth. Strain chicken broth and return to cooking pan. Add processed vegetables and mix. If not very smooth, strain. Heat to boiling.

Whip the egg yolk and cream together. Add about ½ cup of hot soup, stirring constantly. Mix well. Combine egg mixture with very hot soup, stirring constantly until well blended. Keep hot. Do not boil or it will curdle. Serve from soup tureen. Yields 6 servings.

Variations: This is a French cream soup. It may be adapted to make different flavors of soup. Follow the base recipe and substitute 2 pounds of spinach for the broccoli; boil spinach for 10 minutes. Zucchini soup may be made the same way; use 3 cups grated zucchini instead of 1 pound of broccoli, and boil 10 minutes. The green vegetable is always cooked separately from the carrot mixture to insure the bright green color. It should not be overcooked or it will lose the choice color which comes when cooked uncovered for a short period of time.

Easy Cookin' in Nevada

Broccoli-Cauliflower-Cheese Soup

3 chicken bouillon cubes
3 cups water
½ cup diced celery
½ cup diced carrots
¼ cup diced onion
1 cup chopped broccoli

1 cup chopped cauliflower
6 cups milk
½ cup butter, melted
2 tablespoons flour
½ pound Velveeta cheese,
    cubed

Dissolve bouillon cubes in water in a large pot. Add vegetables and cook until tender. Add milk. Cream the melted butter and flour until smooth, add to soup mixture and stir. Simmer. Add cheese; stir until cheese is melted.

Recipes from the Heart

Potato Cheese Soup

2 cups boiling water
2 cups diced potatoes
½ cup sliced celery

½ cup sliced carrots
¼ cup chopped onion
Salt and pepper to taste

Pour water over remaining ingredients in large pot; cover and simmer for 15 minutes or until vegetables are tender. Do not drain.

WHITE SAUCE:
¼ cup butter or margarine
2 cups shredded Cheddar
    cheese

¼ cup flour
2 cups milk
1 cup diced ham

Cook butter, cheese, flour and milk in saucepan, stirring until smooth and thickened. Add to above mixture. Add diced ham and cook, but do not boil, until heated through and of desired consistency. Great with dill bread or French bread.

Feeding the Flock

Mushroom Soup with White Wine

A wonder soup for a first course for company. Keep some in the freezer to serve when entertaining.

6 scallions, trimmed, finely chopped
¼ cup butter
16 ounces mushrooms, finely chopped
3 tablespoons flour

½ teaspoon ground cumin
1 teaspoon salt
½ teaspoon pepper
2½ cups milk, scalded
1 cup dry white wine

Sauté scallions in butter in large saucepan for 7 minutes or until tender. Add mushrooms. Cook for 5 minutes, stirring frequently. Add flour, cumin, salt, and pepper. Cook for 5 minutes or until thickened, stirring constantly. Add milk gradually, stirring constantly. Stir in wine. Bring to a boil; reduce heat. Simmer for 5 minutes. May purée 2 cups at a time in blender for smooth soup. Yields 6 servings.

Approximately per serving: Cal 193; Prot 6g; Carbo 12g; Fiber 2g; Total Fat 11g; 53% Calories from Fat; Chol 35mg; Sod 468mg.

Best Bets

Parsnip Soup

½ cup butter
2 pounds parsnips, peeled and cut into chunks
2 white onions, chopped

1 teaspoon curry powder
2 cups vegetable broth
Fresh dill, snipped, for garnish

Melt butter in a large heavy saucepan. Add parsnips and onions and cook gently, allowing the vegetables just to absorb the butter. Add curry powder and vegetable broth and let simmer until vegetables are soft, about 20 minutes. Purée in a processor or blender in batches. Return to saucepan and reheat just before serving. If too thick, thin with water. Garnish with snipped fresh dill.

The Food You Always Wanted to Eat Cookbook

The Alpine Village Chicken Supreme Soup

ROUX:

½ cup oil   1 cup flour

Heat oil until smoking; add flour and stir constantly with wire whisk.   It should be the consistency of mashed potatoes. Remove from heat when slightly browned.

SOUP:

2½ quarts water   1 medium onion, ground
1 pound ground, cooked   ¼ teaspoon pepper
  chicken   2–3 carrots, ground
2 teaspoons Kitchen Bouquet   2 teaspoons chicken bouillon
2 teaspoons celery salt

Boil all Soup ingredients together for about 30 minutes.   Add Roux to Soup and use whisk to blend. Enjoy.

Feeding the Flock

Chinese Chicken Corn Soup

This soup is served as a first course in Chinese restaurants but also makes a good meal.

5–6 chicken thighs	**Chicken broth or water to cover**
1–2 chicken breast halves	

Cook the chicken in canned chicken broth or water. If using water, add 1 chopped onion and 1 sliced rib of celery with leaves, and salt and pepper to taste. You may also roast the chicken, but be careful not to dry out the meat. Discard skin and separate meat from bones. Cut into bite-size pieces or shred and set aside.

BROTH:

1 tablespoon minced garlic	**¼ pound mushrooms, sautéed**
1 tablespoon minced ginger	**in a little butter or oil**
2 teaspoons vegetable oil	**½ cup peas, fresh or frozen**
1 quart chicken broth	**Soy sauce to taste**
1 (15-ounce) can sweet	**Sugar to taste**
whole-kernel corn (or fresh)	**Salt and pepper to taste**
1 (15-ounce) can creamed	**2 egg whites**
corn	**Chopped cilantro (optional)**

Sauté garlic and ginger in soup pot in a small amount of oil until flavor is released, 1–2 minutes. Add broth, cooked chicken, corn, mushrooms, soy sauce, and sugar. Simmer for 20–30 minutes. Add peas and simmer until they are tender. Adjust seasoning with soy sauce, sugar, salt and pepper, if necessary. Just before serving, scramble the egg whites. Add egg whites to broth in a slow steady stream while stirring broth. Serve with chopped cilantro, if desired.

Note: If using fresh corn, add with the peas so they're not overcooked. Frozen corn also works well in this recipe.

Soup for Our Souls

Portuguese Sopas

1 (5-pound) chuck roast
1 can tomato sauce
½ medium onion, finely
  chopped
½ teaspoon black pepper
1 teaspoon salt
1 cup burgundy wine or
  ¼ cup vinegar
1 cup water
¼ cup ketchup

¼ teaspoon garlic salt
½ teaspoon whole cloves
¼ teaspoon whole cumin seed
½ teaspoon whole allspice
3 or 4 bay leaves
1 stick cinnamon
Sprigs of mint
French bread
Dill pickles

Put roast in heavy roaster (one with a lid) and place tomato sauce, onion, pepper, salt, wine, water, ketchup, and garlic salt around the roast. Put remaining spices in a tea strainer or wrap in cheesecloth. Put container with spices down into the juice. Cover roaster and cook for 3–3½ hours at 350°.

When cooked, remove pan from heat and let cool so that all fat will come to the top of the pan. Remove fat, then add 1½–2 quarts water (to suite taste). Simmer with meat for 30 minutes or so. Pour juice over mint and sliced French bread. Serve meat in separate bowl. Do not forget to serve with dill pickles.

The Great Nevada Food Festival Cookbook

The Comstock Lode helped Nevada become a state. President Lincoln needed the riches of the Comstock Lode to finance the Union's efforts in the Civil War. He also needed the votes of another state to pass the 13th Amendment to abolish slavery. (The fact that Nevada didn't contain enough people to qualify for statehood was conveniently overlooked.) To meet legal requirements, the Nevada Constitution had to be delivered to Washington D.C. in person. The Pony Express didn't exist yet, and sending it by ship would have taken too long. So it was decided by Nevada officials to telegraph the entire constitution to Chicago, where it would be written out in longhand and delivered to Washington. It was the longest telegraph in history. It took Frank Bell over 12 hours to tap it out and it cost over $4,000 to send! It did the trick, and on October 31, 1864, Nevada became the thirty-sixth state.

Ground Beef Soup

1 pound ground beef, browned
  and drained
⅓ cup pearl barley
1½–2 teaspoons seasoning
  salt
5 cups water
2 tablespoons chopped parsley
  (or to taste)

1 tablespoon bouillon granules,
  or 2 beef bouillon cubes
1 cup chopped celery
1 teaspoon basil
Salt and pepper to taste
1 cup sliced carrots
¼ cup ketchup
1 bay leaf

Add all ingredients to meat in a large pot; cover and simmer for approximately 1 hour, stirring occasionally.

Feeding the Flock

Fast and Easy Tortilla Soup

This soup, like all soups, is better the next day.

2 tablespoons olive oil
1 medium onion, diced
2 celery ribs, diced
2 carrots, diced
3 cloves fresh garlic, diced
1 quart homemade chicken
  stock, or 2 (14.5-ounce) cans
  low-sodium chicken broth

1 (14.5-ounce) can stewed
  tomatoes
1 teaspoon chili powder
1 teaspoon Mexican oregano
1 teaspoon dried cumin powder
Salt and pepper to taste
Tortilla chips and cilantro for
  garnish

In a saucepan, heat olive oil over medium heat. Add onions, celery, and carrots. Sauté for 5–7 minutes, until onions start to turn transparent. Add garlic and continue to sauté for 2 minutes, stirring often. Add remaining ingredients. Simmer for 20–30 minutes. Taste and adjust seasoning. Add cayenne or hot pepper sauce if you prefer a spicier soup. To serve, top with tortilla chips and fresh cilantro. Feel free to add meat, such as leftover shredded roasted chicken, turkey, steak, etc.

Home Cooking

Mexican Chicken Chile Pepper-Tortilla Soup

1 large onion, cut into
  medium dice
3 tablespoons olive oil
8 cups chicken stock
4 roasted Anaheim or
  California green peppers,
  peeled, stemmed, seeded,
  and diced
2½ cups finely chopped
  chicken

2 teaspoons dried oregano
6 corn tortillas, halved and cut
  into ½-inch-wide strips
Salt and pepper to taste
1 large tomato, cored and diced
1 avocado, diced
¾ cup chopped fresh cilantro

In heavy-bottomed, 4-quart saucepan, cook onion in olive oil over moderate heat for 10 minutes, stirring frequently. Add stock, chiles, chicken, and oregano; bring to boil over high heat. Reduce heat to moderate and simmer for 15 minutes or until chicken is cooked through. Add tortillas and cook 5 minutes. Season with salt and pepper. Garnish each portion with tomato, avocado, and cilantro before serving.

Lake Tahoe Cooks!

Festivals and food fairs are popular events in Nevada. A few of the most popular ones include: World's Championship Chili Cook-Off held in early October at the Reno Hilton; Las Vegas Greek Food Festival held in May; Italian Festivals held every October in Reno and Las Vegas; Genoa Candy Dance held in Genoa in October; National Basque Festival held in Elko on the first weekend in July; Best in the West Nugget Rib Cook-Off held in Sparks in September; Portuguese Festas held in May in Fallon.

Taco Soup

Easy, but oh so good! With a green salad and French bread, this makes a tasty and fun meal, great for a tree-trimming supper, a tailgate party, or skiing.

1–1½ pounds hamburger
1 package taco seasoning mix
1 or 2 onions, sliced
1 (32-ounce) can chopped
  tomatoes
1 (15-ounce) can dark red
  kidney beans
1 (15-ounce) can chicken
  broth

1 (10-ounce) box frozen corn
1–2 cups grated Cheddar
  cheese
1 bag tortilla chips
1 (4-ounce) can sliced black
  olives
1 pint sour cream
1 avocado, chopped

In a large soup kettle, sauté meat until all pink is gone, breaking it up with a fork. While meat is cooking, add seasoning, onions, tomatoes, beans including liquid, chicken broth, and corn. (If you expect to keep this cooking for a long time, you may wait to add corn 15 minutes before serving.) Let everything simmer slowly for as little as ½ hour, or up to a few hours.

Serve with cheese, chips, olives, and sour cream in separate bowls. The avocado should be prepared at the last moment, to prevent darkening. Serve the soup in bowls ⅔ full, then pass the toppings.

NSHSRA High School Rodeo Cookbook

A scenic by-product of Hoover Dam is the gigantic reservoir of Lake Mead, a stunningly beautiful water recreation wonderland. Lake Mead backs up 110 miles behind Hoover Dam, thus creating America's largest man-made reservoir. Lake Mead can store nearly two years of average Colorado River flow, about 28.5 million acre-feet of water. (An acre-foot of water is 325,851 gallons, or enough to cover an acre to a depth of one foot.) This water is released in a regulated, year-round flow as needed.

Gift of the Sea Chowder

2 tablespoons butter
1 cup chopped yellow onion
1 cup chopped celery
2 garlic cloves, minced
3 cups peeled and cubed red
  potatoes
2 tablespoons all-purpose
  flour
2½ cups 1% low-fat milk
1 tablespoon thyme
1 teaspoon black pepper

¼ teaspoon nutmeg
1 (14½-ounce) can cream-style
  corn
1 (14-ounce) can fat-free,
  low-sodium chicken broth
6 ounces lump crabmeat,
  picked through
4 ounces salad shrimp
2 teaspoons chopped fresh
  parsley leaves
½ teaspoon salt

Melt butter in a large saucepan. Sauté onion, celery, and garlic until softened. Add potatoes and sauté lightly. Sprinkle with flour and stir to coat. Stir in milk, thyme, pepper, and nutmeg. Add corn and broth. Reduce heat and simmer covered for about 15 minutes until potatoes are tender. Stir in crab, shrimp, parsley, and salt. Cook 5 minutes, stirring occasionally, until seafood is heated through. Serves 6.

Nutritional values: One serving equals 1½ cups: Calories 225; Protein 16g; Fat 6g; Carbohydrates 35g; Sodium 968mg; Cholesterol 47mg.

Easy Gourmet for Diabetics

A Cowboy's "Real Chili Got No Beans in It, Ma'am" Chili

1 cup diced yellow onions
3 cloves garlic, minced
2 tablespoons oil
2 pounds beef sirloin, cubed into ¼-inch squares
2 cups chopped, peeled ripe tomatoes
1 cup tomato sauce
1 (12-ounce) bottle beer
1 cup strong brewed coffee
2 (6-ounce) cans tomato paste
½ cup low-salt beef broth

½ cup packed brown sugar
3 tablespoons chili powder
1 teaspoon cumin
1 teaspoon unsweetened cocoa powder
1 teaspoon dried oregano
1 teaspoon ground cayenne pepper
1 teaspoon salt
½ teaspoon black pepper
4 fresh jalapeño chile peppers, seeded and chopped

Sauté onions and garlic in oil. Add sirloin and lightly brown in oil for about 8–10 minutes. Mix tomatoes, tomato sauce, beer, coffee, tomato paste, beef broth, brown sugar, chili powder, cumin, cocoa powder, oregano, cayenne pepper, salt, and black pepper. Reduce heat to low and simmer for about 1½ hours. Stir in jalapeños and simmer for another 30 minutes. Authentic chili should not be thick. Serves 2 cowboys or about 6 tender-foot sissies.

A Cowboy Cookin' Every Night

Peggy's Chili

1 pound ground round
1 medium piece salt pork
1 green pepper, cut in small
  pieces
1 clove garlic, minced
1 small onion, chopped

1 (14½-ounce) can crushed
  tomatoes with juice
3 (15-ounce) cans chili beans
Cumin to taste
Salt and pepper to taste

In frying pan, brown meat with salt pork, green peppers, garlic and onion. Add tomatoes with juice, beans, cumin, salt and pepper to taste. Simmer for ½ hour or more, until thickened.

Our Daily Bread

Chili Con Carne

1½ cups red chili beans, or
  2½ cups kidney beans
1 large onion, diced
1 green pepper, chopped
1½ pounds ground round
2 tablespoons fat (optional)
1 (27- to 29-ounce) can whole
  tomatoes

1 teaspoon salt
⅛ teaspoon paprika
⅛ teaspoon cayenne
3 whole cloves
1 bay leaf
4 teaspoons chili powder

Soak chili beans overnight. Cook in salted water until tender (or use canned beans). Brown onion, green pepper, and meat in hot fat. Add tomatoes and seasonings. Simmer 2 hours, covered. Add beans; heat thoroughly. Serves 6.

Timbreline's Cookbook

Choice Chili with Venison

½ pound dry pinto beans
4 cups chopped tomatoes
1 cup chopped green bell
  peppers
2 tablespoons olive oil
2 yellow onions, chopped
2 cloves garlic, minced
½ cup chopped parsley

½ cup butter
2 pounds ground venison
1 pound ground pork
6 tablespoons chili powder
1 teaspoon salt
1 teaspoon black pepper
½ teaspoon cumin
½ teaspoon oregano

Rinse beans, checking for and removing stones. Soak beans in water to cover overnight.

Drain beans, cover with cold water and simmer until tender, about 1 hour. Add tomatoes; simmer 5 minutes. Sauté green peppers in oil until tender. Add onions and cook until tender, stirring often. Add garlic and parsley. In separate skillet, melt butter and add venison and pork. Cook 15 minutes, stirring often, until crumbly and brown. Add meat to onion mixture and stir in chili powder. Cook 10 minutes. Add meat mixture to beans along with salt, pepper, cumin, and oregano. Simmer, covered, for 1 hour. Remove cover and simmer 30 minutes. Serves 8–10.

Wild Man Gourmet

Doc's Secret Remedy

This prescription is good for what ails ya! It is known to cure lumbago, mange, dry rot, blind staggers, and a bad hangover. As a precaution for those stomach burners, keep something to prevent acid reflux handy.

3 pounds cubed or coarsely
  ground sirloin or tri-top
6 ounces sausage (Italian,
  spicy, or otherwise)
2 (14½- ounce) cans beef
  broth, divided
1 (8-ounce) can tomato sauce
1 (6-ounce) can Snap-E-Tom
  tomato juice

11 tablespoons chili powder,
  divided
1 teaspoon garlic powder
1 tablespoon onion powder
1 teaspoon cumin
2 teaspoons Tabasco, divided
Salt to taste

Sauté beef. Fry sausage until done and drain well. Place beef, sausage, and ½ can beef broth in chili pot and bring to a slow simmer. Add tomato sauce, tomato juice, 6 tablespoons chili powder, garlic powder, onion powder, and 1 teaspoon Tabasco sauce. Simmer slowly for about an hour and 30 minutes or until meat is tender. Add remaining broth and chili powder, cumin, and remaining teaspoon Tabasco sauce. Simmer for 30 minutes. Salt to taste. This will serve 6–8 hungry interns.

The Great Nevada Food Festival Cookbook

Parts of the rest of the nation called for the recension of Nevada's statehood when gambling was legalized in Nevada in 1931 in order to stimulate economic growth during the Great Depression. But that was not the first time people called for a recall of Nevada's statehood. It first happened in the 1890s, when the state allowed prizefighting for money, which was against the law in every other state.

Basque Stew

1 pound oxtails	2 tablespoons flour
2 pounds beef stew meat	2 quarts water
Oil for braising	½ head white cabbage, in
2 medium carrots, sliced	chunks
1 medium onion, sliced	3 zucchini, sliced
2 stalks celery, chopped	Salt and pepper to taste

Preheat oven to 450°. Cut oxtails at the joints. Place in oven roasting pan with beef stew meat and a little oil. Place pan in oven and brown meat, stirring often. It will cook fast. When meat has browned, remove and turn off oven. Add carrots, onion, and celery to pan and return to hot oven for about 10 minutes to allow the vegetables to brown slightly. Remove from oven.

Stir in flour. Add water to pan and simmer on top of stove, covered for about 2 hours or until oxtail joints and meat are tender. Add cabbage and zucchini. Check for seasoning and add salt and pepper if necessary. Cook another 20–25 minutes or until done. Serve with side dishes of carrots, potatoes, and peas. Yields 8 servings.

Easy Cookin' in Nevada

Salads

There's no place on earth like the Las Vegas Strip. At night, The Strip comes alive with miles of colored neon and millions of dancing, pulsating lights—giving it the distinction of being just as scenic at night as it is by day. It is a never-in-the-dark neon city!

Juanita's Green Salad

2 large cloves garlic, coarsely
  chopped
1½ tablespoons olive oil
¼ teaspoon salt

1 tablespoon wine vinegar
1 head romaine or butter
  lettuce
1 ripe avocado, mashed

Place garlic in glass or wooden bowl (do not use metal or plastic) and mash against bottom and sides of bowl with your thumb (or a wooden spoon). Remove garlic. Place olive oil and salt in bottom of bowl and mix with fingers till salt is almost dissolved. Add wine vinegar. Continue to mix till salt is dissolved. Tear lettuce into bite-size pieces, and add to mixture in bowl. Adjust seasoning as needed. Add mashed avocado and mix well. Yields 6 servings.

Chorizos in an Iron Skillet

Caesar Salad

Large head romaine
1 egg
½ tube anchovy paste
3 cloves garlic, crushed
1 splash Worcestershire sauce
1 splash Tabasco
1 heaping tablespoon Dijon
  mustard

1 cup olive oil
1 splash lemon juice
1 splash wine vinegar
1 cup freshly grated Parmesan
  cheese
½ cup toasted croutons

Wash lettuce and tear in bite-size pieces. Boil egg for 30 seconds and cool immediately with cold water. Mix together anchovy paste, crushed garlic, Worcestershire sauce, Tabasco, mustard, and egg. Whisk well. Add olive oil to mixture along with lemon juice and wine vinegar. Blend well. Toss salad with dressing right before you are ready to eat, adding the grated cheese and croutons last.

The Fruit of the Spirit

Spinach Salad
with Black Pepper Dressing

BLACK PEPPER DRESSING:

⅓ cup low-fat mayonnaise
2 tablespoons honey
1 tablespoon rice or white
  wine vinegar
½ teaspoon freshly ground
  black pepper

¼ teaspoon garlic powder
¼ teaspoon salt
1 tablespoon water

Whisk ingredients together. Set aside.

SALAD:

¾ pound fresh spinach
2 tomatoes, cut in thin wedges
2 avocados, cubed
¼ pound mushrooms, thinly
  sliced

2 hard-boiled eggs, diced
3 thin slices red onion
¼ cup bacon bits
1 cup croutons

Wash spinach in cold water to remove dirt, and dry in a salad spinner. Discard stems; tear spinach leaves into bite-size pieces. Place in large bowl with other Salad ingredients except croutons.

Keep Salad, croutons, and Dressing separate until serving time. At serving time, toss Salad and croutons with Dressing.

Lake Tahoe Cooks!

The Air Force Thunderbirds call Nellis Air Force Base (outside of Las Vegas) home, and the Fallon Naval Air Station is the new home of the Top Gun Competition. The Air Force, Army, Coast Guard, Marines, and Navy contribute to the 70,000 plus members temporarily and permanently stationed in Nevada.

Greek Salad

2 medium heads romaine
  lettuce, chopped
2 tomatoes, peeled and sliced
  in quarters
20–25 ripe kalamata olives,
  pitted
¼ cup sliced green onions
¼ cup sliced red onion
¼ cup sliced cucumber
⅔ cup olive oil
⅓ cup balsamic vinegar
½ teaspoon salt
¼ teaspoon dried oregano
¼ teaspoon pepper
3 ounces feta cheese, cubed

Toss greens in a large bowl. Add tomatoes, olives, onions (both green and red) and cucumbers. In a jar, add olive oil, vinegar, salt, oregano, and pepper. Cover; shake well. Pour over salad. Top with feta cheese. Serves 12.

Family and Friends Favorites

India Slaw Salad

1 small head cabbage
1 cup chunk pineapple,
  drained
1 (2-ounce) jar diced pimento,
  drained
1 cup golden raisins
1 (11-ounce) can Mandarin
  oranges, drained
⅔ cup sliced pitted black
  olives, drained
1 cup honey roasted peanuts

Chop cabbage medium-fine, put in colander, and rinse. Drain well. Cut pineapple chunks in half. Mix all ingredients together, except nuts.

DRESSING:

½ cup mayonnaise
1 tablespoon dill weed
1½ teaspoons curry
½ teaspoon ginger
1 tablespoon sugar
1 tablespoon vinegar
1 teaspoon dry mustard
1 tablespoon mustard

Mix ingredients well and pour over salad. Mix well. Add nuts to salad just before serving. Serves 4–6.

Timbreline's Cookbook

Avocado Salad

½ cup olive oil or vegetable oil
¼ cup red wine vinegar
1 clove garlic, crushed
1 teaspoon salt
¼ teaspoon pepper
¼ teaspoon dry mustard
3 avocados
1 onion, sliced
Lettuce leaves
Pimento strips for garnish

Shake oil, vinegar, garlic, salt, pepper, and mustard in covered jar. Cut avocados lengthwise in half and remove pits and peel. Arrange avocado halves and onion on lettuce leaves. Pour dressing over avocados. Garnish with pimento strips. Makes 6 servings.

NSHSRA High School Rodeo Cookbook

Spicy Avocado Salad

1 teaspoon salt
1 clove garlic, minced
1 teaspoon Worcestershire sauce
½ teaspoon Tabasco sauce
Juice of ⅓ lemon
3 tablespoons olive oil
3 ripe tomatoes, diced
2 ripe avocados, diced
Freshly ground pepper to taste
1 green chile, seeded, minced
3 tablespoons minced cilantro
3 tablespoons (heaping) diced Monterey Jack cheese
3 tablespoons (heaping) crumbled crisp-fried bacon
2 tablespoons (heaping) minced onion
½ green bell pepper, diced

Mash salt and garlic in bowl with fork until smooth paste forms. Whisk in Worcestershire sauce, Tabasco sauce, lemon juice, and olive oil until well blended. Pour over mixture of tomatoes, avocados, pepper, green chile, cilantro, cheese, bacon, onion, and green pepper in bowl; mix well. Marinate in refrigerator for 30 minutes. Serve on bed of mixed salad greens. Yields 4 servings.

Approximately per serving: Cal 306; Prot 5g; Carbo 15g; Fiber 12g; Total Fat 28g; 76% Calories from Fat; Chol 6mg; Sod 631mg.

Best Bets

Pat's Cauliflower Salad

1 head cauliflower, cut into
  bite-size pieces
½ cup fried and crumbled
  bacon
½ cup shredded Cheddar
  cheese
4 green onions, chopped
2 teaspoons Lawry's Seasoned
  Salt

¼ cup vinegar
1 teaspoon black pepper
2 tablespoons sugar
1 cup mayonnaise
1 cup sour cream
2 tablespoons milk

Place cauliflower, crumbled bacon, cheese, and onions in a large
bowl. Mix together in another bowl the seasoned salt, vinegar,
pepper, sugar, mayonnaise, sour cream, and milk. Pour just
enough of the sauce over the cauliflower mixture to moisten
slightly. Keep chilled.

Kitchen Chatter

In the Hopi religion, everything in the world
has two forms, the visible object and the spirit
form. An example of the spirit form is the
steam rising above hot food, which departs into the
clouds without changing the form of the food.
Kachina dolls are reincarnations of the spirit form
returned from the clouds. Usually made from the
roots of the cottonwood tree, Kachina dolls were
important to the Hopi tribe because they were a part
of their religion.

Elegant Rosemary Green Bean and Potato Salad

3 pounds red boiling potatoes
⅓ cup olive oil
1 red onion, thinly sliced
2 pounds fresh green beans, washed, trimmed, and cut

24 kalamata olives, pitted, halved
Rosemary sprigs for garnish

Preheat oven to 425°. Wash potatoes and let dry on paper towels. Do not peel. Cut potatoes into 1-inch wedges. Toss potatoes in oil to coat. Place in a roasting pan and roast in oven for about 30 minutes until tender. Let potatoes cool.

Soak onion slices in ice water for 5 minutes. Drain on paper towels. Cook green beans in boiling water for about 5 minutes until medium tender. Drain. Rinse green beans under cold water and pat dry. Combine potatoes, onion, green beans, and olives. Pour Dressing over vegetables and toss gently. Serve warm or at room temperature garnished with rosemary sprigs. Serves 8.

DRESSING:
¼ cup red wine vinegar
1 tablespoon fresh rosemary leaves

3 garlic cloves
¼ teaspoon salt
½ cup olive oil

In a food processor, blend together vinegar, rosemary leaves, garlic, and salt. With the motor running, add oil in a stream and blend until emulsified.

All American Meals Cookbook

Saucy Cowgirl's
Deviled Red Potato Salad

3 pounds unpeeled red
  potatoes
4 hard-boiled eggs
1½ cups mayonnaise
2 tablespoons balsamic vinegar
1 teaspoon chili powder
½ teaspoon salt

¼ teaspoon ground black
  pepper
¼ teaspoon cayenne pepper
1 cup sliced celery
1 cup diced scallions
2 jalapeño peppers, diced

Cook potatoes until tender but firm. Drain, cool and cut into cubes. Cool, peel, and dice hard-boiled eggs. In a bowl, whisk together mayonnaise, vinegar, chili powder, salt, black pepper, and cayenne pepper. Pour mixture over potatoes and toss. Add eggs, celery, scallions, and jalapeños and toss. Cover and chill at least 2 hours before serving. Serve with cold beer. Serves 3 chili-head wranglers or 6 sissy greenhorns.

Authentic Cowboy Cookery Then & Now

Mom's Potato Salad

10 potatoes, boiled and cooled
  (day ahead), cubed
½ onion, sliced
3 hard-boiled eggs, sliced
2 stalks celery, sliced in small
  pieces
½ pound bacon, chopped
  and fried until crisp
  (reserve grease)

1 cup lite regular mayonnaise
  or Miracle Whip
½ cup Durkee dressing
1 egg
¼ cup sugar
2 tablespoons bacon grease

Slice cooled potatoes. In large bowl, gently combine potatoes, onion slices, eggs, celery, and bacon. In a bowl, mix mayonnaise, Durkee dressing, egg, sugar, and bacon grease. Pour over salad and refrigerate for several hours. Serves 6.

Recipes from Sunset Garden Club

German Potato Salad

4 pounds cooked salad
  potatoes
6 slices bacon, diced
½ cup bacon drippings
½ cup sugar
3 tablespoons flour

2 teaspoon salt
¼ teaspoon pepper
1 cup cider vinegar
1 cup water
4 green onions, sliced

Peel and cut cooked potatoes in thin slices. Fry bacon at 330° until golden brown. Remove from drippings. Blend sugar, flour, salt, and pepper. Stir into ½ cup bacon drippings to make smooth paste. Add vinegar and water. Boil 2–3 minutes. Stir constantly. Combine sauce, potatoes, and onions in skillet and turn skillet to off. Let stand at room temperature 3–4 hours. Sprinkle with crisp bacon just before serving. Makes 10–12 servings.

Traditional Treasures

Slimscrumptious
Chinese Chicken Salad

2 chicken breasts, skinned
  and boned
2 slices fresh ginger
1½ cups water or chicken
  broth
3 cups shredded romaine
  lettuce
3 cups shredded cabbage
1 cup bean sprouts
½ cup chopped cucumber

½ cup pea pods, stringed
  and cut into strips
¼ cup chopped celery
¼ cup chopped green onion
½ cup shredded carrot
½ of 1 package ramen
  noodles, broken up

1 tablespoon shredded
  beni shoga (pickled ginger)

Place chicken breasts in skillet with fresh ginger pieces and water or chicken broth. Bring to a boil. Reduce heat to low, simmer and cook partially covered for 10–15 minutes or just until chicken is done. Drain chicken. Cool and cut into very thin slices. Arrange lettuce on 3 dinner plates. Then arrange cabbage, chicken, and vegetables over salad. Sprinkle uncooked ramen noodles over top.

DRESSING:
3 tablespoons rice or regular
  vinegar
¼ cup water
1 tablespoon sesame oil

1 tablespoon soy sauce
2 teaspoons sugar
⅛ teaspoon salt

Shake Dressing ingredients together in a covered jar, pour over salad and toss very well. Serve at once.

Bless This Food

Mark Twain once called Lake Tahoe "the fairest picture the whole earth affords." His older brother, Orion Clemens served as secretary of the Nevada Territory for more than three years and designed the first territorial seal in 1861.

Mandarin Chicken Salad

3 cups chopped, cooked
  chicken
1 tablespoon minced onion
1 teaspoon salt
2 tablespoons lemon juice
1 cup chopped celery
1 cup seedless grapes

1/3 cup mayonnaise
1 (11-ounce) can Mandarin
  oranges, drained
1/2 cup toasted almonds
Lettuce leaves
Orange sections, almonds, and
  ripe olives for garnish

Combine chicken, onion, salt, lemon juice, and celery, and refrigerate several hours. Before serving, mix with other ingredients and serve on lettuce leaves. Garnish with orange sections, almonds, and ripe olives.

Tasteful Treasures

Baked Chicken Salad

2 cups chopped celery
1 small onion, chopped
1 tablespoons butter
4 cups chopped cooked
  chicken (about 5–6 breasts)
3/4 cup mayonnaise
4 hard-boiled eggs, chopped

1 teaspoon salt
2 tablespoons lemon juice
1 cup crushed potato chips
2/3 cup grated cheese
1/3 cup chopped slivered
  almonds

Sauté celery and onion in butter until soft. Mix with chicken, mayonnaise, eggs, salt, and lemon juice. Put into greased 9x13-inch pan. Combine potato chips, cheese, and almonds and sprinkle on top. Bake, uncovered, in 350° oven for 35–40 minutes.

The Fruit of the Spirit

Chicken Salad Cassidy

David Cassidy is a visible force in Las Vegas, both in the showrooms and in the community. His high-energy performances have been witnessed by many in EFX at the MGM Grand and At the Copa at the Rio. He has also served as Grand Marshal in the Henderson Industrial Days Parade. He organized a celebrity charity golf tournament to give back to the community that he and his family call home—Las Vegas.

2 tablespoons Dijon mustard
⅓ cup tamari
Splash of balsamic vinegar
2 whole chicken breasts,
   cut into small strips
1 teaspoon butter
1 teaspoon olive oil
Salt to taste
1–2 heads romaine lettuce
Assorted mixed greens
1 green onion, chopped

Raisins (optional)
Sunflower seed kernels
   (optional)
Sliced beets (optional)
1 hard-cooked egg, sliced
   (optional)
Equal parts olive oil, Dijon
   mustard, and tarragon
   vinegar
½ teaspoon (or less) salt

Mix mustard, tamari, and balsamic vinegar in a medium bowl. Add chicken strips and stir to coat. Let marinate for 15 minutes. Melt butter with 1 teaspoon olive oil in a skillet. Season with salt to taste. Heat until hot and add the chicken and marinade mixture. Cook until chicken is browned and cooked through. Set aside and keep warm.

Combine the romaine lettuce, mixed greens, green onion, raisins, and sunflower seeds. Top with sliced beets and sliced egg. Cover with chicken and pan juices. Whisk the olive oil, mustard, tarragon vinegar, and ½ teaspoon salt in a small bowl until creamy. Pour over salad and toss to coat. Yields 2–4 servings.

Las Vegas Glitter to Gourmet

Creamy Chicken Salad

DRESSING:

1 medium orange
1/3 cup plain low-fat yogurt

1 teaspoon honey
1/2 teaspoon poppy seed

Finely shred peel from orange. Peel and section orange over the bowl to catch juices (I use scissors to cut up the sections). Set orange sections aside. Reserve 1 teaspoon juice. Mix together with yogurt, honey, and poppy seed; cover and chill.

SALAD:

1 cup cubed cooked chicken
 or turkey
1/2 cup halved seedless grapes

1/4 cup chopped pecans
Thinly sliced celery
Torn fresh spinach

Toss together the orange sections, chicken, grapes, pecans, and celery. Spoon onto spinach-lined plates. Spoon Dressing on top. Chill remaining Dressing. This will serve 2 people.

CASA Cooks

Groom Lake, a dry lake bed north of Las Vegas, known worldwide to some as the infamous Area 51, is an installation once so secret, its existence was denied by the government agencies and contractors that had connections there. By late 1955, the facility had been completed for flight testing of Lockheed's U-2 spyplane. Since that time, Area 51 has hosted flight testing of the aforementioned Lockheed U-2, the SR-71 Blackbird, the F-117 stealth fighter, Northrop's B-2 stealth bomber, and the mysterious Aurora Project. The Groom Lake facility has been known by many names since its construction. In June 1958, it was officially designated Area 51 by the Atomic Energy Commission (AEC). The adjacent AEC proving grounds became known as the Nevada Test Site and divided into numbered areas.

American Southwest Corn Salad

⅓ cup fresh lime juice
½ cup olive oil
2 garlic cloves, minced
1 teaspoon salt
⅛ teaspoon ground cayenne
  pepper
2 (15-ounce) cans black beans,
  rinsed and drained
2 (15-ounce) cans yellow corn,
  rinsed and drained

1 avocado, pitted, peeled, and
  diced
1 red bell pepper, diced
2 ripe tomatoes, chopped
¾ cup diced red onion
½ cup chopped fresh cilantro
  leaves

Whisk together lime juice, olive oil, garlic, salt, and cayenne pepper. In a bowl, combine beans, corn, avocado, bell pepper, tomatoes, onion, and cilantro. Pour dressing over salad and toss to coat. Chill. Serves 6.

All American Meals Cookbook

Black Bean and Corn Salad

This is even better the next day. Very good with grilled chicken or fish.

2 cans black beans, rinsed and
  drained
2 cups fresh corn cut off cob
  (frozen can be substituted)
1 small red pepper, diced

½ cup diced purple onion
6 green onions with tops,
  chopped
2 medium tomatoes, chopped
½ cup chopped fresh cilantro

DRESSING:
½ cup fresh-squeezed lime
  juice
⅛ teaspoon cayenne pepper
2 teaspoons ground cumin
1 teaspoon sugar

1 tablespoon Dijon mustard
½ cup olive oil
¼ cup rice vinegar
Salt and pepper to taste

Whisk Dressing ingredients together, pour over salad, and refrigerate before serving.

God, That's Good!

Spicy Southwestern Taco Salad

⅔ cup chopped yellow onion
1 pound boneless, skinless
   chicken breast, cut into
   1-inch cubes
1 cup black beans, drained
¾ teaspoon turmeric
¼ teaspoon cayenne pepper

¼ teaspoon black pepper
½ cup diced red bell pepper
4 scallions, diced, divided
4 cups shredded iceberg lettuce
4 tablespoons no-oil salsa
4 tablespoons nonfat sour
   cream

Spray a nonstick skillet with nonfat cooking spray. Sauté onion 5–7 minutes or until golden. Add chicken and sauté 3–4 minutes or until chicken is browned. Stir in black beans, turmeric, cayenne, and pepper, and sauté 3–4 minutes. Reduce heat to medium low. Stir in half the scallions. Sauté 2–3 minutes until scallions are softened. Serve hot taco salad over lettuce. Top with remaining scallions, salsa, and sour cream.

Nutritional analysis per serving: Calories 306; Protein 39g; Fat 9g; Carbohydrates 16g.

The Protein Edge

Mexican Treat

A treat for young folk—taco-flavored salad.

1 pound lean ground beef
1 (¼-ounce) package dry
  taco mix
½ cup water
⅔ cup vegetable oil
¼ cup vinegar
3 ounces dry Italian seasonings
  salad dressing mix
1 small onion, chopped

1 small green pepper, chopped
1 (15-ounce) can chili beans,
  meatless
1 head lettuce, chopped
1 (3-ounce) package taco-
  flavored corn chips, crushed
1 cup grated Monterey Jack
  cheese
1 ripe avocado, chopped

The night before, sauté the beef; add taco mix and water; simmer until dry. Drain off any grease. Combine oil, vinegar, and seasonings in a glass jar; shake well. Place meat in a glass bowl; add salad dressing, onion, green pepper, and beans. Stir and cover. Marinate overnight.

Just before serving time, add chopped lettuce, corn chips, cheese, and avocado. Toss and serve. Yields 6 generous servings.

Easy Cookin' in Nevada

Tarragon Beefsteak Salad

2 pounds beef sirloin, cut
  ¾–1 inch thick
1 cup salad oil (part olive oil,
  if desired)
⅓ cup red wine vinegar
1 tablespoon tarragon leaves
1 teaspoon salt
¾ teaspoon sugar
½ teaspoon dry mustard
½ teaspoon freshly cracked
  pepper

¼ teaspoon garlic powder
2 large red onions, sliced and
  separated into rings
½ pound fresh mushrooms,
  sliced (optional)
Romaine or other lettuce leaves
½ cup chopped fresh parsley
2 tablespoons capers

Grill sirloin (on BBQ or under broiler) for 3–4 minutes on each side. Cook just to rare. Cool slightly for handling. Using a very sharp knife, carve steak into very thin strips, 2–3 inches long. Combine oil, vinegar, tarragon, salt, sugar, mustard, pepper, and garlic powder in large bowl. Add beef strips, onion rings, and mushrooms, tossing lightly to combine. Cover and refrigerate at least 2 hours or overnight, if desired.

To serve, arrange lettuce leaves on large platter or in salad bowl. Place steak salad on leaves. Sprinkle with parsley and capers.

A Gathering of Recipes

On the average, approximately 230 marriage licenses are issued per day in Las Vegas, which is known as the "Wedding Capital of the World." Greater Las Vegas issues more than 110,000 wedding licenses per year.

Crab-Rice-Cucumber Salad

1 cup crabmeat	2 hard-boiled eggs, chopped
1 teaspoon lemon juice	¾ cup mayonnaise
¾ cup cooked rice	3 lettuce cups
¼ cup diced cucumber	3 stuffed olives for garnish

Flake crabmeat; add lemon juice, rice, cucumbers, and eggs. Mix mayonnaise with the first mixture. Place on lettuce cups and garnish with stuffed olives.

Hoover Dam Cooks, 1933

Casablanca Salad

½ cup plus 1 tablespoon extra virgin olive oil, divided	1½ pounds medium shrimp, shelled and deveined
2½ tablespoons sherry vinegar	¼ cup mint leaves, torn in half
Kosher salt and black pepper to taste	3 tablespoons golden raisins
1 medium onion, finely chopped	¼ teaspoon ground cumin
	1 pound mesclun salad greens

In a small bowl, whisk 7½ tablespoons olive oil with the sherry vinegar. Season with salt and pepper. Heat remaining 1½ tablespoons olive oil in large skillet. Add onion and cook over moderate heat, stirring, until softened and just beginning to brown, about 7 minutes. Add shrimp, mint, raisins, cumin, and a pinch of kosher salt and black pepper. Sauté, stirring, until shrimp are pink, about 7 minutes. In a large bowl, toss the mesclun with dressing and mound on 10 plates. Scatter shrimp over salads and serve. Yields 10 servings.

Never Trust a Skinny Chef...II

Shrimp Tomato Aspic

1 (3-ounce) package lemon
  Jell-O
2 cups tomato juice, heated
Pinch of salt, dash pepper,
  and paprika
1 can deveined shrimp

Juice of 1 lemon
1 tablespoon sweet pickle juice
1 cup sliced ripe olives
½ cup chopped sweet pickles
½ cup chopped celery

Dissolve Jell-O in hot tomato juice. Add seasonings. Add shrimp
and remainder of ingredients. Chill until set. Serves 4–6.

Timbreline's Cookbook

Acini di Pepe Salad

½ cup sugar
1 tablespoon flour
1 cup pineapple juice
¼ teaspoon salt
2 egg yolks
¾ cup acini di pepe pasta
1 can crushed pineapple,
  undrained

1 can Mandarin oranges,
  drained
1 (8-ounce) container Cool
  Whip
½ small package miniature
  marshmallows

One day or several hours ahead of serving, combine sugar, flour,
pineapple juice, salt, and egg yolks in a saucepan and cook until
thick, stirring frequently, but not boiling. If using the
microwave, cook in 2-minute increments, stirring after each
until mixture is thickened. Boil the pasta according to package
instructions. Rinse and cool slightly, then combine with above
mixture and add the crushed pineapple, oranges, Cool Whip,
and marshmallows. Refrigerate overnight or for several hours.

Church Family Recipes

Pearls and Pineapple

2 (20-ounce) cans pineapple
  chunks or tidbits
1 (8-ounce) can crushed
  pineapple
2 (11-ounce) cans Mandarin
  oranges
3 quarts water
1 teaspoon vegetable oil
2 teaspoons salt
1 package acini di pepe

¾ cup sugar
2 tablespoons flour
Salt to taste
3 egg yolks, beaten
1½ teaspoons lemon juice
1 cup miniature marshmallows
¾ cup coconut
8 ounces (or more) whipped
  topping

Drain pineapple chunks and crushed pineapple, reserving 1¾–2 cups juice. Drain 1 can of the oranges. Chill the drained fruit in refrigerator. Bring water, oil, and 2 teaspoons salt to a boil in a large saucepan. Add pasta and cook until tender; rinse, drain, and cool. Mix sugar, flour, and salt to taste in saucepan. Stir in reserved pineapple juice and egg yolks. Cook until thickened and smooth, stirring constantly.

Stir in lemon juice. Cool to room temperature. Combine with pasta in large bowl and mix gently. Chill for 8 hours or longer. Add oranges, pineapple chunks, crushed pineapple, marshmallows, and coconut. Fold in the whipped topping. Yields 12–16 servings.

From Sunrise to Sunset

Though known as "The Silver State," the semiprecious gemstone, Nevada Turquoise, "Jewel of the Desert," is found in many parts of the state. The Virgin Valley Black Opal is found in northern Nevada.

Cranberry Fluff Salad

2 cups chopped fresh
  cranberries
½ cup sugar
3 cups miniature
  marshmallows
1 cup heavy cream

¼ cup mayonnaise
2 cups diced, red apples
½ cup seedless red grapes
½ cup pineapple tidbits,
  drained
½ cup chopped nuts

Combine cranberries and sugar. Mix well. Add marshmallows and refrigerate overnight. Whip cream. Fold mayonnaise into whipped cream. Combine diced apples, grapes, pineapple, and nuts. Fold cranberry and apple mixture into whipped cream. Chill.

Church Family Recipes

Fruit Salad

1 (20-ounce) can chunky
  pineapple, reserve juice
1 (3-ounce) box vanilla
  pudding (not instant)
1 (11-ounce) can Mandarin
  oranges

3 or 4 bananas, sliced
Miniature marshmallows
Chopped nuts (optional)

Drain fruit, reserving 1 cup juice. Mix juice with pudding mix and cook until thick. Cool. Add pineapple chunks and oranges and chill. Before serving, add bananas and marshmallows. Add nuts or other fruit, if desired.

Recipes from the Heart

Zucchini Pickles

5 pounds zucchini, finely
   sliced
2½ pounds onions, thinly
   sliced
1 cup chopped green pepper
1 cup chopped red pepper
¾ cup salt
2 quarts ice cubes

5 cups vinegar
5 cups sugar
2 teaspoons celery seed
1 teaspoon peppercorns
1½ teaspoons turmeric
½ teaspoon whole cloves
2 teaspoons mustard seed

Combine zucchini and onion slices, chopped peppers, and salt. Add ice cubes and cover in large container. Set aside for 3 hours. Drain.

In saucepan, combine vinegar, sugar, celery seed, peppercorns, turmeric, cloves, and mustard seed; heat to boiling. Add drained squash mixture. Reheat just to boiling. Put in jars and seal. Let stand at least 2 weeks.

Timbreline's Cookbook

Vegetables

Virginia City is one of the largest federally designated Historical Districts in America, and is maintained in its original condition. "C" Street, the main business district, is lined with buildings constructed in the late 1800s, now housing specialty shops of all kinds, rather than the boisterous saloons of yesteryear.

Nevada Heat Chili Fries

1 teaspoon chili powder
1 teaspoon cumin powder
1 teaspoon crushed red
  pepper flakes
½ teaspoon salt
6 large baking potatoes,
  scrubbed (about 3 pounds)

Preheat oven to 500°. In a bowl, combine chili powder, cumin powder, crushed red pepper flakes, and salt. Cut potatoes into sticks. Spray a baking sheet and place potatoes in a single layer. Sprinkle with spices. Bake 10 minutes, then turn over potato slices. Bake another 10–15 minutes, until potatoes are browned and fork-tender. Serves 6.

A Cowboy Cookin' Every Night

Twisted Taters

2 teaspoons coarse salt
1 teaspoon cayenne
1 teaspoon paprika
1 teaspoon ground coriander
8 cups vegetable oil
6 medium russet (baking)
  potatoes (about 12 ounces
  total)

In large bowl, stir together salt, cayenne, paprika, and coriander. In a deep frying pan, heat enough oil to cover fries at 325° or use a deep-fryer at 325°. Cut potatoes into ¼-inch thick sticks. Fry potatoes in oil 1½ minutes (potatoes will not be golden), and with a slotted spoon, transfer to paper towels to drain. Heat oil to 350°; return potatoes to oil and fry until golden and crisp, about 5 minutes. Toss fries in spice mixture. Spices may be adjusted to taste. Serve with fried fish dishes.

The Hooked Cook

Silver State Potatoes

2 cups sour cream
1 tablespoon salt
¼ cup milk
¼ cup butter
1 (10¾-ounce) can cream of
  chicken soup
½ cup chopped onion

½ cup grated Cheddar cheese
4 medium potatoes, boiled,
  peeled, and grated, or hash
  browns
1 cup crushed cornflakes
2 tablespoons melted butter

Combine sour cream, salt, milk, butter, soup, onion, and cheese and simmer on low heat until cheese melts. Then add potatoes. Put in 9x13-inch baking dish that has been sprayed with non-stick spray. Combine crushed cornflakes with melted butter and sprinkle on top. Bake in 350° oven for 35–45 minutes.

Our Daily Bread

Parisian Style Potatoes

1 tablespoon plus 1 teaspoon
  olive oil, divided
1 pound potatoes, boiled,
  peeled and sliced
½ teaspoon salt

¼ teaspoon dried marjoram
¼ teaspoon black pepper
1 cup sliced red onion
2 garlic cloves, diced
¼ cup chicken broth

Heat 1 tablespoon oil in a large skillet and add potatoes. Season with salt, marjoram, and pepper, and cook 10 minutes turning as they brown. In a separate skillet, heat remaining oil and add onion. Sauté 3–4 minutes; add garlic, and sauté 2 minutes longer. Add broth and cook 5–7 minutes, until onions are softened. Add onions to potatoes and toss together. Serve hot. Makes 4 servings.

Nutritional values: One serving equals ½ cup: Calories 143; Protein 3g; Fat 3g; Carbohydrates 23g; Sodium 243mg; Cholesterol 0mg.

Easy Gourmet for Diabetics

Twice-Baked Parmesan-Chive Potatoes

5 pounds russet potatoes
1 cup milk
½ cup butter
2 eggs, beaten
¾ cup grated Parmesan
  cheese, divided

½ cup snipped fresh chives
½ teaspoon salt
½ teaspoon pepper
⅛ teaspoon ground nutmeg
Paprika to taste

Pierce potatoes several times with fork. Place on baking sheet. Bake at 400° for 50–60 minutes or until tender; cool for 15 minutes. Cut into halves lengthwise. Scoop out centers into mixer bowl, leaving ¼-inch shells; set 18 shells aside. Heat milk and butter in saucepan until butter is melted. Pour over potatoes and beat with electric mixer until smooth. Add eggs, ½ cup Parmesan cheese, chives, salt, pepper, and nutmeg. Whip until smooth. Spoon mixture into reserved shells. Sprinkle with remaining Parmesan cheese and paprika. Place on baking sheet. Bake at 350° for 30 minutes or until puffed and lightly browned. Yields 18 servings.

Approximately per serving: Cal 215; Prot 6g; Carbo 33g; Fiber 3g; Total Fat 7g; 30% Calories from Fat; Chol 42mg; Sod 188mg.

Best Bets

The California gold rush of 1849 brought prospectors from the East. As they passed through Nevada's Carson Valley en route to California, some of them panned for gold. Few found anything except a heavy, bluish sand that they found to be a nuisance. Someone finally had the sand assayed in 1859 and found that it was silver sulfide, mixed with gold, and worth about $4,000 a ton. News spread rapidly. During the peak of what was termed the Comstock Lode, Virginia City was a boisterous town with about 25,000 residents. It now has only about 800.

That Old Goat's Cheesy Potato Cakes

1 cup toasted sourdough
  bread crumbs
1 pound russet potatoes,
  shredded
8 ounces goat cheese,
  crumbled

1 cup diced yellow onions
1/4 cup minced fresh chives
6 garlic cloves, minced
1 cup canola oil
Salt to taste

Toast sourdough bread and crumble into fine crumbs. Shred potatoes with a food processor. Combine bread crumbs, potatoes with potato juices, goat cheese, onions, chives, and garlic. Form into 1/4-inch thick cakes. Heat enough oil to cover bottom of frying pan. Place a few potato cakes at a time in hot oil and fry until brown. Salt to taste. Serves 6–8.

The Hooked Cook

Virginia City Creamy Goat Cheese Mashed Potatoes

3 pounds russet potatoes,
  peeled, washed, and
  quartered
3/4 stick unsalted butter,
  softened

1 1/2 cups heavy cream
1/2 cup crumbled goat cheese
1/2 teaspoon salt
1/2 teaspoon black pepper

Bring a large pot of salted water to a boil. Add potatoes to water and return to boil. Cook potatoes until tender, about 15–20 minutes. Drain in a colander. Mash potatoes in a large bowl with a potato masher. Add butter and blend. Add 1 cup cream and blend into potatoes thoroughly. Blend in goat cheese, salt, pepper, and more cream, if necessary, to achieve desired consistency. Serves 8.

A Cowboy Cookin' Every Night

Bacon-Cheese Mashed Potatoes

4 baking potatoes (russet), approximately 3 pounds, peeled, cut into 1-inch pieces
1¾ teaspoons salt, divided
½ cup heavy cream
4 tablespoons butter
¼ teaspoon ground black pepper

8 slices bacon, cooked crisp and crumbled
½ pound sharp Cheddar, grated
¼ cup sour cream
¼ cup chopped fresh chives
Freshly ground black pepper

Place the potatoes and 1 teaspoon salt in a heavy 4-quart saucepan and cover with water by 1 inch. Bring to a boil. Reduce heat to a simmer and cook until the potatoes are fork-tender, about 20 minutes. Drain in a colander and return to the cooking pot. Add cream, butter, remaining ¾ teaspoon salt, and black pepper. Place the pan over medium-low heat and mash with a potato masher to incorporate the ingredients and achieve a light texture, about 4–5 minutes. Add bacon, grated cheese, sour cream, and chopped chives, and stir until thoroughly combined. Season to taste. Serve immediately. Yields 4–6 servings.

CASA Cooks

Garlic Cream Cheese Mashed Potatoes

2 pounds unpeeled new
potatoes, cut into 1-inch
cubes
1¾ teaspoons salt, divided
½ cup (1 stick) butter, cut
into pieces
4 ounces cream cheese, cut
into pieces, softened
5 (or more) garlic cloves,
minced

½ cup finely chopped fresh
parsley
¼ cup grated Parmesan or
Romano cheese
¼–½ teaspoon white pepper
2 ounces Monterey Jack cheese,
shredded

Place potatoes in a saucepan. Add 1 teaspoon salt and enough
water to cover the potatoes by 3 inches. Bring to a boil and boil
until tender. Drain and place in a large bowl. Mash by hand for
home-style potatoes or use an electric mixer for smoother potatoes.

Add butter, cream cheese, garlic, parsley, Parmesan cheese,
remaining ¾ teaspoon salt, and white pepper to the potatoes
and mix well. Spoon potatoes into a greased 12-inch baking
dish. Top with Monterey Jack cheese. Bake at 450° for 10 minutes or until top is lightly browned. Yields 10–12 servings.

Variation: Use minced chives or green onions in place of parsley. Add
¼ cup sautéed onion.

Las Vegas Glitter to Gourmet

Nevada's "Lost City," officially known as Pueblo Grande de Nevada, is a series
of Anasazi Indian ruins situated along the Muddy and Virgin River Valleys in
southern Nevada. The site area is located at the northern end of man-made
Lake Mead and continues up both valleys for a distance of approximately 30 miles.

Hoppin' John Squares

½ cup chopped green bell
  pepper
1 tablespoon finely chopped
  onion
2 tablespoons butter
2 tablespoons flour
¾ teaspoon chili powder
¼ teaspoon ground cumin

1¼ cups milk
1 cup shredded Cheddar
  cheese, divided
1 (16-ounce) can black-eyed
  peas, drained
1 cup cooked brown rice
¾ cup diced lean cooked ham
2 large eggs, beaten

Cook pepper and onion in butter till tender; stir in next 3 ingredients. Stir in milk; cook and stir until bubbly. Remove from heat. Stir in ¾ cup of the cheese and remaining ingredients. Turn into a well-greased 8x8x2-inch baking pan. Bake in 350° oven for 30 minutes or till set. Top with remaining cheese. Let stand 5 minutes. Cut into squares to serve. Yields 6 servings.

Still Cookin' After 70 Years

Grandma's Beans

1 onion, chopped
2 (16-ounce) can kidney beans,
  drained
2 (16-ounce) cans lima beans,
  drained
2 (16-ounce) cans pork and
  beans
8 ounces bacon, crisp-fried,
  crumbled

1 cup packed brown sugar
1 cup ketchup
1 tablespoon prepared mustard
1½ teaspoons Tabasco sauce
1 teaspoon Worcestershire
  sauce
2 teaspoons garlic juice

Sauté onion in a nonstick skillet until tender. Combine with kidney beans, lima beans, pork and beans, and bacon in a large bowl and mix gently. Combine brown sugar, ketchup, mustard, Tabasco sauce, Worcestershire sauce, and garlic juice in a bowl and mix well. Add to the bean mixture and mix gently. Spoon into a large baking dish. Bake at 300° for 2 hours. Yields 12–15 servings.

From Sunrise to Sunset

Ezkualdun Itarrak

(Basque Beans)

1 pound dried pinto beans
½ pound bacon, cut into
  1-inch lengths
½ pound chorizo sausage,
  sliced
1 large green pepper, diced
1 large onion, diced
5 cloves garlic, finely chopped
2 teaspoons Worcestershire
  sauce

1 teaspoon crushed red pepper
  (can substitute chili powder)
1 bay leaf
1 teaspoon thyme
½ teaspoon rosemary
1 tablespoon chopped parsley
2 teaspoons rock salt, or to
  taste

Clean and rinse beans. Put beans in large stockpot with enough water to cover. Bring to a boil; reduce heat to simmer. As beans simmer, fry bacon and sausage over medium heat until sausage is cooked through. Add green pepper, onion, and garlic; cook until vegetables are soft. Add Worcestershire sauce, crushed red pepper (or chili powder), bay leaf, thyme, rosemary, and parsley. Mix thoroughly. Add to beans; cover and continue simmering until beans are soft (you might have to add about a cup of water). Add salt; remove bay leaf. Serves 4.

Home Cooking

Low Fat Stir-Fried Veggies

½ head red cabbage
1 large onion
½ red or orange bell pepper
1 crown fresh broccoli
1 tablespoon canola oil
Mrs. Dash Spicy Seasoning to
    taste

Garlic powder to taste
Black pepper to taste
2 tablespoons Tamarind sauce
½ pound bean sprouts

Cut all vegetables into bite-size pieces except the bean sprouts. Heat oil in a large skillet or wok. Put in cabbage and onions and cook on medium heat until they are done but cabbage is still crunchy. Add seasonings and then add broccoli. Cook for another few minutes. Add bean sprouts and cook for another 2 minutes, stirring occasionally to be sure it does not stick. Serve and enjoy.

Variation: You may stir-fry a seasoned chicken breast or beef strips separately and add at the end.

The Best of Down-Home Cooking

Sweet and Sour Stuffed Cabbage

3 heads cabbage
3 pounds ground beef
3 eggs
Minced onion
Salt and pepper
Garlic powder
Bread crumbs
1 large can crushed tomatoes

¾ large bottle ketchup
2 cans tomato mushroom sauce
½ box brown sugar
5 pieces sour salt (citric acid
    crystals)
½ cup lemon juice
Garlic powder

Boil cabbage until leaves are soft. Mix beef, eggs, onion, seasonings, and bread crumbs. Place some beef mixture on a cabbage leaf; roll up and tuck in ends. Combine other ingredients in casserole dish. Add rolled cabbage leaves and bake, uncovered, at 350° for 3–3½ hours. Enjoy.

Traditional Treasures

Rome by Candlelight
Sausage and Peppers

5 ounces Italian turkey sausage, 90% fat-free, cut into ¼-inch slices
1 cup julienne cut red bell pepper
1 cup julienne cut green bell pepper
1 cup julienne cut yellow bell pepper
½ cup sliced yellow onion
¼ cup chicken broth
4 garlic cloves, minced
¼ teaspoon red pepper flakes
¼ teaspoon dried oregano

Spray a skillet with nonfat cooking spray and cook sausage, stirring frequently to break up and until no longer pink. Add bell peppers, onion, broth, garlic, pepper flakes, and oregano. Sauté, stirring frequently, 5–8 minutes, until liquid has reduced and peppers and onion are tender. Makes 4 servings.

Nutritional values: One serving equals ½ cup: Calories 92; Protein 7g; Fat 4g; Carbohydrates 7g; Sodium 256mg; Cholesterol 29mg.

Easy Gourmet for Diabetics

Portobello Mushrooms with Ratatouille and Spinach

1 cup chopped onion
5 teaspoons minced garlic, divided
2 tablespoons extra virgin olive oil, divided
1 (1-pound) eggplant, trimmed, peeled, cut into ½-inch pieces
2 cups ½-inch diced zucchini pieces
1 cup ½-inch diced red bell pepper pieces
2 tablespoons tomato paste
2 teaspoons red wine vinegar
1 teaspoon chopped fresh thyme
Pinch of cayenne pepper
Salt and black pepper to taste
4 (5-inch-diameter) portobello mushrooms, stems removed
¼ cup chopped flat-leaf parsley
1 (10-ounce) package ready-to-use spinach leaves

Preheat oven to 350°. Mix onion, 3 teaspoons garlic, and 1 tablespoon oil in large oven-proof pot. Cover; cook over medium-low heat until onion is very tender, stirring often, about 15 minutes. Stir in eggplant; cover and cook 10 minutes, stirring often. Stir in next 6 ingredients. Season with salt and pepper. Cover; bake until vegetables are very tender, about 30 minutes.

Heat 2 teaspoons oil in large nonstick skillet over medium heat. Add mushrooms, rounded-side-down. Cook until bottoms are golden, about 10 minutes. Turn mushrooms over; cook until just tender, about 6 minutes. Sprinkle with parsley and remaining 2 teaspoons garlic; cook until mushrooms are very tender, about 5 minutes.

Meanwhile, heat remaining 1 teaspoon oil in large nonstick skillet over medium heat. Add spinach; stir until wilted, about 2 minutes. Divide spinach among 4 plates. Top each with 1 mushroom, rounded-side-down. Fill mushrooms with ratatouille. Yields 4 servings.

Never Trust a Skinny Chef...II

Drunken Mushrooms with Brandy

1¼ cups heavy cream
1 garlic clove, crushed
2 tablespoons mustard seeds
1 tablespoon green
  peppercorns in brine,
  drained,
1 teaspoon Worcestershire
  sauce
4 cups mixed mushrooms
  (such as button, oyster,
  chanterelle, shiitake or
  crimini, sliced or halved)

2 tablespoons coarse-grained
  mustard
2 tablespoons brandy
12 small portobello mushrooms
1 tablespoon olive oil
Salt and pepper to taste
Italian parsley for garnish

Combine cream, crushed garlic, mustard seeds, green pepper-corns, and Worcestershire sauce in a saucepan. Bring to a boil. Stir in mixed mushrooms. Cook for 10 minutes or until the mushrooms are tender and sauce has thickened.

Stir the mustard and brandy into the sauce. Season to taste. Keep warm over very low heat. Brush portobello mushrooms with oil, then cook in a hot frying pan, turning once, until browned. Divide among 4 plates and spoon the creamy mush-rooms and their sauce on top. Garnish with Italian parsley and serve.

Elko Ariñak Dancers Cookbook

Highway 375, known as the Extraterrestrial Highway, has sightings that some believe to be not of this earth. A glint of light off a shiny desert rock becomes a signal from "The Mothership." Joshua Trees, with their arms reaching to the sky, become giant aliens on the march.

Mushrooms Stuffed with Buttered Walnuts

32 whole fresh mushrooms
½ cup margarine, softened, divided
2 teaspoons chopped walnuts
4 scallions, chopped

¼ teaspoon garlic powder
2½ teaspoons chopped fresh parsley
Salt and pepper to taste

Wash and dry mushrooms; remove stems and reserve. Arrange caps in well-greased, shallow baking pan. In a small skillet, melt 2 teaspoons margarine; add chopped mushroom stems and sauté lightly. In a small bowl, mix remaining margarine, walnuts, onion, garlic, parsley, salt and pepper; mix thoroughly. Stir in mushroom stems. Fill each cap with a rounded teaspoonful of mushroom mixture. Broil stuffed mushroom caps for 5 minutes until bubbly and serve at once. Makes 6 servings of 5 caps per serving.

Nutritional analysis: Calories 183; Carbohydrates 6g; Fat 18g; Sodium 196mg; Cholesterol 0.

Sharing Our Diabetics Best Recipes

Baked Tomatoes

1 large or 2 small tomatoes
  per person
Olive oil

Bread crumbs
Parmesan cheese

Preheat oven to 375°. Place tomatoes on cookie sheet, drizzle the oil, then sprinkle with bread crumbs and cheese and bake 10 minutes.

The Food You Always Wanted to Eat Cookbook

Baked Tomatoes and Zucchini Provençal

5 ripe plum tomatoes
(1 pound)
2 medium zucchini (1 pound)
½ teaspoon salt
¼ teaspoon freshly ground
pepper
Pinch of red pepper flakes
3 tablespoons extra virgin
olive oil
1 tablespoon minced garlic

2 tablespoons chopped fresh
basil
½ teaspoon chopped fresh
thyme
¼ teaspoon chopped fresh
oregano
2 tablespoons grated Parmesan
cheese
2 tablespoons dry bread
crumbs

Preheat oven to 400°. Cut tomatoes and zucchini diagonally into ½-inch slices. In shallow 1-quart glass baking dish, alternate tomato and zucchini slices on edge in tight rows. Sprinkle with salt, pepper, and red pepper flakes. Cover and bake 20 minutes.

Meanwhile, in a skillet, heat oil; add garlic and sauté 30 seconds. Reserve 1 tablespoon oil and drizzle remaining evenly over vegetables. Bake, uncovered, 10 minutes more or until set. In bowl, mix reserved oil with herbs, cheese, and bread crumbs. Sprinkle over vegetables. Baste vegetables with pan juices. Bake 10 minutes more. Serve hot or at room temperature with grilled meats. Makes 4–6 servings.

MICROWAVE VERSION:

Cut tomatoes and zucchini into ¼-inch slices. In a 10-inch microwave pie plate, arrange zucchini in a single layer, overlapping slightly. Season with ¼ teaspoon salt and ⅛ teaspoon pepper; cover with waxed paper. Microwave on HIGH for 5 minutes; set aside.

In small microwave bowl, combine oil, garlic, and herbs. Microwave on HIGH for 1 minute. Top zucchini with tomato slices. Season with remaining salt and pepper. Drizzle oil mixture over tomatoes. Cover with wax paper. Microwave on HIGH for 6 minutes. Uncover and baste with pan juices. Top with cheese and bread crumbs. Microwave, uncovered, on HIGH for 2 minutes. Let stand 5 minutes before serving.

Still Cookin' After 70 Years

Italian Zucchini Crescent Pie

4 cups thinly sliced zucchini
1 cup chopped onion
½ cup margarine
½ cup chopped parsley, or
  2 tablespoons dried parsley
  flakes
½ teaspoon salt
½ teaspoon pepper
¼ teaspoon garlic powder

¼ teaspoon basil
¼ teaspoon oregano leaves
2 eggs, beaten
8 ounces shredded mozzarella
  cheese
1 (8-ounce) can refrigerated
  crescent dinner rolls
2 teaspoons mustard

Cook and stir zucchini and onion in margarine for 10 minutes. Stir in parsley, salt, pepper, garlic powder, basil, and oregano leaves. Combine eggs and mozzarella cheese. Stir into zucchini mixture.

Separate an 8-ounce can refrigerated crescent dinner rolls into 8 triangles. Place in ungreased 10-inch pie pan; press over bottom and up sides to form crust. Spread crust with mustard. Pour vegetable mixture into crust. Bake in 375° oven for 20 minutes or until center is set. Cover crust with foil during last 10 minutes of baking to prevent over-browning. Let stand 10 minutes before serving. Serves 6.

Still Cookin' After 70 Years

Zucchini Corn Bread Casserole

4 cups shredded zucchini
½ onion, chopped
2 eggs, beaten
1 (8.5-ounce) package dry
corn muffin mix
½ teaspoon salt
¼ teaspoon ground black
pepper
½ pound Cheddar cheese,
grated, divided

Preheat oven to 350°. Grease a 2-quart casserole dish. In a large bowl, mix together the zucchini, onion, eggs, muffin mix, salt, and pepper. Stir in 4 ounces of the cheese. Spread mixture into greased casserole dish; top with remaining 4 ounces cheese. Bake in a preheated oven for 60 minutes.

Elko Ariñak Dancers Cookbook

Posh Squash

2 pounds summer squash
(crookneck)
Boiling, salted water
2 eggs
1 cup mayonnaise
1 small onion, finely chopped
¼ cup chopped green pepper
¼ teaspoon thyme leaves
Salt and pepper
¾ cup grated Parmesan
cheese
1 tablespoon butter

Cut off stem and blossom ends from squash; wash. Cut squash into ½-inch slices and cook in a small amount of boiling water until just tender when pierced, 4–5 minutes. Drain well and set aside. Beat eggs, then blend in mayonnaise, onion, green pepper, and thyme. Stir in well drained squash and season to taste with salt and pepper. Spoon mixture into a greased, shallow 2½-quart casserole; sprinkle evenly with cheese and dot with butter. Cover and chill if made ahead. Bake, uncovered, in 375° oven for 25 minutes (30 minutes if refrigerated) or until puffed and lightly browned. Serves 6–8.

Partyline Cook Book

Walnut Broccoli

2 pounds fresh broccoli
½ cup plus 6 tablespoons
  butter, divided
4 tablespoons flour
1½ teaspoons powdered
  chicken bouillon

2 cups milk
⅓ cup water
2 cups seasoned bread stuffing,
  crumbled
½ cup chopped walnuts

Cook broccoli until crisp tender. Drain, cut in bite-size pieces, and put in greased 2-quart casserole. Melt ½ cup butter; blend in flour and cook gently over low heat. Add chicken bouillon. Gradually stir in milk. Cook until thick and smooth. Pour over broccoli. Heat water and remaining 6 tablespoons butter until melted. Combine with stuffing and nuts; spread on top of casserole. Bake at 350° for 30 minutes.

Virginia City Alumni Association Cookbook

Broccoli Rice Casserole

1 onion, diced
½ stick margarine
1 (10-ounce) package frozen
  chopped broccoli
½ cup cheese sauce or
  pasteurized mild cheese

1 (10¾-ounce) can cream of
  chicken soup
⅛ cup water
¼ cup milk
1 cup precooked rice

Sauté onion in margarine. Cook broccoli as directed on package and drain well. Add remaining ingredients, using the precooked rice dry from package. It will cook in the sauce. Pour into casserole and bake 45 minutes at 350°. Serves 6.

Recipes from Sunset Garden Club

Quick and Easy Broccoli Potluck

2 (10-ounce) packages frozen chopped broccoli, thawed
2 (10-ounce) cans cream of mushroom soup
1 (8-ounce) can sliced water chestnuts, drained

1 (8-ounce) can bamboo shoots, drained
1 cup shredded Cheddar cheese, divided
1 (3-ounce) can French-fried onions, divided

Combine broccoli, soup, water chestnuts, bamboo shoots, half the cheese, and half the onions in bowl; mix well. Add enough water for desired consistency. Spoon into 1½-quart baking dish. Bake, covered, at 350° for 20 minutes. Sprinkle with remaining cheese and onions. Bake, uncovered, for 10 minutes longer. May substitute green beans for broccoli and cream of chicken or celery soup for mushroom soup. Yields 8 servings.

Approximately per serving: Cal 234; Prot 8g; Carbo 18g; Fiber 4g; Total Fat 15g; 57% Calories from Fat; Chol 16mg; Sod 752mg.

Best Bets

Creamed Onions

18–20 medium onions, thickly sliced
⅓ cup salad oil
3 tablespoons flour

½ cup milk
1 cup shredded American cheese
½ cup chopped peanuts

Peel onions and cook in large amount of boiling, salted water until tender. Drain. Blend salad oil and flour. Stir in milk and slowly cook until thick. Add cheese and stir until melted. Add onions and heat through. Place in bowl and top with chopped peanuts.

Let Freedom Ring

Eggplant Soufflé

1 eggplant	½ cup grated cheese
2 tablespoons butter	¾ cup soft bread crumbs
2 tablespoons grated onion	1 tablespoon tomato ketchup
2 tablespoons flour	1 teaspoon salt
1 cup milk	2 eggs, separated

Peel and cube eggplant, cook until tender, and mash fine. Melt butter; add onion and flour and blend till smooth. Then add milk, stirring to prevent lumping. Add eggplant, cheese, bread crumbs, ketchup, salt, and beaten yolks of eggs. Lastly fold in stiffly beaten egg whites. Pour into greased baking dish, put in pan of hot water and bake at 375° about 45 minutes or until set.

Hoover Dam Cooks, 1933

Corn Pudding

2 eggs, separated	1 cup shredded cheese
1 (15-ounce) can creamed	1 cup corn muffin mix
corn	Paprika
¾ cup milk	Butter
½ cup salad oil	

Beat egg whites; set aside. Combine egg yolks with corn, milk, oil, cheese, and corn muffin mix, and beat. Fold in beaten whites. Grease 1½-quart casserole and pour in mixture. Sprinkle with paprika. Dot with butter. Bake 1 hour in 350° oven.

Twentieth Century Club Cook Book

 Boulder City is the only town in Nevada where gambling is illegal.

Turnip and Collard Greens

1 pound ham hocks (or
  smoked turkey)
7 cups water
1 bunch fresh collard greens
  (about 5 pounds)
1 bunch fresh turnip greens
  (about 5 pounds)

1 teaspoon salt
1 small whole red pepper
  (optional)
Pepper to taste

Combine ham hocks and water in a large pot. Bring to boil.
Cover and reduce heat to simmer for about one hour or until
meat is tender. In the meantime, wash greens thoroughly and
drain. Cut into bite-size pieces. Add greens, salt, and pepper to
boiled meat. Bring to a boil. Cover; reduce heat and simmer for
1–1½ hours or until greens are tender.

The Best of Down-Home Cooking

Spinach Pie

3–4 pounds spinach
Sea salt and pepper to taste
1 tablespoon olive oil
2 cloves garlic

2 Bermuda onions, chopped
Bread dough, enough to line
  a pie pan

Preheat oven to 375°. Wash spinach; squeeze out all the water,
and add a little sea salt and pepper. Heat olive oil and add garlic and onions; sauté until tender. Add spinach and cook down
until it is limp. Prick dough in pie pan and add spinach mixture
and bake about 30–45 minutes, or until the dough is golden
brown.

The Food You Always Wanted to Eat Cookbook

Carrot Cutlets

1 cup mashed, boiled carrots	1 teaspoon minced onion
2 cups cold boiled rice	1 teaspoon pimento
1 egg, beaten	1 teaspoon celery salt
Paprika	Salt to taste

Mix all ingredients well. Form into balls, then flatten in shape of cutlets. Fry in deep fat, 395°, till brown. Place a cube of tart jelly on each cutlet and garnish with parsley.

Hoover Dam Cooks, 1933

Brown Sugar Carrots

1½ cups water	½ stick margarine
8 or so carrots, scraped and diced	½ cup brown sugar

In a 6-quart pressure cooker, put water and diced carrots. Slice margarine and place over carrots, sprinkle brown sugar over all. Cook for 6 minutes after pressure builds up. If you don't have a pressure cooker, cook carrots in water in saucepan until tender. Add margarine and sugar; cook awhile longer.

Partyline Cook Book

 The longest running show in Las Vegas is the Follies Bergere at the Tropicana Hotel and Casino. It opened in 1959.

Yam and Apples in the Microwave

5 large red yams
5 large Granny Smith apples
Pan spray
2 tablespoons pumpkin pie
  spice

Brown sugar substitute to
  equal 1 pound regular brown
  sugar
½ cup reduced-fat margarine

Cut yams in half crosswise. Place cut-side-down in microwave-safe dish in ½ inch of water; cover with clear plastic. Cook on HIGH 8–10 minutes or until fork goes in smoothly. Set aside to cool.

Peel apples and core; slice and place in a bowl. Skin yams and slice crosswise and place in the bowl. In a 9x13x2-inch baking dish prepared with pan spray, alternate yams with layers of apples; sprinkle with pumpkin spice and brown sugar substitute. Dot layers with margarine. Continue layering until pan is full. Cover with clear plastic wrap. Cook on HIGH 10–15 minutes or until apples are opaque and mixture is bubbling evenly. Serves 6–8.

Nutritional analysis: Calories 165; Carbohydrates 35g; Fat 2g; Sugar 9g; Sodium 44mg; 2 starch and ½ fruit exchange

Sharing Our Diabetics Best Recipes

Sweet Potato Balls

4 large sweet potatoes
2/3 cup brown sugar
1 teaspoon grated orange peel

4–6 tablespoons orange juice
8 large marshmallows
2 cups toasted flaked coconut

Wash sweet potatoes; place in large Dutch oven and cover with water. Simmer 25–30 minutes or until tender. Let cool to the touch. Peel, mash, and measure 4 cups potatoes. Stir in brown sugar, orange peel, and orange juice; mix well.

Shape ½ cup potato mixture around a marshmallow; roll in coconut. Place potato balls in 9x13-inch baking dish and bake at 350° for 15–20 minutes. Potato balls may be frozen (unbaked), if desired. Thaw before baking.

Still Cookin' After 70 Years

Spiced Pineapple

This a great accompaniment for ham or chicken.

1 cup vinegar
1 cup sugar
½ teaspoon cinnamon

8 whole cloves
1 (20-ounce) can sliced pineapple, drained

Combine vinegar and sugar; stir in cinnamon and cloves. Pour over sliced pineapple and cook slowly for ½ hour. Cool to serve.

Hoover Dam Cooks, 1933

Pasta, Rice, Etc.

The Bristlecone Pine is the state tree of Nevada. These trees are the oldest living things on earth and are found at higher elevations. Great Basin National Park is home to groves of these ancient pines, some noted to be as old as 4,000 years!

Dante Blue's Alfredo Blue

16 ounces fettuccini
3 garlic cloves, diced
1 tablespoon olive oil
6 ounces Stiltson blue cheese,
    crumbled
¼ cup grated Parmesan
    cheese
2 cups heavy cream

1½ cups crabmeat, picked
    over
1 tablespoon chopped fresh
    basil
1 tablespoon chopped fresh
    oregano
Salt and black pepper to taste

Cook pasta in boiling water until al dente. Drain and keep hot.
Sauté garlic in oil until golden. Reserve garlic and oil. In
saucepan over medium heat, combine blue cheese, Parmesan
cheese, and cream. Stir until cheeses are melted. Add crabmeat
and heat through, about 2–3 minutes. Do not overcook crabmeat. Stir in reserved garlic and olive oil. Season with basil,
oregano, salt and pepper. Toss sauce with hot pasta and let
stand 5 minutes before serving. Serves 8.

Chef's Note: If you cannot find Stiltson blue cheese, be careful to substitute only high quality blue cheese such as Midnight Blue brand blue
cheese from Finlandia. Avoid using creamy blue cheese, as the sauce
will turn out relatively bland. Do NOT substitute imitation crab for
real crabmeat.

Use Your Noodle!

Fettuccini with Bay Scallops and Shrimp

4 tablespoons butter, divided
1 tablespoon olive oil
½ cup chopped shallots
8 ounces uncooked medium
   shrimp, peeled, deveined
8 ounces bay scallops
1 teaspoon chopped fresh
   basil

1 tablespoon chopped fresh dill
¾ cup white wine
1 cup half-and-half
1 pound uncooked spinach
   fettuccini
Salt to taste
½ cup grated Parmesan
   cheese

Melt 2 tablespoons butter with the olive oil in a large skillet. Add shallots and sauté 2–3 minutes or until tender but not browned. Add shrimp and scallops and sauté for 1 minute. Stir in the basil, dill, and wine. Reduce heat and simmer until mixture is reduced by ½. Add half-and-half and cook until mixture thickens, stirring constantly. Remove from heat and keep warm.

Cook fettuccini in boiling salted water in a stockpot until al dente. Drain and toss with remaining 2 tablespoons butter and Parmesan cheese in a serving bowl. Add seafood mixture and toss to mix. Serve with warm sourdough bread. Yields 4–6 servings.

Las Vegas Glitter to Gourmet

Sand carried by the wind from beaches of a prehistoric inland sea that once covered much of Nevada created Sand Mountain, over a period of thousands of years. Located about an hour from Reno, this 600-foot-high mound of sand is one-mile wide and stretches for two miles. You can sandboard down this massive sand dune at speeds exceeding 40 miles per hour.!

Basil Shrimp Fettuccine

8 ounces uncooked fettuccine
½ cup chopped onion
¼ cup chopped sweet yellow
  pepper
¼ cup chopped sweet red
  pepper
2 cloves garlic, minced
2 tablespoons olive oil

1 (12-ounce) can evaporated
  milk or half-and-half
¼ cup flour
½ teaspoon salt
1 pound uncooked, peeled, and
  deveined shrimp
2 tablespoons minced fresh
  basil (must be fresh)

Cook pasta; set aside. In a fry pan, cook onion, both peppers, and garlic in oil until tender. In a bowl, mix milk and sifted flour; blend well. Pour over vegetables. Bring to a boil; cook 2 minutes longer. Reduce heat; add salt, shrimp, and basil. Cook about 3 minutes or until shrimp is pink. Pour over pasta. Makes 6 servings.

Family and Friends Favorites

Herbed Chicken Pasta

1 teaspoon vegetable oil
1½ cups sliced mushrooms
½ cup chopped onion
1 garlic clove, minced
1 pound skinned, boned
  chicken breasts, cut into
  1-inch pieces, divided
½ teaspoon salt

½ teaspoon dried basil
¼ teaspoon pepper
2 cups coarsely chopped
  tomatoes
4 cups cooked fettuccine
¼ cup grated Parmesan
cheese

Heat oil in a large skillet over medium-high heat. Add mushrooms, onion, and garlic; sauté 2 minutes. Add chicken, salt, basil, and pepper; sauté 6 minutes or until chicken is done. Add tomatoes; sauté 2 minutes. Serve over pasta; sprinkle with cheese. Makes 4 servings.

Recipes from the Heart

Chicken with Spinach-Pasta Sauce

1 (1-pound) package fusilli
pasta or spaghetti
3 tablespoons salad oil

2 pounds boneless chicken
breasts (6 halves)

Cook pasta as package label directs; drain and return to pot. Meanwhile, in large skillet, heat 3 tablespoons oil. Sauté chicken breasts (which have been pounded thin) for about 8 minutes on each side or until tender; keep chicken and pasta warm.

SAUCE:

1 tablespoon salad oil
¼ cup chopped onion
3 cloves garlic, minced
1 (10-ounce) package frozen
chopped spinach, thawed
and drained
1 cup (½ pint) heavy cream

½ cup chicken broth
¼ cup grated Parmesan
cheese
¼ teaspoon salt
¼ teaspoon pepper
¼ teaspoon ground nutmeg

In small saucepan, heat oil; sauté onion and garlic for 3 minutes, or until tender. Add spinach, cream, broth, cheese, and seasonings. Bring to boiling; reduce heat and simmer, uncovered, for 3 minutes, or until sauce thickens slightly. Pour sauce into blender or processor and purée until smooth. Pour Sauce over pasta, tossing to coat well on serving platter. Arrange chicken over pasta. Makes 6 servings.

Virginia City Alumni Association Cookbook

Nevada has an estimated 314 mountain ranges—more than any other state—all of which have a northeast/southwest orientation. The tallest are the 13,145-foot Boundary Peak near the west-central border and the 13,063-foot Wheeler Peak in Great Basin National Park. There are 51 peaks above 9,000 feet. Mountains crisscross the state, and no matter where you travel, these natural Nevada wonders are visible.

Fettuccine Gorgonzola

½ pound Gorgonzola cheese
1 tablespoon unsalted butter
1 cup whipping cream
1 tablespoon lemon juice

1 pound fettuccine
Fresh ground pepper
Basil leaves (optional)

Cut cheese into small pieces. Melt cheese and butter in top of double boiler over simmering water, whisking occasionally. Stir in cream. Remove sauce from heat and allow to thicken. Add lemon juice to boiling water and cook pasta. Drain pasta and toss with sauce. Serve with pepper and garnish with basil, if desired. Yields 6–8 servings.

CASA Cooks

Mo Mo Noodles

4 cups flour
Salt to taste
6–8 eggs

1 (3- to 4-pound) chicken
Parsley (optional)

Sift flour onto cutting board; add salt. Make a hole in flour; add eggs and mix well. Roll dough out on well-floured surface, cut, and dry most of the day, 4–6 hours.

Boil chicken in seasoned water. Bone chicken and pull apart or cut in chunks. Add noodles and parsley, if desired, to boiling chicken broth for about 15 minutes. Add chicken and heat thoroughly. Enjoy.

Feeding the Flock

Simply Sublime Noodles

10 ounces egg noodles
⅛ cup unsalted butter, melted
⅛ cup chicken stock
⅛ cup freshly grated
  Parmigiano-Reggiano
¼ cup diced fresh chives
1 teaspoon lemon zest
½ teaspoon salt
¼ teaspoon black pepper

Cook noodles in lightly salted boiling water until tender, about 10–12 minutes. Drain, and while still hot, toss with remaining ingredients. Serve immediately. Serves 8–10.

Use Your Noodle!

Iva Cuneo's Szechuan Style Noodles

½ cup light sesame oil
½ cup tahini (sesame paste)
½ cup smooth peanut butter
¼ cup soy sauce
¼ cup dry sherry
⅛ cup sherry vinegar
¼ cup honey
6 garlic cloves, minced
2 tablespoons fresh ginger,
  minced
½ teaspoon hot chili oil
½ teaspoon black pepper
⅛ teaspoon cayenne pepper
1 pound Ramen or Asian
  noodles
1 red bell pepper, cut in
  julienne strips
1 yellow bell pepper, cut in
  julienne strips
4 scallions, cut in julienne
  strips

Add sesame oil, tahini, peanut butter, soy sauce, sherry, sherry vinegar, honey, garlic, ginger, chili oil, black pepper, and cayenne to a food processor and blend well. Cook noodles in lightly salted boiling water until al dente. Drain and while still hot; toss with ¾ of the sauce. Add bell peppers and scallions and toss. Serve immediately. Remaining sauce may be served on the side to moisten salad. Serves 6–8.

Use Your Noodle!

Million Dollar Spaghetti

A good casserole to do ahead; just refrigerate and remove from refrigerator 20 minutes before baking. Good with green salad and French bread.

1 (7-ounce) package thin spaghetti	1 (8-ounce) package cream cheese, softened
1½ pounds ground beef	¼ cup sour cream
1 tablespoon butter	⅓ cup chopped scallions
2 (8-ounce) cans tomato sauce	1 tablespoon minced green pepper
Salt and pepper to taste	
½ pound cottage cheese	2 tablespoons melted butter

Heat oven to 350°. Cook spaghetti according to directions on package; drain. Sauté beef in 1 tablespoon butter till brown; add tomato sauce, salt and pepper. Remove from heat. Combine cottage cheese, cream cheese, sour cream, scallions, and green pepper.

In a greased square 2-quart casserole, spread ½ of the spaghetti, cover with cheese mixture. Add remainder of spaghetti and pour melted butter over spaghetti. Spread tomato-meat sauce over the top. Bake for 45 minutes or until hot and bubbly.

Tasteful Treasures

Pizza Spaghetti

7 ounces broken spaghetti
  (break into thirds)
2 eggs
1 cup milk
2 pounds hamburger, browned
  and drained

Onion or garlic powder
1 (32-ounce) jar spaghetti sauce
Sugar
Pepperoni slices
Mozzarella cheese

Cook and drain spaghetti. Beat eggs and milk together. Put spaghetti in the bottom of a 9x13-inch greased pan. Pour egg-milk mixture over the spaghetti. Brown hamburger and onion or garlic powder. Mix jar of spaghetti sauce into hamburger; sprinkle a little sugar in. Put on top of spaghetti. Place pepperoni slices on top. Cover with a good layer of mozzarella cheese on top. Bake in 350° oven for 45 minutes, covered, then uncover 10 minutes to set before serving. Serve with garlic toast.

A Gathering of Recipes

Baked Spaghetti (For a Crowd)

1 (16-ounce) package spaghetti
4 pounds ground beef
2 large onions, chopped
1 large green pepper, chopped
2 teaspoons salt
2 (10¾-ounce) cans cream of
  mushroom soup

4 (10¾-ounce) cans tomato
  soup
1 quart milk
4 cups shredded sharp
  processed American cheese,
  divided

Break spaghetti into 3-inch lengths. Cook in salted water; drain. In a Dutch oven or kettle, cook meat, onions, and green pepper until meat is browned. Sprinkle with salt. Gradually stir in soups, milk, and 2 cups cheese. Divide cooked spaghetti evenly between 2 (9x13-inch) baking dishes. Into each pan, stir half of soup-meat mixture. Sprinkle remaining cheese on top of casseroles. Bake, uncovered, in a 350° oven for 1 hour or until hot. Makes 20 servings or more.

The Ruby Valley Friendship Club Cookbook I

Spaghetti Casserole

1 pound ground beef
½ medium onion, chopped
1 small green bell pepper,
  chopped
1 pound spaghetti noodles
1 (8-ounce) can tomato sauce
1 small can chopped ripe
  olives

1 (20-ounce) can diced
  tomatoes, with most of juice
1 (11-ounce) can cream-style
  corn
½ teaspoon chili powder
1 teaspoon salt
¼ pound sharp Cheddar
  cheese, grated

Sauté beef, onion, and green pepper in frying pan. Boil spaghetti according to directions on package. Do not overcook. When done, drain and place in large bowl with meat mixture, tomato sauce, olives, tomatoes, corn, chili powder, and salt. Mix together and place in large buttered casserole dish. Cover with grated cheese and bake in 350° oven for 45 minutes.

The Fruit of the Spirit

Spaghetti Pie

6 ounces spaghetti
2 tablespoons margarine
⅓ cup shredded Parmesan
  cheese
2 eggs, beaten
1 pound ground beef or
  Italian sausage
½ cup chopped onion
¼ cup chopped bell pepper

1 (6-ounce) can tomato paste
1 tablespoon sugar
1 teaspoon dried crushed
  oregano
½ teaspoon garlic salt
1 cup cottage cheese
½ cup shredded mozzarella
  cheese

Cook spaghetti and drain. Add margarine, Parmesan cheese, and beaten eggs. Press mixture into buttered 10-inch pie pan. Brown meat, onion, and pepper; mix well and add tomato paste, sugar, oregano, and garlic salt to meat mixture. Spread cottage cheese on top of spaghetti crust. Fill with meat mixture. Bake uncovered in 350° oven for 20 minutes. Sprinkle mozzarella cheese on top. Bake 5 minutes longer.

Kitchen Chatter

Sweet Sausage Bowties

Vegetable oil
1 pound sweet Italian sausage,
　casings removed, crumbled
½ teaspoon crushed red
　pepper
½ cup finely chopped onion
3 garlic cloves, minced
2 cups chopped, seeded,
　peeled Roma tomatoes, or
　1 (28-ounce) can tomatoes,
　drained, coarsely chopped
1½ cups heavy cream

½ teaspoon salt
2 teaspoons pesto (optional)
Freshly ground black pepper to
　taste
12 ounces uncooked farfalle
　(bowties)
Salt to taste
3 tablespoons finely chopped
　fresh parsley
¾–1 cup grated Parmesan
　cheese

Heat a small amount of vegetable oil in a heavy skillet over medium heat. Add the sausage and red pepper. Sauté for 7 minutes or until sausage is no longer pink. Add onion and garlic and sauté until onion is tender and sausage is lightly browned. Stir in tomatoes, cream, ½ teaspoon salt, and pesto. Season with black pepper. Simmer for 4 minutes or until mixture is slightly thickened and flavors have blended.

Cook the pasta in boiling salted water in a stockpot until al dente. Drain and add to sausage mixture in the skillet. Cook for 2 minutes, stirring occasionally. Add parsley and Parmesan cheese. Toss to mix well. Yields 6–8 servings.

Las Vegas Glitter to Gourmet

Pioche's mining town was considered Nevada's wildest in the mid-1800s. Once home to twelve thousand people, Pioche was practically a ghost town by the turn of the century. Today, people come from near and far to visit The Million Dollar Courthouse, which got its nickname for a good reason. Violence in the streets distracted attention from the activities of corrupt public officials, who kept refinancing the courthouse's 1876 cost of $26,000 until it ended up costing nearly $1 million when finally paid off in 1938.

Lasagne Rosettes with Marinara and Pesto Sauce

PESTO SAUCE:

1 cup olive oil, divided
6 cloves garlic
2 cups fresh basil leaves,
   tightly packed, divided
½ cup toasted pine nuts
   (pignoli)

½ cup grated fresh Parmesan
   cheese
Sea salt to taste

In a blender or processor, purée ¼ cup oil, garlic, and 1 cup basil. Add another ¼ cup oil and the rest of the basil and the nuts. Then drizzle in the remaining oil and alternate with the cheese. Add sea salt to taste.

MARINARA SAUCE:

1 small onion, grated
1 clove garlic, pressed
1 (12-ounce) can tomato sauce
1 tablespoon olive oil
¼ teaspoon ground oregano,
   or ½ teaspoon fresh, minced

¼ teaspoon dried basil, or ½
   teaspoon fresh, minced
1 tablespoon honey

In heavy saucepan, sauté onion and garlic in oil until transparent. Then add the remaining ingredients and simmer for about 30–45 minutes. Let rest, then reheat before using so that the flavors come out.

LASAGNE:

2 heads cauliflower
½ bunch fresh parsley,
   chopped
¼ cup water
¼ cup wheat germ
½ teaspoon sea salt

½ teaspoon dried basil, or
   1 teaspoon fresh, minced
½ teaspoon dried oregano, or
   1 teaspoon fresh, minced
¼ cup Parmesan cheese
1 package lasagne noodles

Steam cauliflower, then purée in processor or blender. Return to a heavy saucepan and add remaining ingredients except noodles and keep warm. Cook lasagne noodles in salted water until

(continued)

(Lasagne Rosettes with Marinara and Pesto Sauce continued)

al dente. Then remove from hot water and place in cool water to stop the cooking process and make it easier to handle. Lay out the noodles flat and spread mixture on it about ¼ inch thick, leaving about 1½ inches without mixture.

Roll the noodle starting from the end with the mixture and sealing the end with the unspread end. Then place the rosettes, standing up on one end in a lightly oiled baking pan, and fill to about 1½–2 inches of water; cover with foil. Bake at 325° for about 30 minutes. Keep sealed so the water will steam-cook the rosettes. Place on serving plate and serve both sauces, ½ cup of each, on top of every rosette.

The Food You Always Wanted to Eat Cookbook

College Lasagna

1 pound ground beef
½ cup water
1 (32-ounce) jar spaghetti
   sauce (garden-style is best)
Mushrooms, canned or fresh
1 teaspoon salt
Lasagna noodles (8 ounces)

1 pint cottage cheese
1 (16-ounce) package grated
   mozzarella cheese (reserve
   some for top)
1 (8-ounce) package Parmesan
   cheese (reserve some for top)

Brown beef and drain. Add water, spaghetti sauce, mushrooms, and salt. Bring to a boil. In a baking dish, layer this hot sauce, uncooked noodles, cottage cheese, and mozzarella and Parmesan cheeses. Repeat layers, ending with sauce. Top with reserved cheese (both types). Cover with foil and bake in 375° oven for 1 hour. Set dish on a cookie sheet covered in foil to help with cleanup of overflow.

Partyline Cook Book

Easy Lasagna

1 pound beef or ground
  turkey
1 onion, chopped
1 tablespoon salt
½ tablespoon pepper
2 tablespoons Italian
  seasonings
2 (26-ounce) jars pasta sauce

1 (1-pound) box lasagna
  noodles
2 cups shredded mozzarella
  cheese, divided
1 (16-ounce) container ricotta
  cheese
1 egg
¼ cup Parmesan cheese

Preheat oven to 375°. Cook ground beef or turkey and onion in a 10-inch skillet until brown. Drain. Stir in salt, pepper, and Italian seasoning. Stir in both jars of pasta sauce. Heat to boiling and cook about 10 minutes.

Cook lasagna noodles according to package directions (minus about 1–2 minutes). Drain noodles. In a bowl, mix together 1 cup mozzarella cheese, ricotta cheese, egg, and Parmesan cheese. Set aside.

Spread 1 cup of sauce on bottom of an ungreased rectangular 9x13-inch baking dish. Arrange 4 lasagna noodles over sauce, each overlapping the previous one (don't leave any gaps). Spread 1 cup of cheese mixture over noodles. Spread 1 cup sauce mixture over cheese. Repeat with noodles, cheese, and sauce 2 more times. Arrange 4 noodles and cover with remaining sauce. Sprinkle with rest of mozzarella cheese. Cover with foil and cook in oven for 30 minutes. Uncover and cook for 10 minutes or until cheese is melted. Let stand for 30 minutes before cutting. Cut into 12 servings.

The Melting Pot

That Old Italian Guy's Fast Pesto Sauce

4 cups fresh basil
4 garlic cloves
¼ stick unsalted butter
¼ cup olive oil
¼ cup toasted pine nuts

¼ cup grated Parmesan
  cheese
⅛ cup grated Romano cheese
¼ teaspoon salt

In a food processor, combine all ingredients for 60–90 seconds. Scrape ingredients down from sides of processor and continue combining until thick and smooth. Makes about 1 cup.

Use Your Noodle!

Brown Rice Casserole

1 cup brown rice
Boiling water
3 tablespoons chopped onion
3 tablespoons bacon drippings
1 pound ground beef
1 (10¾-ounce) can chicken
  rice soup, condensed

1 (4-ounce) can sliced
  mushrooms
½ cup water
⅛ teaspoon each: celery salt,
  onion salt, garlic salt, paprika
  and pepper
1 bay leaf, crumbled

Preheat oven to 325°. Place brown rice in a pot and cover with boiling water; cover the pot and let stand 15 minutes. While rice is sitting, sauté onion in bacon fat until lightly browned, then add ground beef, stirring until brown and crunchy. In a large bowl, combine chicken rice soup, mushrooms, water, and spices. Combine ground beef mixture and rice, then add them to the soup and spices mixture; mix thoroughly. Pour mixture into a buttered or greased casserole dish. Bake, covered, at 325° for 1 hour. Serves 4–6.

God, That's Good!

Three Colored Rice

6 tablespoons butter, divided
1 large onion, minced
2 cups Arborio rice
8 cups vegetable stock
Sea salt to taste
4 tablespoons chopped fresh
  parsley
1 tablespoon chopped fresh
  basil
2 tablespoons tomato paste
½ cup freshly grated
  Parmesan cheese

Melt 3 tablespoons butter in a large saucepan, then add onions and sauté until pale yellow. Add rice and mix well. Add stock one cup at a time, stirring until it is absorbed; continue to cook for 5 minutes. Divide rice in 3 equal portions, putting each portion into separate saucepans. Add the parsley and basil to one pan; the tomato paste to another, and nothing to the third. Continue to cook the rice till tender but firm. To the third pan of rice add remaining butter and half the Parmesan cheese. Add remaining cheese to the other 2 rice pans and mix to blend.
To serve, place equal portions of each rice next to each other in rows on the plate.

The Food You Always Wanted to Eat Cookbook

Minerva Rice

A wonderful main dish to serve with a green salad and rolls.

¼–½ pound bulk sausage
1 onion, chopped
½ green pepper, chopped
1 cup chopped celery
1 cup raw rice
2 cans bouillon or broth
1 can mushroom soup

Brown first 4 ingredients in a frying pan. Combine remaining ingredients and mix with sausage mixture. Place in a greased casserole; cover and bake 1½–2 hours at 350°.

Twentieth Century Club Cook Book

Chorizo Paella

1½ pounds chorizo (sausage), skin removed
1 large yellow onion, chopped
1 cup short-grain rice
1 cup cooked and chopped ham
1 (2-ounce) can sliced olives, drained
⅓ cup chopped pimentos
3 cups chicken broth
2 cloves garlic, pressed
1 cup chicken
1 pinch of saffron
1 chicken bouillon cube

Crumble chorizo and cook with chopped onion in 3-quart saucepan over medium heat. Stir often. Preheat oven to 350°. When onion becomes soft, add remaining ingredients all at once and bring to boil. As soon as mixture boils, pour into 3-quart casserole. Bake covered for 40 minutes.

Elko Ariñak Dancers Cookbook

Taco Rice

1 pound hamburger
1 package taco seasoning
1 (15-ounce) can tomato sauce
2½ cups cooked rice
1 pound shredded Colby cheese
1 bag taco chips

Brown hamburger. Add seasoning and tomato sauce. Mix; add rice. In large baking dish, layer rice mixture, cheese, and chips until gone. Bake at 350° until cheese is melted. Can be made ahead and kept in refrigerator until ready to bake.

Recipes from the Heart

Mexican Quiche

1 (10-inch) unbaked pie shell
2 tablespoons melted butter
1 (8-ounce) package cream
  cheese, chopped
2 (4-ounce) cans chopped
  green chiles, drained

1 cup shredded Swiss, Cheddar,
  or Monterey Jack cheese
5 eggs
1½ cups whipping cream
½ teaspoon salt
Pepper to taste

Brush pie shell with melted butter and arrange cream cheese in the shell. Chill until the butter sets. Spread drained green chiles on paper towels and pat dry. Sprinkle green chiles and shredded cheese in pie shell. Beat eggs, cream, salt, and pepper in a bowl until smooth. Pour into prepared pie shell. Bake at 425° for 15 minutes. Reduce oven temperature to 350°. Bake for 30 minutes longer or until a knife inserted in center comes out clean. Cool for 5–10 minutes before serving. Yields 6–8 servings.

From Sunrise to Sunset

Crustless Quiche

3 eggs, slightly beaten
1½ cups milk
½ cup Bisquick
1 cup grated Cheddar cheese
2 tablespoons melted butter

¼ cup chopped onion
¼ pound sliced mushrooms
1 medium zucchini, grated
½ cup diced cooked ham or
  bacon

Mix eggs, milk, Bisquick, cheese, and butter. Add any or all of the remaining ingredients and pour into buttered pie pan or quiche dish. Bake at 350° for 45 minutes or until golden brown.

Note: You may use egg beaters, buttermilk, 1 (10-ounce) package frozen spinach, well drained.

God, That's Good!

Meats

Started in 1919 by a group of community leaders, the Reno Rodeo has grown to a nine-day extravaganza featuring a purse in excess of $1 million. Dubbed the "Wildest, Richest Rodeo in the West," it has been called the greatest outdoor rodeo in the world.

Nevada Ranch Woman's Charcoal Broiled Blue Cheese Steaks

4 ounces blue cheese
1 teaspoon Worcestershire
  sauce
1 tablespoon heavy cream
6 (8-ounce) sirloin steaks
½ teaspoon black pepper

Crumble blue cheese and blend with Worcestershire sauce and cream. Broil steaks over charcoal to desired doneness. Spread cheese mixture over steaks and broil 1–2 minutes to melt cheese. Sprinkle with pepper. Serve hot. Serves 6 regular guys or 3 working cowgirls.

Authentic Cowboy Cookery Then & Now

Bourbon Street Style Flank Steak

⅛ cup bourbon whiskey
⅛ cup water
1 tablespoon brown sugar
¼ teaspoon cayenne pepper
4 (5-ounce) flank steaks,
  trimmed of fat

Combine whiskey, water, sugar, and cayenne. Place steaks in a shallow baking dish. Pour whiskey marinade over steaks, cover, and marinate in refrigerator about one hour, turning over once. Drain steaks of excess marinade. Grill steaks to desired doneness. Makes 4 servings.

Nutritional analysis per serving: Calories 243; Protein 29g; Fat 11g; Carbohydrates 7g.

The Protein Edge

Perfect Hostess Beef Medallions with Cognac Sauce

1 cup chopped shallots
6 tablespoons butter, divided
1 tablespoon brown sugar
2 cups low-sodium chicken
  broth
1½ cups low-sodium beef
  broth

1¼ cups cognac
1½ cups whipping cream
8 (4-ounce) beef tenderloin
  steaks, about 1 inch thick
Salt and pepper to taste
8 tablespoons chopped fresh
  chives

Sauté shallots in 4 tablespoons butter until tender, about 4 minutes. Add brown sugar and stir in. Add broth and cognac. Simmer until reduced to ½ cup, about 20 minutes. Add cream. Cover and chill.

Season steaks with salt and pepper. Melt remaining 2 tablespoons butter in skillet. Add steaks and cook to desired doneness, about 4 minutes per side for rare. Place steaks on a platter and let rest. Add sauce to skillet and bring to boil, scraping up any browned bits. Season with salt and pepper to taste. Slice steaks and fan out slices on plates. Top with sauce and garnish each with one tablespoon chives. Serves 8.

All American Meals Cookbook

It is illegal to pick many types of wildflowers in Nevada, as well as to gather rocks. Tossing away lighted cigarette butts is also illegal in this dry land.

Pepper Steak

2 tablespoons oil
1 medium onion, minced
1 clove garlic, minced
2½ pounds round steak,
    1 inch thick, cut into 1-inch
    strips
1 teaspoon salt
1 teaspoon freshly ground
    pepper

2 green peppers, diced
1 teaspoon meat glaze
    (dissolved in 2 tablespoons
    hot water)
1 cup drained tomatoes
1 tablespoon cornstarch
2 teaspoons soy sauce
¼ cup water

Place oil, onion, and garlic in a heavy skillet and simmer a few minutes. Add steak strips; season with salt and pepper. Add peppers and meat glaze solution, cover, and cook ½ hour. Add tomatoes and simmer 5 minutes longer. Combine cornstarch and soy sauce with water and add to steak mixture; cook 5 minutes, stirring constantly.

The Ruby Valley Friendship Club Cookbook II

Stir-Fried Steak and Vegetable Sandwiches

1 pound beef round tip steak,
  cut ⅛ to ¼ inch thick
2 teaspoons olive oil, divided
1 medium zucchini, cut into
  ¼-inch slices
1 medium onion, thinly sliced
1 medium red bell pepper,
  cut into thin strips
1 teaspoon Italian seasoning,
  crushed

¼ teaspoon salt
¼ teaspoon pepper
4 crusty hoagie rolls,
  approximately 6 inches long,
  split
4 (¾-ounce) slices mozzarella
  cheese

Stack beef steaks, cut lengthwise in half, then crosswise into 1-inch wide strips; set aside. In large skillet, heat 1 teaspoon olive oil over medium-high heat until hot. Add zucchini, onion, bell pepper, and Italian seasoning. Stir-fry 3–4 minutes or until crisp-tender. Remove from skillet.

In same skillet, heat remaining 1 teaspoon oil until hot. Stir-fry beef in 2 batches, 1–2 minutes each, or until outside surface is no longer pink. (Do not overcook.) Return beef to skillet. Season with salt and pepper. Stir in zucchini mixture; heat through. Arrange ¼ of beef mixture on bottom of each roll and top each with 1 cheese slice. Place on rack in broiler pan so surface of cheese is 4 inches from heat. Broil 1–2 minutes or until cheese is melted. Close sandwiches.

NSHSRA High School Rodeo Cookbook

Swiss Steak

2 tablespoons flour
¾ teaspoon salt, divided
¼ teaspoon pepper, divided
1 pound beef round steak

1 tablespoon shortening
1 (8-ounce) can whole tomatoes
1 medium onion, chopped
½ green pepper, chopped

Mix flour, ¼ teaspoon salt, and ⅛ teaspoon pepper. Sprinkle one side of steak with half of flour mixture and pound it. Do same to other side. Cut beef into 4–5 servings. Heat shortening until melted. Cook beef over medium heat about 15 minutes until browned. Mix in tomatoes and remaining ingredients. Heat to boiling; cover, reduce heat, and simmer until beef is tender, about 45 minutes.

Bless This Food

Persian Style Beef Kabobs

2 pounds beef tenderloin
1 cup diced white onion
1 teaspoon salt
1 teaspoon black pepper
¼ cup water

⅛ cup fresh lime juice
½ cup bite-size green bell
  pepper chunks
½ cup bite-size white onion
  chunks

Cut beef into bite-size cubes. Combine onion, salt, black pepper, water, and lime juice in a shallow pan. Add beef cubes, cover, and refrigerate at least 1 hour.

Preheat grill to high. If using wooden skewers, soak in water to prevent burning. Thread beef and vegetable chunks onto skewers. Place kabobs on grill for about 4 minutes per side, to desired doneness. Makes 8 servings.

Nutritional values: One serving equals 1 skewer with 4 ounces beef and ⅛ cup vegetables: 170 calories; 19g protein; 7g fat; 7g carbohydrates; 560mg sodium; 113mg cholesterol.

Easy Gourmet for Diabetics

Deep-Dish Beef Pie

PASTRY:

¾ cup all-purpose flour
½ teaspoon baking powder

3 tablespoons margarine
3 tablespoons cold water

Combine flour and baking powder. Cut in margarine until mixture resembles coarse crumbs. Sprinkle with cold water, one tablespoon at a time, stirring with a fork until mixture holds together. Form into a ball. On a floured surface, roll dough into a circle 1 inch larger than top of casserole.

1 pound lean boneless beef
   for stew, trimmed of fat and
   cut into ½-inch pieces
1 teaspoon cooking oil
1 cup chopped onion
1 cup chopped celery
1 cup sliced carrots
1 cup cubed, peeled turnip
1½ cups tomato juice
¾ teaspoon crushed dried
   thyme or basil

¼ teaspoon salt
⅛ teaspoon pepper
1 cup plus 2 tablespoons water,
   divided
1 tablespoon all-purpose flour
2 cups fresh or frozen cut
   green beans
1 teaspoon skim milk

Spray a large skillet with nonstick coating. Preheat over medium-high heat. Brown half the meat in skillet. Remove. Add oil. Brown remaining meat. Return all meat to skillet. Stir in onion, celery, carrots, turnip, tomato juice, thyme, salt, pepper, and 1 cup water. Cover and simmer 50–60 minutes or until meat is nearly tender. Combine flour and remaining 2 tablespoons water. Stir into skillet mixture. Cook and stir until thickened and bubbly. Stir in green beans. Spoon into a 1½-quart casserole. Cover with Pastry; flute edges. Brush with milk. Cut vents for steam. Bake in a 400° oven for 30 minutes or until Pastry is lightly browned and meat and vegetables are tender. Serves 6.

Bless This Food

Shepherd's Pie

1 pound cooked beef or lamb
2 onions, chopped
2 carrots, peeled and chopped
3 tablespoons butter, divided
1 tablespoon cooking oil

1 cup gravy
2 pounds potatoes, boiled and
   mashed
1 egg yolk, beaten

Dice meat. Cook onions and carrots in 1 tablespoon butter and the oil over medium heat until they are tender but not brown. Stir in gravy. (If you do not have gravy, stir the 1 tablespoon flour into onions and carrots in pan and cook slowly for 7 minutes, then add 1 tablespoon tomato paste, and 1 cup bouillon.) Stir and cook until gravy thickens. Stir in diced meat.

With 1 tablespoon butter, grease well a 2-quart shallow oven-proof dish. Spread half the mashed potatoes in the bottom of the dish. Spoon meat and gravy over the potatoes and top with a layer of remaining potatoes. Paint the top of the potatoes with egg yolk. Dot with remaining 2 tablespoons butter. Bake, uncovered, in a 350° oven for 30 minutes. The potatoes should be golden brown on top when the dish is done.

A Gathering of Recipes

Cornish Pasty

PASTY:

3 cups flour
1 cup vegetable shortening
1 teaspoon salt
Ice water

Sift flour in a bowl and cut in shortening with 2 forks or a pastry blender; add salt. Add about ⅓ cup of ice water or enough to form a ball. Let stand a few minutes in refrigerator. Then roll out into 6 (4-inch) circles. Separate circles with wax paper and chill in refrigerator until filling is ready.

FILLING:

1 pound round steak, cut in
   cubes
Small bunch leeks or
   green onions
2 potatoes
⅛ cup chopped parsley
Salt and pepper to taste

Cut up meat, leeks or onions, potatoes, and parsley and season with salt and pepper. Divide mixture into 6 portions. Preheat oven to 350°. To the circle of dough add Filling on one side of dough; fold over dough and seal edges with a fork. Cut a couple of slits in each Pasty. Repeat until all dough and Filling are used up. Bake on greased baking sheets for 40–55 minutes or until Pasty is golden brown and vegetables are tender. Yields 4–6 servings.

Easy Cookin' in Nevada

Monkey Meat

This is a dish we affectionately call Monkey Meat. This is an excellent dish that you can make up in large quantities and freeze in quart-size freezer bags, to be used later as the main filling in tacos, taco salad, chili dishes, or with scrambled eggs (or make up your own). I recommend that you buy the brisket when it's on sale and do a big pot. I usually end up with 10–12 freezer bags full and it never goes to waste!

1 (10-pound) brisket
3 pounds ground beef (90%)
1 package sweet Italian sausage (about 5 links)
1 package hot Italian sausage (about 5 links)
2 bay leaves
4 tablespoons chili powder
3 tablespoons ground cumin seed
2 teaspoons salt
3 teaspoons pepper
5–7 medium garlic cloves, crushed
2 (28-ounce) cans crushed tomatoes
4 medium onions, chopped
3 (7-ounce) cans green chile peppers
3 bunches cilantro
3 raw jalapeño peppers, chopped

Cook brisket in covered roaster for 8 hours (overnight, 11pm to 7am) at 250°. Let meat cool to handle and save juices after skimming fat. Meat will be tender and stringy; pull apart and cut into shorter strips, trimming all fat.

In large stew pot, put in the cut-up brisket. In separate pan, brown ground meat; drain and add to pot. Remove casings from Italian sausage (both); brown and add to pot. Add bay leaves, chili powder, cumin, salt, pepper, garlic, crushed tomatoes, chopped onions, diced green chile, and all the juice drippings from roasting the brisket.

Simmer and stir frequently. Chop cilantro and add to pot. Dice 2 jalapeño peppers and add to pot. Taste and add more of any seasonings to correct. Some prefer a lot more cumin and chili powder.

Serve with flour tortillas; use meat as main addition to tortilla. Add condiments of grated cheese, sour cream, chopped lettuce, tomato, jalapeño, and chopped onion; or use the same condiments over meat on a bed of lettuce. To freeze, package into quart-size bags. Cool before putting into freezer.

Feeding the Flock

Corned Beef

1 (3-pound) beef brisket	1 (1-ounce) package au jus mix
1 large carrot, chopped	2 cups water
1 large onion, chopped	2 tablespoons tomato paste
1 clove garlic, minced	1 bay leaf
¼ cup vegetable oil	¼ teaspoon thyme
Salt and pepper	1 pound carrots, peeled

Trim excess fat from brisket. Heat oil in Dutch oven. Shallow fry chopped carrot, onion, and garlic in oil. Remove vegetables and add brisket; brown well and season with salt and pepper. Combine au jus mix with water; add to brisket with tomato paste, bay leaf, thyme, and sautéed vegetables. Cover and bake in a 350° oven for 1½ hours. Drain off cooking juices into saucepan. Keep meat hot. Sieve vegetables into sauce; taste and adjust seasonings. Keep hot.

Cut carrots in quarters lengthwise. Cook in boiling, salted water until just done. Carve brisket. Arrange overlapping slices on platter. Cover with hot sauce and garnish with carrots. Makes 4 servings with enough meat left for another meal.

Virginia City Alumni Association Cookbook

The Black Rock Desert Playa (ply-yah, Spanish for intermittent dry lake) is a basin surrounded by several mountain ranges. Driving on the playa is an amazing experience—it's so smooth that one has the feeling of being in a boat on a lake with no waves or resistance. Black Rock was the site in 1997 of the first breaking of the sound barrier—763.035 miles per hour—by a vehicle on land by the rocket-powered thrust SSC (super sonic car).

Roast, Dutch Oven Style

1 (4-pound) beef roast
3 onions
4–6 potatoes
3 bell peppers

6 carrots
1 clove garlic
1 (18-ounce) bottle barbecue
   sauce

Prepare pit (see below). Lightly oil a large Dutch oven. Place roast in oven. Peel and quarter onion and potatoes and place in the oven. Seed bell peppers, then cut into quarters and add with whole carrots. Pour entire bottle of barbecue sauce over the top. Place lid firmly on the oven and carefully lower it into the pit. Cook for about 2 hours.

TO PREPARE PIT:

Dig a hole about 2 feet deep and approximately 8 inches bigger around than your Dutch oven. About 2 hours before cooking, heat the hole by burning wood in it. You should use a wood that makes lots of ashes (sagebrush and smaller pine limbs are good). It takes a large fire to heat the ground. After heating the ground, take out the ashes, leaving 3 or 4 inches of ashes in the bottom of the hole. After setting the Dutch oven in the hole, put the ashes back in, surrounding the pan on all sides, and with 3 or 4 inches of ashes on top. Cover the ashes with 1 or 2 inches of dirt to hold the heat in, and you are cooking.

The Great Nevada Cookbook

Greek Moussaka

MEAT SAUCE:

2 (1-pound) eggplants, washed and dried
2 tablespoons butter or margarine
1 cup finely chopped onion
1½ pounds ground chuck or lamb
1 clove garlic, crushed
½ teaspoon dried oregano leaves
1 teaspoon dried basil leaves
½ teaspoon cinnamon
1 teaspoon salt
Dash of pepper
2 (8-ounce) cans tomato sauce
Salt
½ teaspoon sugar
½ can water
½ cup butter or margarine, melted

Peel and slice eggplants ¼ inch thick or less. Fry in margarine until golden brown on both sides. Line an ungreased 9x13-inch baking dish with half the eggplant slices. Mix all other ingredients together and spread over eggplant slices. Top with remaining slices. Pour Cream Sauce over top. Bake, uncovered, for 1 hour at 350°. Serves 4–6. Serve with salad and rice for a complete meal.

CREAM SAUCE:

2 tablespoons butter or margarine
2 tablespoons flour
½ teaspoon salt
Dash of pepper
2 cups milk
2 eggs
½ cup grated Parmesan cheese
½ cup Cheddar cheese
2 tablespoons dry bread crumbs

In saucepan on medium heat, combine ingredients until well blended. Pour over Meat Sauce.

Note: You may want to sauté onion, meat, and garlic in Meat Sauce before adding other ingredients.

Traditional Treasures

Skillet Tamale Pie

Tamale Pie is great for a crowd and especially tasty in cold weather. A tossed salad and light dessert is a nice accompaniment for this dish.

Olive oil
5 pounds lean ground beef
(give or take a pound)
4 medium onions, chopped
2 bell peppers, chopped (any
colors)
5 cloves garlic, chopped
2 (15-ounce) cans whole-
kernel or shoe peg corn
with liquid (or fresh
frozen corn)
1 (6-ounce) can tomato paste

2 (14½-ounce) cans diced
tomatoes with liquid
¼–½ cups hot chili powder
1½ teaspoons seasoned salt
1 teaspoon garlic salt
Plenty of freshly grated pepper
2 (15-ounce) boxes corn bread
mix
2 cups grated sharp Cheddar

cheese

GARNISHES:
½ cup freshly grated sharp
cheese
½ cup freshly chopped cilantro
½ cup sliced jalapeño
peppers

1 (4½-ounce) can sliced black
olives, drained
Chopped green onions with
tops
Cherry tomato slices

Lightly oil a large hot skillet and stir-fry the ground beef and onions. When onions are soft, add chopped bell pepper and minced garlic; cook 5 minutes longer. Add all the canned ingredients, chili powder, and seasoning, and stir. Bring to a simmer. Mix the corn bread according to directions on package. Sprinkle 2 cups cheese over meat mixture before spooning on the corn bread. (You may reserve ½ of the grated cheese and sprinkle it over the corn bread top before baking.) Spread the batter evenly over the meat mixture, smoothing it to the edges of the skillet. Place skillet in 400° oven and cook for about 35 minutes or until center of corn bread springs back when touched. Garnish as desired and serve hot from the skillet. Serves 8–10.

A Gathering of Recipes

West Coast Wrangler's Camp-out Quickie

1 pound ground beef
1 packet chili mix
1 (15-ounce) can Mexican
 corn, drained

3 (15-ounce) cans chili beans
1 (15-ounce) can Mexican-style
 tomatoes

Fry ground beef in a large skillet or Dutch oven until browned. Add contents of chili mix packet and the cans of vegetables to beef and heat through. Feeds 2 or 3.

A Cowboy Cookin' Every Night

Buffet Beans

3 pounds ground beef
2 medium onions, chopped
2 celery ribs, chopped
2 teaspoons beef bouillon
 granules
2/3 cup boiling water
2 (28-ounce) cans baked beans
 with molasses

1½ cups ketchup
¼ cup prepared mustard
3 cloves garlic, minced
1½ teaspoons salt
½ teaspoon pepper
½ pound sliced bacon, cooked
 and crumbled

In Dutch oven over medium heat, cook beef, onions, and celery until meat is no longer pink and vegetables are tender. Drain. Dissolve bouillon in water. Stir into beef mixture. Add the beans, ketchup, mustard, garlic, salt, and pepper. Mix well. Cover and bake at 375° for 60–70 minutes or until bubbly. Stir. Top with bacon. Makes 12 servings.

The Fruit of the Spirit

Meat Loaf

1 pound round steak
½ pound lean pork
1 cup cracker crumbs
3 eggs
2 teaspoons salt

Pepper to taste
1 tablespoon chopped onion
1½ cups sweet milk
4 slices bacon

Grind round steak and pork together. Mix ground meat, cracker crumbs, beaten eggs, salt, pepper, onion, and sweet milk. Place 2 slices of bacon in the bottom of loaf pan; pour in the mixture; place 2 slices on top. Bake 1¼ hours in hot (400°) oven.

Hoover Dam Cooks, 1933

Chili Chip Casserole

1 pound ground round
1 cup chopped onion
1 package Lawry's chili
  seasoning mix
1 (6-ounce) can tomato paste
¾ cup water

1 (6-ounce) bag corn chips
1 (1-pound) can pinto beans
2 (2½-ounce) cans sliced ripe
  olives
2 cups grated Cheddar cheese

Brown beef until crumbly. Mix in onion, chili seasoning mix, tomato paste, and water and simmer 10 minutes.

Place ½ bag of corn chips in bottom of buttered 2-quart casserole. Spoon ½ chili meat mixture over corn chips. Spread ½ can pinto beans over meat mixture followed by 1 can sliced olives. Sprinkle with 1 cup grated cheese. Repeat meat, pinto beans, olive layers. Arrange remaining corn chips over top, sprinkle with remaining cheese. Cover casserole and bake at 350° for 30–35 minutes. Uncover and bake an additional 15 minutes. Serves 6–8.

Twentieth Century Club Cook Book

Hearty Basque Style Casserole

1 pound extra lean ground beef

1 pound extra lean ground lamb

1 cup chopped yellow onion

1 (29-ounce) can tomato sauce

4 cups chopped green cabbage

2 cups chopped purple cabbage

1 cup uncooked white rice

$\frac{1}{2}$ teaspoon rosemary

$\frac{1}{2}$ teaspoon salt

$\frac{1}{2}$ teaspoon black pepper

2 (14-ounce) cans low-sodium nonfat beef broth

Preheat oven to 350°. Spray a large skillet with nonfat cooking spray and brown beef and lamb. Drain fat. In a large bowl, combine meat, onion, tomato sauce, cabbage, rice, rosemary, salt, and pepper. Pour mixture into a 9x13-inch baking dish; pour broth over mixture and bake, covered, for about 1 hour. Makes 8 servings.

Nutritional values: One serving equals 1¾ cups. Calories 415; Protein 25g; Fat 8g; Carbohydrates 33g; Sodium 875mg; Cholesterol 80mg.

Easy Gourmet for Diabetics

Dad's World Famous Goulash

1 pound hamburger

1 medium onion, chopped

$\frac{1}{2}$ green pepper, chopped

1 (16-ounce) can diced tomatoes

1 (8-ounce) can tomato sauce

$\frac{1}{2}$ teaspoon chili powder

Salt and pepper to taste

1 (8-ounce) package macaroni or penne pasta, cooked as directed on package

Several slices American cheese

Brown hamburger, onion, and green pepper in electric skillet. Add tomatoes, tomato sauce, and seasonings. Add cooked pasta and cheese. Allow cheese to melt. Serve and enjoy.

Still Cookin' After 70 Years

John Cuneo's Spaghetti Sauce

1 pound sweet Italian sausage, casings removed, cut in chunks
1 pound sirloin steak, cut in strips
3 tablespoons olive oil, divided
1 cup chopped yellow onion
6 garlic cloves, minced
4 (15-ounce) cans tomato sauce
1 (32-ounce) can whole tomatoes

4 (6-ounce) cans tomato paste
1 cup good dry red wine (Chianti is excellent)
1 teaspoon dried oregano
1 teaspoon dried basil
½ teaspoon salt
½ teaspoon black pepper
½ pound smoky links, sliced ½ inch thick
½ pound pepperoni (optional)
Cooked spaghetti

Brown Italian sausage and steak in 2 tablespoons olive oil. You may need to use 2 skillets. In a 6-quart saucepot, sauté onion and garlic in remaining oil until softened. Add Italian sausage, steak, tomato sauce, tomatoes, tomato paste, wine, oregano, basil, salt, and black pepper. Simmer, covered, stirring occasionally for 1 hour. Sauce should bubble a little between stirring. Add smoky links and pepperoni (if you can't take spicy sauce, omit the pepperoni) and simmer 15 minutes. Serve over spaghetti. Serves about 20.

Use Your Noodle!

The amazing expanses of large, old Joshua trees are perhaps one of the most impressive stands of their sort in the country. Certainly, they make for one of the most thrilling natural spectacles in all of Nevada. Scientists have learned that Joshua trees often grow as little as a half-inch per year, and many of them in the Wee Thump Joshua Tree Wilderness stand over 30 feet tall—which makes them over 720 years old!

Braised Beef Short Ribs

5 pounds beef short ribs,
  cut into 1-rib pieces
All-purpose flour, seasoned
  with salt and pepper
¼ cup rendered bacon fat
4 cloves garlic, chopped
3 onions, chopped

6 carrots, sliced
½ teaspoon crumbled dried
  rosemary
Salt and pepper to taste
Mushrooms (optional)
1 cup red wine
3 cups beef broth

Preheat oven to 350°. Dredge ribs in flour, knocking off excess. Heat bacon fat in a 6-quart Dutch oven over moderately high heat until hot but not smoking. Brown the short ribs. Transfer ribs to a large plate. Pour off all but about 2 tablespoons bacon fat remaining in Dutch oven, and in it cook garlic, onions, carrots, and rosemary with salt and pepper to taste over moderate heat, stirring until browned lightly; add mushrooms, if desired. Cook mixture about 6 more minutes.

Deglaze the pot with red wine. Add beef broth to the vegetable mixture and bring to a boil, stirring. Return ribs to the pot and cover. Cook (braise) in the oven until tender, about 2 hours.

The Best of Down-Home Cooking

Silver State Beef Short Ribs

4½ pounds beef short ribs
12 garlic cloves, sliced
1 red onion, sliced

3 quarts water
3 cups good red wine
Salt and pepper to taste

Place ribs, garlic cloves, and onion slices in large pot and cover with water and red wine. Bring to a boil. Reduce heat and simmer uncovered until meat is cooked through, about 50 minutes. Sprinkle with salt and pepper; set aside.

TOMATO CHILE SAUCE:

3 garlic cloves
½ red onion, sliced
3 ripe tomatoes
4–6 mild chiles, stemmed,
   halved, seeded

1–2 ancho chiles, stemmed,
   halved, seeded
2 teaspoons ground cumin
1 teaspoon dried oregano
¼ cup red wine vinegar

Combine garlic, onion, tomatoes, chiles, spices, and vinegar in a food processor. Blend until chunky. Grill ribs, slathering with about half the Sauce. Serve ribs with remaining Sauce. Serves 4–6.

A Cowboy Cookin' Every Night

Jealous Bourbon BBQ Sauce

1½ onions, chopped
12 cloves garlic, minced
2¼ cups bourbon whiskey
1½ teaspoons black pepper
2 teaspoons salt
6 cups ketchup
1 cup tomato paste
1 cup apple cider vinegar
¼ cup liquid smoke flavoring
¼ cup Worcestershire sauce
1½ cups brown sugar
1½ teaspoons Louisiana hot
  pepper sauce

In a large skillet over medium heat, sauté onions, garlic, and whiskey 5–10 minutes, until onion is translucent. Add black pepper, salt, ketchup, tomato paste, vinegar, liquid smoke, Worcestershire sauce, brown sugar, and hot pepper sauce. Mix well and bring to a boil. Reduce heat and simmer for 20 minutes.

A Cowboy Cookin' Every Night

Barbecue Sauce

1 (14-ounce) bottle ketchup
1 (6-ounce) jar chili sauce
⅙ cup prepared mustard
1½ teaspoons dry mustard
¾ cup brown sugar
1 tablespoon coarse black
  pepper
¾ cup wine vinegar
½ cup fresh lemon juice
¼ cup thick steak sauce
Dash Tabasco sauce
1½ teaspoons soy sauce
1½ tablespoons Worcestershire
  sauce
2 tablespoons Mazola oil
6 ounces beer

Mix all ingredients well. This sauce should be made ahead of time for the flavors to blend. It keeps very well refrigerated. Makes about 3 pints.

Historical Boulder City Cookbook

Independence Day Barbecue Spare Ribs

5 pounds pork spareribs,
  cut into sections
1 cup brown sugar
½ cup chili sauce
½ cup ketchup
¼ cup Worcestershire sauce
¼ cup rum

⅛ cup soy sauce
4 cloves garlic, crushed
1 teaspoon dry mustard
1 teaspoon ground black
  pepper
½ teaspoon cayenne pepper
  (optional)

Preheat oven to 350°. Wrap ribs in double thickness of foil and bake for 45 minutes. Unwrap and drain. Combine brown sugar, chili sauce, ketchup, Worcestershire sauce, rum, soy sauce, garlic, mustard, black pepper, and cayenne, if desired. Pour over ribs. Marinate refrigerated overnight.

Preheat grill. Grill ribs for 30 minutes, turning once and basting with marinade. Serves 10.

All American Meals Cookbook

Barbecued Pork Chops

BARBECUE SAUCE:

½ small onion, finely chopped
1 (10¾-ounce) can condensed
  tomato soup
1½ cups water
3 tablespoons vinegar
2 tablespoons Worcestershire
  sauce

1 teaspoon salt
1 teaspoon paprika
1 teaspoon chili powder
½ teaspoon pepper
¼ teaspoon cinnamon
Dash ground cloves

Combine all ingredients in a pan. Bring to a boil, lower heat, and simmer 20 minutes. Set aside.

CHOPS:

6 thinly sliced pork chops
5 tablespoons olive oil

Flour

Wipe off pork chops with damp cloth. Heat oil. Dredge chops in flour and sear them in oil. Pour half the Barbecue Sauce over chops. Cover, reduce heat, and cook slowly for 20 minutes. Turn chops over. Pour remaining sauce over chops and continue to cook slowly for another 30 minutes. Add small amounts of water if sauce dries up. Yields 3–6 servings.

Chorizos in an Iron Skillet

The array of wildlife—which includes numerous birds, desert tortoise, desert bighorn sheep, and wild burros—isn't the only thing that makes Red Rock Canyon unique; the multi-colored rock formations contribute to a geologic wonderland composed almost entirely of Aztec Sandstone (found also in the Valley of Fire State Park and very few other areas in the Southwest United States).

Marinated Pork Tenderloin

MARINADE:

½ cup lemon juice
½ cup soy sauce
½ cup Marsala or red wine

½ teaspoon pressed garlic
2 teaspoons ground ginger
3 pork tenderloins

Combine lemon juice, soy sauce, wine, garlic, and ginger, and marinate pork tenderloins overnight.

ORANGE SAUCE:

⅔ cup sugar
1 tablespoon cornstarch
½ teaspoon salt
20 whole cloves, tied in
  cheesecloth

½ teaspoon cinnamon
1 tablespoon orange rind
1 cup orange juice

Combine in saucepan sugar, cornstarch, salt, cloves, cinnamon, orange rind, and orange juice. Cook over medium heat until thick and clear. Remove cloves and rinds and remove from heat. Cover pot. Barbecue pork on hot fire 12–20 minutes, depending on thickness and desired doneness. Serve topped with Orange Sauce and garnished with orange slices.

Tasteful Treasures

With mostly mountainous and desert terrain, altitudes vary in Nevada from above 13,000 feet to below 1,000 feet.

Darned Good Skillet Supper

¼ cup olive oil
2 slices bacon, cut in small
  pieces
3 medium onions, peeled and
  sliced into rings
1 or 2 teaspoons paprika
Salt and coarsely ground
  pepper
8 boneless pork loin chops,
  about ½ inch thick
1½ cups fresh carrots, cut in
  chunks
8 fresh turnips, peeled and
  cut into eighths
16 baby boiling potatoes
  (unpeeled)

2 cloves fresh garlic, minced
  (or ½ teaspoon garlic
  powder)
2 or 3 sprigs fresh thyme (or
  1½ teaspoons dry, crushed)
3 tablespoons chopped fresh
  parsley (or ½ teaspoon dry)
1 generous sprig fresh mint
  (or ½ teaspoon dry)
1 sprig fresh bay leaf (or 1 dry
  leaf, crushed)
1 (14-ounce) can beef broth
½ cup white wine

Add olive oil to hot skillet and cook bacon pieces till clear, not crisp. Remove and set aside. Add onions and cook till soft. Remove and set aside with bacon. Rub paprika, salt and freshly ground pepper on both sides of pork chops. Brown in same skillet. Cook about 5 minutes on each side to medium-well. Remove chops and set aside.

Arrange carrots, turnips, and potatoes in the skillet. Add onions, bacon, and minced garlic. Lay fresh thyme, parsley, mint, and bay leaf over vegetables (or sprinkle dry herbs). Mix beef broth and wine and pour into skillet. Cover with a tightly fitted lid and simmer vegetables until tender, about 35–40 minutes. Uncover and correct seasoning. Arrange the browned chops around the vegetables; cover and reheat chops about 5 minutes longer; remove lid.

For a stunning presentation, place hot skillet supper in the center of the table, accompanied by a tossed salad with vinaigrette dressing.

A Gathering of Recipes

Ben Cuneo's Sicilian Succo

5 cloves garlic, chopped
3 (32-ounce) cans tomato
  sauce
4 (6-ounce) cans tomato paste
3 tablespoons chopped fresh
  parsley, divided
1 tablespoon chopped fresh
  basil

2 pounds ground sirloin
1 pound ground pork
1 cup bread crumbs
1 cup grated Parmesan cheese
1 teaspoon black pepper
½ teaspoon garlic salt
2–4 tablespoons olive oil

In a large pot, mix together garlic, tomato sauce, tomato paste, 1 tablespoon parsley, and basil. Bring sauce to a boil, then turn down the heat and simmer 30 minutes.

Combine ground sirloin, ground pork, bread crumbs, Parmesan cheese, remaining parsley, black pepper, and garlic salt. Shape into 3-inch wide meatballs.

In a skillet, fry meatballs in hot olive oil until brown. Add to sauce mixture. Simmer over low heat for about 1½ hours until meatballs are cooked thoroughly. We serve this with pasta or on crusty bread. Serves about 12.

Use Your Noodle!

"Cowboy Life is Peachy" Ham

1 (5-pound) boneless country
  ham
¾ cup peach preserves or jam

1 tablespoon lemon juice
1 teaspoon cinnamon
½ teaspoon ground cloves

Skewer ham on spit. Cook one hour over medium fire or coals. Mix jam, lemon juice, cinnamon, and cloves. Baste ham with peach sauce often and cook about 45 minutes to 1 hour longer until meat thermometer reads 185° and ham is well glazed. Serves 4–5 loafing cowpokes on a Sunday afternoon or 6–8 church ladies in loose knickers.

Authentic Cowboy Cookery Then & Now

Ham Puff

1 pint milk
1 cup flour
½ cup butter

Salt and pepper to taste
6 or 8 eggs, separated
1½ cups ground ham, cooked

Make white sauce of milk, flour, and butter; let cool. Add salt and pepper to taste. Beat egg yolks and add to white sauce, then add ham and stiffly beaten egg whites. Bake in buttered baking dish set in a pan of water for ¾ of an hour. Serve at once.

Hoover Dam Cooks, 1933

The Silver Terrace Cemeteries are a series of terraces dramatically located on the steep, windswept hillside of Virginia City. Nearly every plot is fenced or bordered, a typical practice of the Victorian period. Very few of the adults buried in these cemeteries were born in Nevada. The birthplaces noted throughout the grounds provide a glimpse of the scope of immigration and the makeup of the settlement that supported the Comstock mining industry.

All American Marmalade Glazed Ham

GLAZE:

1 cup orange marmalade

¼ cup Dijon mustard

2 tablespoons orange juice

Melt marmalade in saucepan. Whisk in mustard and orange juice. Boil until thickened, about 5 minutes. Set aside.

1 (20-pound) smoked bone-in
  ham
30 whole cloves
1 cup orange juice
2 cups water
4 orange spice-flavored
  tea bags
1 cup low-sodium chicken
  broth

4 tablespoons orange
  marmalade
1 tablespoon Dijon mustard
1 tablespoon cornstarch,
  dissolved in 1 tablespoon
  water
Black pepper to taste

Preheat oven to 325°. Score fatty side of ham in a crisscross pattern. Insert a clove into cross sections of score pattern. Place ham on a rack in a roasting pan with orange juice. Bake 3 hours for 45 minutes.

Increase oven temperature to 425°. Baste ham with Glaze and bake until Glaze is set and begins to caramelize, about 20 minutes. Transfer ham to cutting board and let set at least 15 minutes. Reserve pan juices and pour into a saucepan.

In another saucepan, bring water to a boil. Add tea bags and remove from heat. Let steep 10 minutes. Discard tea bags. Add chicken broth and orange marmalade to tea. Bring to a boil; reduce heat. Whisk in mustard and reserved pan juices until blended. Whisk in cornstarch mixture and stir until thickened. Boil until sauce thickens slightly, about 4 minutes. Season with black pepper to taste. Carve ham and serve with sauce. Serves 12.

All American Meals Cookbook

Veal Rolls Divan

3 slices bacon
1½ cups packaged herb
  seasoned stuffing mix
6 thin veal steaks, pounded
  ⅛-inch thick
1 tablespoon salad oil
2 (10-ounce) packages frozen
  broccoli spears, thawed

1 chicken bouillon cube
1 (10-ounce) can frozen
  condensed cream of shrimp
  soup, thawed
⅓ cup milk

In skillet, cook bacon till crisp; drain, reserving drippings. Prepare stuffing mix according to package directions, using bacon drippings and melted butter to make ¼ cup. Crumble bacon; stir into stuffing.

Sprinkle veal steaks with salt. Place ⅓ cup stuffing on each steak; roll and tie each securely. Add 1 tablespoon salad oil to same skillet; brown veal rolls. Arrange meat and broccoli spears in 7½x12x2-inch baking dish.

Dissolve crushed bouillon cube in ½ cup boiling water; pour over meat. Cover with foil; bake at 350° for 1 hour. Combine soup and milk; heat through. Before serving, remove ties from meat; pour soup mixture over. Makes 6 servings.

Let Freedom Ring

A popular saying in Virginia City: "Samuel Clemens was born in Missouri, but Mark Twain was born in Virginia City." Samuel Clemens had recently taken the pen name of Mark Twain when he began his 22-month stint as a young reporter for the Virginia City *Territorial Enterprise,* Nevada's first newspaper.

Chopstick Veal Bake

1½ pounds veal steak,
  ½ inch thick
2 tablespoons salad oil
1½ cups sliced celery
1 cup chopped onion
1 cup diced green pepper
3 tablespoons chopped canned
  pimiento

½ cup uncooked long-grain
  rice
1 (10¾-ounce) can condensed
  cream of mushroom soup
1 cup milk
2 tablespoons soy sauce
1 (3-ounce) can chow mein
  noodles (2 cups)

Cut meat in 2x½-inch strips. Brown in hot oil. Add remaining ingredients except noodles. Turn into 2-quart casserole. Cover; bake at 350° for 1¼–1½ hours; stir occasionally. Last 5 minutes of baking, uncover; sprinkle with noodles. Serves 8.

Let Freedom Ring

Six Mile Canyon Rattlesnake

5 tablespoons butter, divided
4 (1½-inch) fillets rattlesnake
  meat
3 large portobello mushrooms,
  sliced
2 tablespoons minced red
  onion

½ cup burgundy wine
1 tablespoon flour
1 teaspoon cumin
½ teaspoon garlic powder
½ teaspoon salt
½ teaspoon pepper

Heat 2 tablespoons butter in a fry pan; sauté fillets 5 minutes per side. Remove fillets. Add 2 tablespoons butter to pan; sauté mushrooms and onion until soft. Add red wine; cook over low heat until contents are reduced by half.

    Mix remaining 1 tablespoon butter and flour to form a paste. Add to vegetables. Cook, stirring constantly until blended. Add cumin, garlic powder, salt, and pepper. Pour vegetables and sauce over snake meat; serve.

A Cowboy Cookin' Every Night

Firefries

Lamb, mutton, and beef are staples on many dining tables in the Silver State. One culinary interpretation—based on the precept that one should not waste any part of the animal—is the "mountain oyster" or "lamb fry."

2 tablespoons butter
4 slices bacon, diced
1 onion, chopped
4 garlic cloves, chopped fine
½ cup fresh parsley
2 pounds lamb fries (slit, soaked, peeled, parboiled, and cut into halves lengthwise)
½ cup tomato sauce

½ cup dry white wine
½ cup beef stock
½ teaspoon rosemary
Salt
Freshly ground pepper
1 dried hot red chile (stemmed, seeded, finely chopped)
2 tablespoons Madeira

In a large skillet, melt butter over low heat. Add bacon and cook gently until the bacon fat begins to melt. Add onion, garlic, and parsley. Increase heat and sauté for about 5 minutes. Add fries and brown, stirring occasionally. Combine tomato sauce, wine, and beef stock, and pour just enough to cover the fries. Add rosemary, salt, pepper, and red chile. Simmer over low heat for 45 minutes or until the fries are firm. Add more of the liquid as necessary to keep fries covered. When fries are firm, add Madeira and simmer for a few minutes. For a stronger flavor, add garlic and more chiles. Serves 6.

The Great Nevada Cookbook

One of the Silver State's most unique desert environments, Valley of Fire State Park near Las Vegas is a fascinating landscape of wind-sculptured red sandstone.

Lamb Stew with Garlic and Pinot Noir

This interpretation of this tummy-warming comfort food has a Lebanese touch. Fresh mint adds an interesting flavor prominent in Lebanese dishes.

½ cup all-purpose flour
Salt and pepper to taste
2 pounds lamb stew meat
  (preferably shoulder)
  trimmed of fat, cut into
  stew-size pieces
3 tablespoons olive oil
1 large head garlic, roasted
  and chopped finely
½ cup chopped yellow onion

¼ cup chopped green pepper
½ cup chopped peeled carrots
½ cup chopped celery
2 cups Pinot Noir (red wine)
½ cup chopped Roma
  tomatoes
2–3 cups lamb stock made from
  the bones and trimmings
3 bay leaves
1 tablespoon fresh mint

Combine flour, salt and pepper in a bowl. Add lamb and stir to coat. Set aside. In a large, heavy-bottomed stainless steel pot, heat the olive oil. Add chopped garlic and cook until slightly golden. (Do not allow it to brown or it will add a bitter taste.) Add onion, pepper, carrots, and celery. Cook for 5–10 minutes, stirring, until onion is slightly translucent. Add the lamb and brown on all sides, approximately 10–15 minutes. Add the Pinot Noir. Cook and reduce the liquid by 25 percent. Add the tomatoes, 2 cups lamb stock, bay leaves, pinch of salt and freshly ground pepper. Reduce by another 25 percent.

Lower heat, cover, and simmer over low heat 1–1½ hours. During the last half hour, uncover and let the stew thicken to a nice velvety thick consistency. If it is too thick, add a little more stock. Use your own judgment on the final consistency of this wonderful dish. Add fresh mint just before serving. Serve with polenta. Serves 4.

God, That's Good!

Rack of Lamb with Mint Stuffing

1 (7-ounce) package herb
  seasoned cubed stuffing mix
1 pound ground lamb
1/4 cup finely chopped onion
1 tart apple, peeled, cored,
  finely chopped
1 teaspoon fresh lemon juice
1 tablespoon finely chopped
  mint leaves, fresh or dried
1 tablespoon water
1/4 teaspoon paprika
1/4 teaspoon pepper

1 teaspoon salt
1 (5- to 6-pound) crown roast
  of lamb
Salt and pepper to taste
1 tablespoon dried mint leaves
1 tablespoon vinegar
1/2 cup red currant jelly
1 tablespoon grated orange
  peel
2 tablespoons finely chopped
  fresh mint leaves

Prepare stuffing mix using package directions. Brown ground lamb with onion in a skillet, stirring frequently. Add apple, lemon juice, 1 tablespoon mint, water, paprika, pepper, and 1 teaspoon salt. Remove from heat. Stir in prepared stuffing. Set aside and keep warm.

Season roast with salt and pepper. Wrap bone ends in foil. Place in a roasting pan on a rack. Bake at 325° for 30 minutes per pound. Remove from oven 45 minutes before roast is done. Fill center with some of the stuffing. Cover top of roast with foil. Place remaining stuffing in a 1½-quart casserole. Place roasting pan and casserole in oven. Bake for 45 minutes.

Mix 1 tablespoon mint and vinegar in a bowl. Let stand for 2 minutes; drain well. Discard vinegar. Break the jelly into pieces with a fork. Stir in orange peel, 2 tablespoons mint, and vinegar-soaked mint.

Remove roast from oven. Let stand for 10 minutes. Cover bone ends with paper frills. Serve the sauce and additional stuffing on the side. Yields 6–8 servings.

Las Vegas Glitter to Gourmet

Elk Enchiladas

2 pounds ground elk
½ cup olive oil
1 (16-ounce) jar picante sauce
1 (7-ounce) can diced green
  chiles, drained
1 (16-ounce) can pinto beans,
  drained
½ pound sharp Cheddar
  cheese, cubed, divided

½ pound pepper Jack cheese,
  cubed
16–20 corn tortillas
1 cup sour cream
1 cup chopped tomatoes
1 cup sliced olives

Preheat oven to 325°. Brown ground elk in oil in skillet and drain grease. Return meat to skillet and add picante sauce and chiles. Simmer 10 minutes; add beans and ¼ of cheese cubes and simmer until cheese is melted. Fill each tortilla with ¼ cup meat mixture; roll and place in baking dish seam-side-down. Bake 25 minutes; top with remaining cheese cubes. Bake 10–12 minutes or until cheese is melted. Top with sour cream, tomatoes, and olives. Serves 6.

Wild Man Gourmet

Starting in the mid 1980s, a period of unprecedented growth began in Las Vegas. Annual population increases averaging nearly 7 percent caused the city's population to almost double between 1985 and 1995, increasing from 186,380 to 368,360 during that time, a 97.6 percent increase. The city's population in 2000 was 478,434. Las Vegas' incorporated population is an understatement of the city's recent population boom, as much of the greater Las Vegas metropolitan area is unincorporated. As of 2001, the greater Las Vegas metropolitan area is the fastest growing population center in the United States and (not including nearby Boulder City) contains 1,337,357 residents. In 2003, the metropolitan area had reached 1,620,748. And the growth continues still. Recent projections are that the Las Vegas Valley will have over two million-plus residents by 2005.

Venison with Blue Cheese Sauce

¼ cup all-purpose flour
¼ teaspoon salt
⅛ teaspoon pepper
6 venison steaks
¼ cup butter, divided
2 tablespoons olive oil
½ cup red wine

¼ cup chopped shallots
2 tablespoons water
1 teaspoon fresh marjoram
½ teaspoon instant beef
   bouillon granules
4 ounces crumbled blue cheese

Combine flour, salt, and pepper. Dredge steaks in mixture to coat. In skillet, heat half the butter and olive oil. Cook steaks for 6–8 minutes, or until desired doneness. Transfer steaks to warm platter. Cover to keep warm. Set aside.

In skillet juices, add red wine, shallots, water, marjoram, and bouillon. Cook over medium-high heat until mixture is reduced by half, stirring constantly. Add remaining butter and blue cheese. Cook over medium heat until sauce is smooth, stirring constantly. Spoon sauce over steaks. Serves 6.

Wild Man Gourmet

Ribs Diablo

8 pounds wild boar spareribs,
  or 10 pounds caribou
  back ribs
Water
1 cup Cabernet Sauvignon
1 Vidalia onion, minced
4 cloves garlic, minced
2 tablespoons butter
1 cup tomato paste

½ cup steak sauce
1 cup honey
1 tablespoon Worcestershire
  sauce
1 bottle dark beer
1 teaspoon cinnamon
½ teaspoon salt
6 shakes Tabasco or to taste

Boil ribs in enough water and wine to cover 1 hour. Sauté onion and garlic in butter. Add tomato paste, steak sauce, honey, Worcestershire sauce, beer, cinnamon, salt, and Tabasco sauce. Bring to boil; reduce heat and simmer 30 minutes. Drain ribs and bake in 350° oven 30–40 minutes or until brown, basting often with sauce until glazed. Serves 6–8.

Wild Man Gourmet

Poultry

Built in just five short years, Hoover Dam contains 4.5 million cubic yards of concrete—enough to pave a two-lane highway from San Francisco to New York. One byproduct of this engineering marvel high above the Colorado River between Arizona and Nevada was the invention of hard hats.

French Country Style Chicken

4 (6-ounce) boneless, skinless
  chicken breasts
Salt and black pepper to taste
1 cup Granny Smith apples,
  unpeeled, cored, sliced
6 scallions, diced
²⁄₃ cup apple cider

1 cube chicken bouillon
1 teaspoon dried sage
½ teaspoon dried ginger
²⁄₃ cup 2% milk
2 teaspoons flour
2 teaspoons Splenda
Parsley as garnish

Spray skillet with nonfat cooking spray. Sauté chicken breasts until browned, about 5 minutes per side. Season to taste with salt and black pepper. Add apples, scallions, apple cider, bouillon, sage, and ginger. Heat to a boil. Reduce heat and simmer, covered, until chicken is tender, 10–12 minutes. Remove chicken and apples to serving platter.

Simmer remaining cider mixture until reduced. Stir in milk, flour, and sugar substitute into skillet. Heat to a boil, stirring constantly, until thickened, about 1 minute. Season to taste with salt and pepper. Pour sauce over chicken and apples. Garnish with parsley and serve hot. Serves 4.

Nutritional values: One serving equals one breast and ¼ apples with ¼ cup sauce: Calories 270; Protein 32g; Fat 2g, Carbohydrates 25g, Sodium 676mg; Cholesterol 66mg.

Easy Gourmet for Diabetics

In the mid-1980s, *Life* magazine ran an article titled "The Loneliest Road," about Highway 50 between Ely and Fernley because there are such few tourist stops in the 287-mile distance. Taking advantage of the publicity, Chamber of Commerce officials soon posted road signs all along the way, deeming it "The Loneliest Road in America."

Raspberry Chicken

1 jar pure raspberry jam
1 cup unsweetened pineapple
  juice concentrate
1 cup low-sodium soy sauce
2 tablespoons rice vinegar
1 teaspoon chili powder
1 teaspoon curry powder

1 teaspoon garlic powder
1 cup fresh raspberries,
  mashed, divided
4 (4-ounce) skinless, boneless
  chicken breasts
1 cup chopped fresh basil, for
  topping

Mix jam, pineapple juice, soy sauce, vinegar, chili powder, curry powder, garlic powder, and ¼ cup mashed raspberries; pour over chicken breasts in baking dish. Marinate in refrigerator for one hour. Top with remaining raspberries and basil. Place in 350° oven for 30–40 minutes.

Let Freedom Ring

Iron Mountain Chicken with Burgundy Sauce

⅔ cup chicken stock
⅓ cup water
⅓ cup red wine, such as
  hearty burgundy
1 teaspoon tarragon
4 (6-ounce) skinless, boneless
  chicken breasts

1 teaspoon cornstarch,
  dissolved in 1 tablespoon
  water
½ teaspoon salt
½ teaspoon black pepper

Bring stock, water, wine, and tarragon to a boil in saucepan. Reduce heat and add chicken breasts. Poach 15–20 minutes until chicken is cooked through. Plate chicken and keep warm. Stir dissolved cornstarch into liquid remaining in saucepan. Bring to a boil, stirring constantly with a wire whisk until sauce thickens. Season with salt and pepper and serve sauce over chicken breasts. Makes 4 servings.

Nutritional analysis per serving: Calories 236; Protein 43g; Fat 3g; Carbohydrates 2g.

The Protein Edge

Grilled Chicken with Herbs

2 tablespoons minced fresh
  parsley
2 teaspoons minced rosemary
2 teaspoons minced thyme
1 sage leaf
3 garlic cloves, minced
¼ cup olive oil
½ cup balsamic vinegar
Salt and pepper
1½ pounds boneless, skinless
  chicken breasts

In a blender, combine all ingredients except chicken. Pour marinade over chicken breasts in a bowl. Cover and place in refrigerator and let marinate for at least 2 hours or up to 48 hours.

Grill or broil chicken for about 6–7 minutes per side until no trace of pink remains. Makes 6 (4-ounce) servings.

Nutritional analysis: Calories 197; Carbohydrates 1g; Sugar 1g; Fat 10g; Sodium 78mg; Cholesterol 69mg; 4 very lean meat and 1 fat exchange.

Sharing Our Diabetics Best Recipes

Crisp Crusted Baked Chicken

6–8 chicken breasts
1 egg
1 tablespoon milk
1 cup instant potato flakes
1 teaspoon garlic powder
¼ cup Parmesan cheese
¼ cup butter

Wash chicken and pat dry. Beat egg and milk together. In another bowl, mix potato flakes, garlic powder, and Parmesan cheese. Roll chicken breasts in egg mixture first, then in potato flakes mixture.

Melt butter in a shallow pan. Roll coated chicken in butter and place in baking pan. Bake at 400° for 50 minutes, or until juices from breasts run clear when pierced by a fork.

Still Cookin' After 70 Years

Chicken Deluxe Casserole

Throw in a side salad and you're set! Delicious.

**4 cups Pepperidge Farm Herb
  Stuffing Mix**
1 cup butter
**2 (10¾-ounce) cans cream of
  mushroom soup**
**1 (13-ounce) can evaporated
  milk**

2 tablespoons minced onion
¼ teaspoon pepper
**2½ pounds cooked chicken,
  cubed**
1 small jar diced pimentos
1 (10-ounce) box frozen peas

Preheat oven to 400°. Use 4 cups stuffing mix and mix with melted butter or margarine. Press ⅔ of the stuffing mixture into the bottom of a 9x13-inch pan. Mix together 2 cans soup, evaporated milk, onion, pepper, approximately 4 cups cooked chicken, pimento, and frozen uncooked peas.

Spoon chicken mixture over dressing mixture that has been pressed into pan; top with remaining ⅓ of dressing mixture. Press dressing down with hands so that you can feel moisture seep through, so that during the baking it will not dry out. Bake 45 minutes at 450°.

Feeding the Flock

Creamy Crockpot Chicken

1 cut-up chicken, or 4 boneless breasts
1 envelope dry Italian dressing mix
1 (8-ounce) package cream cheese
1 (10¾-ounce) can chicken soup

Place all ingredients in crockpot on LOW until chicken is done and gravy is smooth and creamy. Serve over cooked rice or mashed potatoes.

Note: This recipe is very flexible. If you like or need more gravy, add more soup; or try a different "cream of" variety; add more chicken. If you don't have Italian dressing mix, use another dry mix. I have tried lots of different combinations, and they have all been great.

Feeding the Flock

Easy Quick Italian Chicken in Foil

4 bone-in chicken breasts with skin on
4 pieces aluminum foil (enough to wrap each piece of chicken)
1 bottle Wish Bone Italian Salad Dressing or your favorite Italian dressing

Place each piece of chicken, skin-side-up, in a piece of foil. Shake enough salad dressing on chicken to cover; wrap it up. Place in broiler or on BBQ and cook for 15–20 minutes (time varies by breast size). Just before removing, open foil and baste top of chicken and place back in broiler for 3–5 minutes to crisp the skin on top.

The Melting Pot

Gym Rat's Oven Baked Chicken Strips

2 (8-ounce) boneless, skinless
  chicken breasts
2 egg whites, beaten
½ cup whole-wheat cracker
  crumbs
1 teaspoon dried oregano

1 teaspoon dried basil
½ teaspoon dried thyme
1 teaspoon paprika
2 teaspoons grated Parmesan
  cheese

Cut chicken breasts into strips. Dip strips in egg whites. Combine cracker crumbs, spices, and Parmesan in a plastic bag. Add chicken strips and shake bag to coat with crumb mixture. Put chicken strips on a nonstick baking sheet or baking sheet sprayed with nonfat cooking spray. Bake at 350° for 10–12 minutes until golden and crunchy. Great served with marinara sauce. Makes 4 servings.

Nutritional analysis per serving: Calories 197; Protein 29g; Fat 5g; Carbohydrates 6g.

The Protein Edge

Mustard Marinade

¼ cup Dijon mustard
¼ cup whole-seed mustard
¼ cup sweet-hot German
  mustard
¼ cup vinegar
¼ cup olive oil

½ cup apple juice
Juice of ½ lemon
2 tablespoons honey
1 large clove garlic, crushed
2 green onions, sliced
Freshly ground pepper

Combine all ingredients in a bowl. Whisk to emulsify. Marinate chicken 1–3 hours before grilling. Pork or lamb can be marinated 8 hours or overnight before grilling.

Tasteful Treasures

Chicken Stroganoff

4 chicken breast halves,
  skinned and boned
6 tablespoons safflower oil,
  divided
1 small onion, diced
½ cup flour
Pinch of thyme
Pinch of nutmeg

½ teaspoon salt
¼ teaspoon white pepper
2 teaspoons fresh lemon juice
1 cup chicken broth
1 cup sour cream
Cooked buttered spinach
  noodles
Minced parsley for garnish

Cut chicken breasts into bite-size pieces. Heat 2 tablespoons oil in large frying pan. Add onion and sauté until transparent. Remove onion and set aside. Combine flour, thyme, nutmeg, salt, and pepper in bag and dredge chicken pieces. Add remaining 4 tablespoons oil to frying pan. Add chicken pieces and brown over medium heat until light golden in color. Mix in lemon juice and broth and simmer 10 minutes. Reduce heat to low.

Stir 2 tablespoons hot chicken broth into sour cream. Add to pan, stirring constantly, and heat gently to serving temperature. Do not boil or sauce will curdle. Spoon over hot, buttered noodles and garnish with parsley. Serves 4.

Historical Boulder City Cookbook

Red Rock Canyon near Las Vegas is one of the top five rock-climbing destinations in the country. Its name is derived from the striking red sandstone formations found throughout this small valley.

Spicy Garlic Chicken Pizza

½ cup sliced green onions, divided
2 garlic cloves, minced
2 tablespoons rice vinegar or white vinegar
2 tablespoons soy sauce
2 tablespoons olive oil, divided
½ teaspoon crushed red pepper, or ¼ teaspoon cayenne pepper
¼ teaspoon black pepper
12 ounces boneless, skinless chicken breasts, cut into ½-inch pieces
1 tablespoon cornstarch
1 (16-ounce) Boboli Italian bread shell
½ cup shredded Monterey Jack cheese
½ cup shredded mozzarella cheese
2 tablespoons pine nuts or sliced almonds

Combine ¼ cup green onions, garlic, vinegar, soy sauce, 1 table-spoon olive oil, red pepper, and black pepper in a bowl and mix well. Add chicken and stir to coat. Let stand for 30 minutes at room temperature. Drain and reserve the marinade. Stir corn-starch into marinade.

Heat remaining 1 tablespoon olive oil in a large skillet and add chicken. Sauté for 3 minutes or until cooked through. Add reserved marinade to skillet. Cook until thick and bubbly, stir-ring constantly. Spoon chicken mixture evenly onto the bread shell. Sprinkle with Monterey Jack cheese and mozzarella cheese. Bake at 400° for 12 minutes. Top with ¼ cup green onions and pine nuts. Bake for 2 minutes longer. Serve hot. Yields 6 servings.

Las Vegas Glitter to Gourmet

Green Chile Chicken Enchiladas

6 precooked chicken breasts
  chopped
1 green apple, chopped
1 yellow onion, chopped into
  large pieces
1 large can green chile
  enchilada sauce

12 flour tortillas
1 pound shredded Monterey
  Jack cheese
Sour cream for garnish

Put chicken pieces, apple, and onion in pot and cook on medium heat until apple and onion are soft and chicken is warm and has created a good amount of juice.

In a large lasagna pan, pour in enough enchilada sauce to cover bottom of pan. Put approximately 2 tablespoons chicken mixture and 1 tablespoon, or more, cheese into one tortilla. Roll tortilla and place into pan. Repeat process until pan is full. Cover enchiladas with remaining cheese. Cover pan with foil and bake at 350° for 20–30 minutes. Let cool for 5 minutes. Serve. Garnish with sour cream.

The Melting Pot

A Capella Chicken Enchiladas

1 medium onion, chopped
2–3 tablespoons butter
1 (10¾-ounce) can cream of
  chicken soup
1 (10¾-ounce) can cream of
  mushroom soup
1 (4-ounce) can chopped
  green chiles

1 cup chicken broth
1 chicken (or 8 breasts), boiled
  and boned
1 (8-count) package corn
  tortillas
1 pound longhorn cheese,
  grated

In a skillet, sauté the onion in butter. Add soups, chiles, and broth. Add shredded chicken and mix well. In a large baking dish, layer some of the corn tortillas, part of the chicken mixture, and a layer of grated cheese. Repeat layers until the dish is filled, ending with cheese. Let the dish stand for several hours before baking. Bake in a 350° oven for one hour. Serves 10.

Let Freedom Ring

South of the Border Enchiladas

10 (6-inch) corn tortillas,
  halved
3 cups cubed cooked skinless
  chicken breasts
1 cup fresh corn kernels
1 cup chopped yellow onion

1 cup diced green bell pepper
2 cups diced tomatoes, divided
¾ cup diced mild green chiles
1 cup shredded reduced-fat
  Cheddar cheese

Preheat the oven to 350°. Spray a 9x13-inch baking pan with nonfat nonstick cooking spray. Line bottom of pan with half of tortillas and layer with chicken, corn, onion, pepper, and half the tomatoes. Cover with the remaining tortillas. Pour the remaining tomatoes and chiles over the top; cover with foil and bake about 30 minutes. Uncover and sprinkle with the cheese. Bake, uncovered, until cheese melts. Serves 6.

Nutritional values: One serving equals ⅙ of casserole: Calories 286; Protein 27g; Fat 5g; Carbohydrates 35g; Sodium 628mg; Cholesterol 51mg.

Easy Gourmet for Diabetics

Chicken Piccata

2 chicken breasts
2 tablespoons flour
¼ teaspoon salt
⅛ teaspoon pepper
2 tablespoons olive oil
¼ small onion, minced
1 clove garlic, minced
½ cup chicken broth, or
 ½ teaspoon bouillon
 dissolved in ½ cup warm
 water

1 tablespoon butter
1 tablespoon sherry
1 tablespoon lemon juice
1 teaspoon capers
1 slice fresh lemon plus ½
 tablespoon chopped parsley
 for garnish

Pound chicken breasts between 2 sheets of plastic wrap until ¼ inch thick. Set aside. Mix together flour, salt and pepper to form seasoned flour. Dip chicken lightly; shake off excess flour. Heat a large dry frying pan over medium heat until a drop of water sizzles. Then add olive oil. Sauté onion and garlic until golden brown. Remove from heat; set aside. In the same frying pan, sauté chicken breasts until golden, turning only once. Remove from heat; set aside. Place in 250° oven to keep warm.

Make sauce by adding chicken broth to the pan. Add onion mixture, butter, sherry, lemon juice, and capers to the same pan. Stir and cook until syrupy and sauce is slightly thick. Add chicken breasts back to pan; simmer for 2–5 minutes until chicken is thoroughly cooked and piping hot. Place chicken breasts on a serving plate. Spoon sauce neatly on the chicken. Garnish with lemon and parsley. You may substitute fresh prawns (shelled and deveined) or thinly sliced pork for chicken. Serve with noodles, steamed broccoli, and garlic bread for a complete meal. Serves 2.

Tasteful Treasures

Lemonade Chicken

3 pounds cut-up chicken parts
2 tablespoons flour
1 teaspoon salt
1 (6-ounce) can frozen
 lemonade concentrate,
 thawed

3 tablespoons packed brown
 sugar
3 tablespoons ketchup
2 tablespoons salad oil
2 teaspoons vinegar

Toss rinsed and dried chicken parts in flour and salt until well coated. Fry chicken in hot oil until browned on all sides. In a 2-cup measure, combine undiluted lemonade, brown sugar, ketchup, oil, and vinegar; add enough water to make 2 cups. Pour lemonade mixture and another ½ cup water into skillet; cover and cook over low heat 30 minutes or until chicken is fork-tender.

Kitchen Chatter

Korean Chicken

6 pieces chicken
Salt and pepper
2 tablespoons vegetable oil
2 cloves garlic, minced
3 drops hot sauce

¼ teaspoon red pepper flakes
1 tablespoon sesame oil
½ cup soy sauce
⅓ cup sugar
¼ cup chopped green onions

Salt and pepper the chicken pieces. In a large skillet, brown chicken in vegetable oil. While chicken is browning, combine in a medium bowl the garlic, hot sauce, red pepper flakes, sesame oil, soy sauce, and sugar. Mix well. Set aside.

Once the chicken is browned, pour the sauce over the chicken and cook on simmer for about 25 minutes. (Cover skillet for first 15 minutes and then uncover it for the final 10 minutes.) Stir it every so often to ensure it does not burn. To serve, remove pieces of chicken to a serving dish and then pour sauce from skillet over chicken. Garnish with green onions. Serves 4.

God, That's Good!

Chicken with Chocolate

You will be surprised at how truly delicious this chicken is. In the Basque region of Navarra, the use of chocolate, especially in game recipes, is popular.

1 (2½ to 3-pound) fryer,
  cut up
¼ cup cooking oil or olive oil
1 large onion, chopped
2 cloves garlic, minced
1 green bell pepper, chopped
  (1-1½ cups)
2 (8-ounce) cans tomato sauce

1–2 teaspoons crushed dried
  red pepper
1 teaspoon salt
¼ teaspoon Tabasco sauce
2 cloves garlic, chopped
½ ounce unsweetened baking
  chocolate, finely grated

Soak chicken briefly (10–15 minutes) in cold, salted water. Trim off excess fat. Drain chicken pieces in colander. Pat dry with paper towel, if necessary. Heat oil in frying pan or electric skillet to a moderate 300° heat. Brown chicken pieces in oil. When nicely browned, remove pieces to a Dutch oven or casserole with cover.

In the skillet in which you browned the chicken pieces, sauté onion, garlic, and bell pepper for 10 or 15 minutes on low heat. Add remaining 6 ingredients, mixing well. Simmer about 5 minutes. Spoon sauce over chicken pieces in Dutch oven or casserole. Bake at 350° for one hour. Yields 5–6 servings.

Chorizos in an Iron Skillet

The area around Hoover Dam and Lake Mead is the one of hottest and driest regions in the United States. Three of America's four desert ecosystems—the Mojave, the Great Basin, and the Sonoran Deserts—meet in Lake Mead National Recreation Area.

Turkey Tetrazzini

½ cup butter or margarine
½ cup flour
4 cups chicken broth
4 egg yolks
4 tablespoons sherry
1 cup light cream
Salt to taste
½ pound mushrooms, sliced, sautéed in butter

3 cups diced, cooked turkey
2 (10-ounce) packages chopped broccoli, cooked, drained
1 (7-ounce) package spaghetti, cooked, drained
2 tablespoons grated Parmesan cheese
¼ cup slivered, blanched almonds

Melt butter; stir in flour. Gradually stir in chicken broth. Cook over low heat, stirring constantly till mixture thickens. Mix egg yolks, sherry, and cream. Gradually beat flour mixture into egg mixture. Reheat until sauce is thickened, but do not boil. Add salt to taste. Fold in mushrooms and turkey. Reheat.

Put layer of cooked broccoli in bottom of shallow serving dish; top with hot, cooked spaghetti and turkey sauce. Sprinkle Parmesan cheese and almonds on top. Put under broiler and brown until cheese is golden. Serve at once. Serves 6.

Timbreline's Cookbook

Cornish Game Hens

4 Cornish game hens
6 strips bacon, diced
1 cup chopped onion
1 clove garlic, minced
1 cup dry vermouth
1 (12-ounce) can tomatoes

1 (4-ounce) can sliced mushrooms
1 teaspoon salt
1 teaspoon tarragon, crumbled
Croutons

Thaw game hens. Remove giblets. Set aside for other use. Fry bacon; remove from pan. Brown hens in hot bacon drippings. Put in baking dish. Sauté onion and garlic in drippings. Add remaining ingredients, except croutons. Heat to boiling and pour over hens. Cover and bake in 350° oven for 1 hour. Sprinkle crisp bacon and croutons over before serving. Serves 4.

Timbreline's Cookbook

Baked Chukar

1 cup uncooked white rice
½ cup uncooked brown rice
Salt and pepper
6–8 chukar breasts
1 (1-ounce) envelope dry onion
   soup mix

1 (10¾-ounce) can cream of
   celery soup
2 soup cans water

Put white and brown rice in bottom of a 2-quart casserole. Salt and pepper chukar and place on top of the rice. Sprinkle soup mix over chukar and rice. Cover contents of casserole with cream of celery soup mixed with water. Bake uncovered at 425° for 20 minutes. Then cover casserole and bake at 350° for 1½ hours more. Yields 3–6 servings.

Chorizos in an Iron Skillet

Roasted Duck, Nevada Style

6 slices French bread,
   crumbled
½ cup diced yellow onion
5 cloves garlic, sliced
4 tablespoons butter
4 tablespoons chopped cilantro

2 tablespoons diced jalapeño
4 tablespoons chopped
   pine nuts
1 or 2 ducks
1 cup chicken broth
1 cup red wine

Preheat oven to 325°. Combine bread, onion, garlic, butter, cilantro, jalapeño, and pine nuts. Stuff duck(s) with mixture. Rub duck(s) with additional butter. Put in roasting pan; add broth and wine. Bake 4 hours at 325°.

For gravy, add pan juices to a little flour and butter; stir until thick. Serves 1–2 per duck.

Wild Man Gourmet

Seafood

In 1844, explorer John C. Fremont named Pyramid Lake, located north of Reno, after the 500-foot, pyramid-shaped rock off the lake's southeastern shore.

BBQ Salmon
with Potatoes and Peppers

¼ pound red-skinned
   potatoes, scrubbed and cut
   into 1-inch cubes
3 tablespoons olive oil
1 red or yellow bell pepper,
   cut into thin strips

1 medium red onion, sliced
1 tablespoon capers
Salt and pepper to taste
2 (8-ounce) skinless salmon
   fillets or steaks, 1 inch thick

Heat oven to 450°. Partially cook the potatoes by boiling or steaming them for 8 minutes; drain and set aside. In a 9- or 10-inch skillet, heat olive oil over medium heat. Add bell pepper and onion. Cook for 5 minutes or until softened. Remove from heat. In an oven-proof dish, combine bell pepper, onion, and potatoes. Add capers, salt and pepper to taste; toss together. Set aside.

SPICE MIXTURE:
2 teaspoons paprika
2 teaspoons brown sugar
Pinch cayenne or red pepper

½ teaspoon salt
½ teaspoon black pepper

Combine all ingredients and sprinkle on a plate. Coat salmon fillets in the spice mixture on both sides, shaking off excess spices. Put salmon on top of potatoes and peppers and place dish in the oven. Roast for 20–25 minutes, or until salmon is firm to the touch. Makes 2 servings.

CASA Cooks

Lake Tahoe, given its size and depth—22 miles long, 12 miles wide, 72 miles of shoreline, with an average depth of 985 feet—contains an almost incomprehensible amount of water. How much? Enough water evaporates off Lake Tahoe every day to supply the daily water requirements of 3.5 million people.

Salmon with Olive and Bread Crumb Crust

¼ cup chopped kalamata olives
¼ cup chopped green olives
¼ cup chopped sun-dried tomatoes (oil-packed)
3 garlic cloves, minced
2 tablespoons melted butter
1½ teaspoons chopped fresh rosemary
1½ teaspoons chopped fresh thyme
5½ teaspoons Dijon mustard, divided
1 cup panko (Japanese bread crumbs)
4 (6-ounce) salmon fillets

Preheat oven to 400°. Mix olives, tomatoes, garlic, butter, and herbs in medium bowl. Mix in 1½ teaspoons Dijon mustard, then bread crumbs. Butter large baking sheet. Place salmon fillets on sheet. Spread 1 teaspoon mustard over each. Pack ¼ of the bread crumb mixture onto each mustard-coated fillet. Bake until opaque in center, about 15 minutes.

Lake Tahoe Cooks!

Dishwasher Fish

4 (8-ounce) halibut or other fish fillets
1 tablespoon lemon juice
Salt and pepper to taste
Carrots, broccoli, onions, and/or cauliflower, sliced

Arrange fish on a foil-lined baking sheet. Season with lemon juice, salt and pepper. Add vegetables of choice. Cover with foil, sealing completely. Place on top rack of dishwasher. Allow the dishwasher to run through a wash cycle; do not add soap. Yields 4 servings.

From Sunrise to Sunset

North African Coast Tilapia

2 tablespoons light olive oil
1 cup thinly sliced red onion
4 cloves garlic, minced
1 cup chopped tomatoes
½ cup dry white wine
½ cup sliced black olives
2 tablespoons chopped fresh
  parsley
1 tablespoon fresh lemon juice

1 teaspoon chopped fresh basil
1 teaspoon chopped fresh
  oregano
½ teaspoon cumin or
  coriander
½ teaspoon salt
4 (8-ounce) tilapia fillets
  (cod may be substituted)
Lemon slices

In a frying pan, heat oil. Sauté onion and garlic in olive oil until softened. Stir in tomatoes, wine, olives, parsley, lemon juice, and spices. Simmer for 5 minutes. Place fillets in sauce. Simmer until fish turns white. Serve with lemon slices.

The Hooked Cook

Zane's Catfish BLT's

ZANE'S COCKTAIL SAUCE:

¾ cup mayonnaise
3 tablespoons sweet pickle
  relish
1½ tablespoons bottled capers,
  drained and diced
1 tablespoon Dijon mustard

1 tablespoon fresh lemon juice
1 tablespoon bottled cocktail
  sauce
1 teaspoon lemon zest
⅛ teaspoon cayenne
Salt and pepper to taste

In a bowl, combine all ingredients. Chill covered at least one hour.

FISH BLT'S:

2 large eggs, beaten
½ teaspoon salt
¼ teaspoon cayenne
1 cup all-purpose flour,
  seasoned with salt and
  pepper
1 cup cornmeal
2 pounds catfish fillets, cut
  into 8 (4-ounce) portions

Vegetable oil for deep-frying
8 soft sandwich or sourdough
  rolls, split
1 cup shredded iceberg lettuce
2 ripe tomatoes, sliced thin
½ red onion, sliced thin
16 slices bacon, cooked

Beat eggs with salt and cayenne. Place flour, cornmeal, and eggs in 3 separate shallow dishes. Dredge catfish fillets in flour; shake off excess. Then dip fillets in egg mixture, and finally dredge in cornmeal. Transfer the fish to a plate. In a deep-fryer, heat enough oil to cover fillets to 375°, or in frying pan, heat 1 inch of oil to 375°. Fry the fish in batches for 2–4 minutes on each side, or until it is done inside and crispy golden on the outside. Drain on paper towels.

On each bottom half of roll, layer lettuce, tomatoes, onion, 2 slices of bacon, fish, and Cocktail Sauce. Top with upper half of the roll. Serve with fries or potato chips.

The Hooked Cook

Mahi Mahi
with Low-Fat Cucumber Sauce

½ cup peeled, seeded, and
  chopped cucumber
½ cup low-fat plain yogurt
2 tablespoons chopped fresh
  dill or ½ teaspoon dried
2 tablespoons chopped parsley

2 green onions, white part and
  first 2 inches of green,
  chopped
1 teaspoon lemon zest
4 (¼-pound) mahi mahi steaks
1 tablespoon fresh lemon juice

Mix cucumber, yogurt, dill, parsley, green onions, and lemon zest in a bowl and set aside. Arrange mahi mahi on a plate with thickest portions to the outside. Drizzle with lemon juice. Cover with plastic; vent at one corner. Microwave on HIGH for 4–5 minutes until thickest portion is just opaque. Rearrange fish once. If fish is thick, it may need more cooking time. Check frequently, about every 20 seconds, to avoid overcooking. Let stand 5 minutes to finish cooking. Drain. Serve room-temperature yogurt sauce on top of fish.

Recipes from Sunset Garden Club

Sole Sebastian

8–12 fillets of sole
1–1½ cups small shrimp
Lemon juice
3 tablespoons butter
3 tablespoons flour
Salt
1 (10¾-ounce) can
   mushroom soup

1½ pints sour cream
½ pound mushrooms, sliced
Grated Parmesan cheese
Sherry
Paprika
Parsley

Roll each fillet with shrimp. Place in greased casserole. Sprinkle with lemon juice. Melt butter in small pan; add flour and salt to make roux. Cook until blended; stir in soup. Add sour cream just until heated. Sauté mushrooms and place over fish. Pour sauce over fish. Sprinkle generously with Parmesan cheese. Bake 1 hour at 275°. Just before done, sprinkle with sherry and garnish with paprika and parsley.

Virginia City Alumni Association Cookbook

Chopsticks Tuna

1 cup sliced celery
½ cup sliced onion
1 cup water
1 (6½- or 7-ounce) can tuna,
   light meat chunk
1 (10¾-ounce) can cream of
   mushroom soup

1 (8-ounce) can water chestnuts
   (optional)
1 (16-ounce) can Chinese
   noodles
½–1 cup salted cashew nuts

Cook celery and onion in water for 10 minutes. Mix in tuna, mushroom soup, and water chestnuts, if desired. Place layer of Chinese noodles in baking dish; pour tuna mixture over noodles. Sprinkle some noodles and cashews on top. Bake in 350° oven for 15 minutes. Serve with green salad.

Historical Boulder City Cookbook

Twisted Tater Fish Cakes

¾ pound russet potatoes,
  peeled, sliced
2 (6-ounce) orange roughy
  fillets
¼ pound bay shrimp,
  chopped
3 ounces smoked salmon,
  chopped
½ cup chopped leeks
¼ cup chopped fresh dill
2 teaspoons lemon zest

Salt and pepper to taste
1½ cups fresh sourdough
  bread crumbs
1 teaspoon basil
½ cup grated Parmesan
  cheese
1 teaspoon Old Bay Seasoning
1 teaspoon thyme
3–6 tablespoons canola oil
Lemon wedges

Steam potatoes until tender, approximately 10 minutes. Drain and let cool, then mash potatoes in a large bowl. Steam fish until cooked through, about 10 minutes; transfer to plate; cool 5 minutes. Flake fish and add to potatoes. Mix in shrimp, smoked salmon, leeks, dill, and lemon zest. Season to taste with salt and pepper. Using ⅓ cupful per cake, shape fish mixture into ½-inch thick cakes. Season bread crumbs with basil, Parmesan, thyme, and Old Bay. Place bread crumbs in shallow bowl. Coat each cake with bread crumbs, pressing to adhere.

Heat 3 tablespoons oil in large skillet. Working in batches, sauté fish cakes until brown and heated through, adding more oil as needed, about 3 minutes per side. Garnish with lemon wedges. Serve with Twisted Taters (page 90).

The Hooked Cook

The Lahontan Cutthroat Trout, a native trout found in fourteen of the state's seventeen counties, is adapted to habitats ranging from high mountain creeks and alpine lakes to warm, intermittent lowland streams and alkaline lakes where no other trout can live.

Cabo San Lucas Sea Bass with Salsa Verde

SALSA VERDE:

Lime zest
2 limes
4 teaspoons diced, drained
  capers
1 teaspoon minced garlic
Salt and pepper to taste
¼ cup plus 1 tablespoon
  extra virgin olive oil, divided

¼ cup chopped fresh cilantro
  leaves
⅛ cup chopped fresh parsley
  leaves
⅛ cup diced scallions

Grate 1 teaspoon zest from one lime, then squeeze 2 table-spoons of juice. Combine zest, capers, garlic, lime juice, salt and pepper to taste. Add ¼ cup oil in a slow stream, whisking constantly until blended. Whisk in herbs and scallions. Heat an outdoor grill to hot. Or preheat oven to 450°. With remaining oil, lightly oil a baking sheet and place fillets on it.

SEA BASS:

6 (8-ounce) sea bass fillets
4 teaspoons extra virgin
  olive oil
2 tablespoons fresh lemon
  juice
Salt and black pepper to taste

1 tablespoon chopped fresh
  parsley
2 teaspoons chopped fresh
  thyme
2 teaspoons chopped fresh
  oregano

Brush fish with oil; drizzle with lemon juice. Sprinkle fish with salt and pepper, then parsley, thyme, and oregano. Grill or bake fish until opaque, about 10 minutes. Transfer to plates. Spoon several tablespoons of Salsa Verde over fish. Serve any remaining Salsa Verde on the side.

The Hooked Cook

Bacalao

3 or 4 tablespoons olive oil
¾ cup chopped onion
¾ cup chopped green pepper
1 or 2 garlic cloves, finely
  chopped
Salt and pepper to taste

1 (8-ounce) can tomato sauce
½ teaspoon lemon pepper
1½ or 2 pounds codfish,
  cut into serving pieces
Flour
Parsley, fresh or dried

In large skillet, simmer olive oil, onion, green pepper, and garlic for about 10 minutes. Add salt and pepper to taste. Add tomato sauce, lemon pepper, and codfish. Add water to cover and enough flour to thicken slightly. Sprinkle with parsley; cover and simmer 30–40 minutes.

Elko Ariñak Dancers Cookbook

Broiled Herbed Scallops

¼ pound fresh bay scallops
1 green onion, minced
2 tablespoons lemon juice
1 teaspoon vegetable oil

1 teaspoon dried basil
½ teaspoon dried tarragon
Chopped fresh parsley

Put scallops in a bowl. Add remaining ingredients, except the parsley. Toss and marinate at room temperature for 10–15 minutes. Remove scallops from marinade and put on wooden skewers or place in a shallow pan. Broil just until scallops are opaque, being careful not to overcook. Baste with the marinade. Sprinkle on parsley just before serving. Makes 2 servings.

Nutritional analysis: Calories 84; Carbohydrates 0; Fat 3g; Sodium 150mg; Cholesterol 30mg; 2 lean meat exchanges.

Sharing Our Diabetics Best Recipes

Venice Beach Shrimp Verde

2 tablespoons olive oil
2 cloves garlic, chopped
¼ cup chopped green onions
1 pound fresh shrimp, peeled
  and deveined
½ cup chopped Italian
  flat-leaf parsley

½ cup freshly grated
  Parmesan cheese
4 cups spring mix or other baby
  greens

Heat olive oil in a skillet. Sauté garlic and green onions until softened. Add shrimp and sauté until pink. Stir in parsley and grated Parmesan cheese. Remove from heat and serve over salad greens. Makes 4 servings.

Nutritional analysis per serving: Calories 238; Total Fat 11.6g; Carbohydrates 2g.

The Protein Edge

Shorty's Beer Batter Shrimp Poor Boys

1 cup beer
1 cup cake flour
1 teaspoon salt
1 teaspoon cayenne pepper
1 pound uncooked extra large
  shrimp, peeled, deveined

Canola oil for deep-frying
4 French rolls, split, toasted
1 cup shredded iceberg lettuce
1 ripe tomato, thinly sliced

Combine beer, cake flour, salt, and cayenne pepper. Cover shrimp in batter. Heat oil in deep-fryer to 325°. Fry shrimp until golden. Transfer shrimp to paper towels and drain. Slather rolls with Horseradish Spread. Layer bottom half of rolls with lettuce, tomato, and shrimp. Top with upper half of rolls. Serves 4.

HORSERADISH SPREAD:
1 cup mayonnaise
¼ cup prepared horseradish

2 tablespoons fresh lemon juice
2 garlic cloves, minced

Combine well and slather rolls with spread.

The Hooked Cook

Crusty Shrimp and Crab Salad Sandwiches

1 cup diced cooked shrimp
1 cup shredded crabmeat
¼ cup diced black olives
¼ cup diced celery
⅛ cup minced onion
½ cup chopped hard-boiled
  eggs
⅔ cup mayonnaise

2 teaspoons lemon juice
½ teaspoon dill
¼ teaspoon salt
8 teaspoons butter, room
  temperature
8 slices sourdough bread
4 teaspoons chopped fresh
  parsley or watercress

Combine first 10 ingredients. Chill. Spread butter on slices of sourdough bread. Toast sourdough slices under broiler or in toaster oven. Top 4 of the hot bread slices with chilled shrimp and crab salad. Sprinkle with a teaspoon of parsley or watercress. Top with remaining bread slices. Serve immediately while salad is cold and bread is hot. Serves 4.

The Hooked Cook

Tequila Shrimp

1 tablespoon butter
2 tablespoons vegetable oil
¾ pound medium shrimp,
  peeled and split long way
2 teaspoons crushed garlic

½ cup chopped onion
¼ cup chopped cilantro
¾ cup tequila
¾ cup (½-inch cubes)
  avocado

Melt butter with oil in large skillet. Sauté shrimp with garlic and onion until onion is translucent, about 4–5 minutes. Add cilantro, tequila, and avocado. Continue to simmer. Alcohol will evaporate and avocado will thicken the sauce. Don't overcook.

CASA Cooks

Crab Cobbler

½ cup butter
½ cup chopped green pepper
½ cup chopped onion
½ cup flour
1 teaspoon dry mustard
1 teaspoon Ac'cent
1 cup milk
1 cup shredded American
  cheese
1 cup crabmeat
1½ cups drained chopped
  tomatoes
2 teaspoons Worcestershire
  sauce
½ teaspoon salt

In top of a double boiler, add butter, green pepper, and chopped onion; let cook about 10 minutes. Blend in flour, dry mustard, Ac'cent, milk, and cheese; cook and stir until cheese melts and mixture is very thick. Add crabmeat, tomatoes, Worcestershire sauce, and salt. Pour into a greased 2-quart casserole. Drop topping over crab mixture and bake in 450° oven 20–25 minutes.

CHEESE BISQUICK TOPPING:
¼ cup shredded cheese
1 cup Bisquick
½ cup milk

Combine all ingredients and drop by teaspoons on top of crab mixture.

NSHSRA High School Rodeo Cookbook

Because of Nevada's arid land, cattle have to roam over a wide area; therefore, ranches average more than 2,000 acres in size. Most Nevada beef cattle are shipped to California or the Midwest for fattening prior to marketing.

Clam Sauce

¼ cup olive oil
1 clove garlic, minced
¼ cup water
½ teaspoon salt
¼ teaspoon pepper

½ tablespoon chopped parsley
¼ teaspoon oregano
1 (7-ounce) can clams with
juice

Heat oil and garlic together; stir in water slowly. Stir in salt, pepper, parsley, and oregano. Slowly add clams and juice. Cook until heated, and pour over cooked linguine.

Partyline Cook Book

Oysters in Wine Sauce

1½ cups fresh mushrooms,
sliced, or 2 (4-ounce) cans,
drained
1 cup chopped green onions
½ cup butter

1 cup white wine
½ teaspoon Worcestershire
sauce
2½ pints extra small oysters
2 tablespoons flour

Sauté mushrooms and onions in butter. Remove from heat. Add wine and Worcestershire sauce. Rinse and dry oysters. Lightly coat oysters with flour. Into a 9x13-inch baking pan, spoon enough of the sauce to cover the bottom of the dish. Place oysters in pan and pour remaining sauce over them. Bake at 425° for 20 minutes. Serve with rice.

Note: Also wonderful with any white fish, cut into 1-inch pieces, or scallops. Alcohol content bakes out of this sauce.

Church Family Recipes

Cakes

Ward Charcoal Ovens State Historic Park is known for its six historic charcoal ovens. Built in 1873, these beehive-shaped ovens were used in the late 19th century to generate charcoal used for smelting ores in the mines of nearby Ward. Approximately 30 feet high, they were said to contain 35 cords of wood when full.

PHOTO © NEVADA COMMISSION ON TOURISM

Dancing Palomino Spice Cake

3 cups all-purpose flour
4 teaspoons ground ginger
2 teaspoons cinnamon
½ teaspoon ground cloves
½ teaspoon cardamom
2 sticks unsalted butter,
   softened

1 cup brown sugar
1 cup molasses
1 cup boiling water
2 teaspoons baking soda
2 large eggs, beaten

Preheat oven to 350°. Grease a 9x13-inch pan. Combine flour, ginger, cinnamon, cloves, and cardamom. In a separate bowl, beat together butter and brown sugar until fluffy, about 3 minutes. Whisk together molasses and boiling water in another bowl. Whisk baking soda into hot molasses. Combine dry ingredients and molasses, then fold in butter mixture until blended. Whisk eggs into mixture until smooth. Pour batter into cake pan and bake 55–65 minutes until toothpick inserted in center comes out clean. Cool before removing from pan. Prepare frosting.

CREAM CHEESE FROSTING:

2 (8-ounce) packages cream
   cheese, softened
1 stick unsalted butter,
   softened

1 teaspoon orange zest
2 cups powdered sugar

Beat together cream cheese, butter, and orange zest until fluffy. Slowly beat in powdered sugar. Chill frosting before spreading on cooled cake. Serves a couple of cowboys with a sweet tooth or 5 or 6 ranch kids.

Authentic Cowboy Cookery Then & Now

Sock-It-To-Me Cake

STREUSEL FILLING:

2 tablespoons dry cake mix   2 tablespoons cinnamon
2 tablespoons brown sugar   1 cup finely chopped pecans

Combine dry cake mix, brown sugar, and cinnamon in a medium bowl. Stir in pecans and set aside.

BATTER:

1 package Duncan Hines   ⅓ cup oil
  Butter Recipe Cake Mix   ¼ cup water
4 eggs   ¼ cup granulated sugar
1 cup dairy sour cream

Preheat oven to 375°. Combine remaining cake mix, eggs, sour cream, oil, water, and granulated sugar in large bowl. Beat at medium speed with an electric mixer for 2 minutes. Pour ⅔ of Batter into oiled and floured 10-inch tube pan. Sprinkle with Streusel Filling. Spoon remaining Batter evenly over filling and bake 45–55 minutes or until toothpick comes out clean. Cool in pan 25 minutes. Invert onto serving plate. Cool completely.

GLAZE:

1 cup confectioners' sugar   1–2 teaspoons milk

Combine confectioners' sugar and milk in small bowl. Stir until smooth. Drizzle over cake.

The Best of Down-Home Cooking

 Strange but true: You will drive west from Los Angeles, California, to get to Reno, Nevada. (Actually north, then slightly west.)

Basque Tipsy (Sherry) Cake

This delicious cake is excellent plain or served with whipped cream.

CAKE:

⅔ cup sliced almonds
4 eggs
1 teaspoon almond extract
1¾ cups sugar
2 cups flour

2 teaspoons baking powder
¼ teaspoon salt
1 cup boiling water
1 stick (½ cup) butter, melted
(no substitutions)

Preheat oven to 325°. Butter and lightly flour a 10-inch angel food pan. Sprinkle sliced almonds on the bottom. Beat eggs and almond extract till foamy. Continue beating, adding sugar gradually. Sift together flour, baking powder, and salt. Add dry ingredients and boiling water alternately to egg mixture. Stir in melted butter. Spoon or pour batter into pan. Bake for one hour or until cake springs back when touched. Cool cake in pan.

With a wooden or metal skewer, poke holes through cool cake while it is still in the pan. Spoon half the Glaze over the cake. Remove cake from pan, being careful not to disturb the sliced almonds. (You may need to loosen cake by gently running a knife between the cake and sides of pan, as well as between cake and bottom of pan once the side pan had been removed.) Invert cake onto a plate (almonds will be on top of cake). With the skewer, poke holes carefully down from top of cake. Spoon remaining half of Glaze over the cake. Yields 10–12 servings.

GLAZE:

1¼ cups cream sherry
⅓ cup sugar

¼ cup butter
¼ teaspoon almond extract

While cake is cooling, make the Glaze. Heat sherry, sugar, and butter in a saucepan over medium heat till mixture simmers. Lower heat and simmer about 15 minutes. Remove from heat and add almond extract. Cool.

Chorizos in an Iron Skillet

Basque Apple Cake

CAKE:

2 cups sugar
3 eggs
1 cup oil
2 teaspoons vanilla
2¼ cups flour

1 teaspoon salt
2 teaspoons cinnamon
1 teaspoon baking soda
4 cups diced apples
½ cup chopped nuts

Mix sugar, eggs, oil, and vanilla. Add flour, salt, cinnamon, and baking soda. Add diced apples and nuts. Bake in greased 9x13-inch pan at 375° for one hour.

FROSTING:

1 (8-ounce) package cream
  cheese, softened
½ cup powdered sugar

2 tablespoons margarine
1 teaspoon vanilla

Combine cream cheese, powdered sugar, margarine, and vanilla until smooth. Frost cooled cake.

Church Family Recipes

Orange Pineapple Cake

1 (18¼-ounce) yellow cake
  mix
½ cup butter, softened
4 eggs
1 (11-ounce) can Mandarin
  oranges with juice

1 (3-ounce) package French
  vanilla instant pudding mix
2½ cups crushed pineapple
  with juice
1 (9-ounce) container whipped
  topping, thawed

Mix together cake mix, butter, eggs, and oranges with juice. Pour into a 9x13-inch pan that has been sprayed with oil. Bake in 350° oven for 25–30 minutes, or until tested done with toothpick. Put pudding mix in a bowl; add crushed pineapple, juice and all, and fold in whipped topping. Beat together and place a large dollop on each piece of cake when serving. Refrigerate unused topping mixture.

Kitchen Chatter

Tutti-Frutti Cake

3 cups pitted dates
8 ounces candied pineapple
  (4 ounces each: red and
  green)
8 ounces candied cherries
1½ cups shelled whole Brazil
  nuts
1½ cups chopped pecans

½ cup raisins
1¾ cups sifted flour
1½ cups sugar
1½ teaspoons baking powder
½ teaspoon salt
6 large eggs, well beaten
1½ teaspoons vanilla extract
  or rum extract

Halve dates and coarsely chop pineapple. Combine dates, pineapple, whole cherries, Brazil nuts, pecans, and raisins. Sift together the flour, sugar, baking powder, and salt. Add to the fruit and nut mixture and toss to coat mixture generously with flour. Stir in eggs and vanilla extract. Preheat oven to 300°. Line buttered loaf pans with buttered brown paper. Pour in batter. Bake in oven for 30 minutes; reduce heat to 275° and bake another 20–30 minutes. Cool in pans overnight. Remove from pans and wrap well with plastic wrap. Set aside for days. Cut in thin slices and serve. Yields 3 loaf-size fruit cakes.

Note: For longer ripening, wrap in foil and store in covered container or in freezer.

Easy Cookin' in Nevada

Triple Lemon Ripple Cake

FILLING:

1 (8-ounce) package cream
  cheese, softened
⅓ cup sugar

1 egg
2 tablespoons flour
2 tablespoons lemon juice

Beat cream cheese and sugar; beat in egg till fluffy. Add flour. Stir in lemon juice. Set aside.

BATTER:

½ cup butter, softened
1½ cups sugar
3 eggs
3 tablespoons lemon juice

2¼ cups flour
2 teaspoons baking powder
½ teaspoon salt
½ cup milk

Preheat oven to 350°. Spray tube pan with cooking spray. Cream butter and sugar. Beat in eggs till mixture is very light and fluffy. Add lemon juice. Combine dry ingredients and add to creamed mixture alternating with milk.

    Pour ½ the Batter into pan. Cover with Filling, then pour in remaining Batter. Gently swirl knife through batter a few times. Bake 50–60 minutes until cake pulls away from sides of pan. Cool in pan 10 minutes. Turn out and cool completely.

GLAZE:

2 tablespoons lemon juice   1½ cups confectioners' sugar

Stir lemon juice into confectioners' sugar. Drizzle over cake. Makes 10–12 servings.

Still Cookin' After 70 Years

Nevada's name comes from the Spanish word meaning "snow clad"—a reference to the snow-covered peaks of the Sierra Nevada mountain range which has snow for half the year. Nevadans pronounce it Nuh-vad-uh (as in "add," not "odd").

Cherry Chocolate Cake

2 cups flour
3/4 cup sugar
3/4 cup oil
2 eggs, unbeaten
1 teaspoon vanilla
1 teaspoon baking soda
1 teaspoon cinnamon
1/8 teaspoon salt
1 (21-ounce) can cherry pie
  filling
1 (6-ounce) bag chocolate chips
1 cup chopped nuts
Powdered sugar

Combine flour, sugar, oil, eggs, vanilla, baking soda, cinnamon, and salt; mix well. Stir in pie filling, chocolate chips, and nuts. Grease and flour a Bundt pan. Bake at 350° for 45–50 minutes. When thoroughly cool, dust with powdered sugar.

Bless This Food

Red Beet Cake

1 1/2 cups prepared beets
  (about 1 1/2 cans, reserve
  juice)
3 eggs
1 1/2 cups sugar
1 cup oil
1 teaspoon vanilla
1/2 teaspoon salt
6 tablespoons cocoa
1 3/4 cups flour
1 1/2 teaspoons baking soda

Preheat oven to 375°. Prepare beets by putting through a strainer or in blender. Use 2 tablespoons beet juice to aid in blending. In a large bowl, beat the eggs well. Add sugar slowly to the eggs and continue beating until well blended. Add oil, beets, and vanilla to egg mixture and beat until blended. Add salt, cocoa, and part of the flour. Stir to blend and then beat. Add the rest of the flour and baking soda and beat until blended. Bake in a large, greased, oblong pan or in layer pans or 24 cupcakes. Cake is done when toothpick inserted in center comes out clean (about 30–40 minutes.

Our Daily Bread

Strawberry Long-Cake Roll

¾ cup all-purpose flour
1 teaspoon baking powder
½ teaspoon salt
4 eggs, separated
1¼ cups granulated sugar,
  divided

2 teaspoons vanilla, divided
Confectioners' sugar
1 pint whipping cream
2 pints strawberries, sliced

Heat oven to 375°. Lightly coat a jellyroll pan (I use an 11x15-inch pan) with cooking spray. Line the bottom with wax paper. Combine the flour, baking powder, and salt in a small bowl; set aside. Using an electric mixer at high speed, beat egg whites until foamy. Gradually add ½ cup sugar, 1 tablespoon at a time, and continue beating until stiff peaks form.

In another bowl, beat egg yolks and another ½ cup sugar until pale and thick. Beat in 1 teaspoon vanilla. Use a rubber spatula to gently fold the flour mixture and beaten yolks into the egg whites until just blended. Spread in pan. Bake 15 minutes or until cake springs back to the touch. Place a clean dish towel on the counter and dust it lightly with confectioners' sugar. When the cake is done, loosen the edges from the pan with a knife and invert the cake onto the towel. Peel off the wax paper. Roll cake lengthside, along with the towel, and set aside at room temperature to cool.

Whip cream with remaining ¼ cup sugar and 1 teaspoon vanilla until soft peaks form. Unroll the cake and spread with half the whipped cream. Top with half the strawberries, and re-roll without the towel. Serve with remaining whipped cream and strawberries.

CASA Cooks

Strawberry Meringue Cake

1 (2-layer) package yellow
  cake mix
1 cup orange juice
1/3 cup water
4 eggs, separated
1 teaspoon grated orange rind

1/4 teaspoon cream of tartar
1 1/4 cups sugar, divided
2 cups whipping cream
1 quart fresh strawberries,
  sliced

Combine cake mix, orange juice, water, egg yolks, and orange rind in mixer bowl. Beat for 4 minutes. Pour into 2 greased and wax paper-lined round cake pans. Beat egg whites with cream of tartar in mixer bowl until soft peaks form. Add 1 cup sugar gradually, beating constantly until stiff peaks form. Spread gently over batter. Bake at 350° for 35–40 minutes or until layers test done. Cool completely in pans.

Remove from pans, keeping meringue side up. Beat whipping cream and remaining 1/4 cup sugar in mixer bowl until stiff peaks form. Spread 2/3 of the whipped cream over bottom layer. Arrange sliced berries over whipped cream. Add top layer. Spread with remaining whipped cream. Garnish with whole strawberries. Yields 12 servings.

Approximately per serving: Cal 450; Prot 5g; Carbo 63g; Fiber 1g; Total Fat 20g; 40% Calories from Fat; Chol 125mg; Sod 297mg.

Best Bets

Nevada is the seventh largest state (110,540 square miles). It is known by several nicknames; The Silver State, The Sagebrush State, and The Battle Born State.

Pudding Cake

1 cup flour
2 tablespoons sugar
1 stick butter or margarine,
  softened
¼ cup chopped nuts
1 (8-ounce) package cream
  cheese, softened
¾ cup powdered sugar

1 (10-ounce) container Cool
  Whip, divided in half
2 (3.9-ounce) packages instant
  pudding (pistachio or
  chocolate)
2½ cups milk
Chopped nuts for garnish

Mix the first 4 ingredients. Pat into an oblong cake pan. Bake at 350° for 15 minutes. Cool. Mix cream cheese, powdered sugar, and half of Cool Whip. Spread over first layer. Blend pudding and milk. Pour over second layer. Top with remaining Cool Whip and nuts. Refrigerate until ready to serve.

The Ruby Valley Friendship Club Cookbook I

Ugly Duckling Pudding Cake

1 (18¼-ounce) package lemon
  cake mix
1 (3-ounce) package lemon
  instant pudding
1 (16-ounce) can crushed
  pineapple with juice
1 cup flaked coconut

4 large eggs, beaten
½ cup flour
¾ cup water
¼ cup oil
½ cup brown sugar
½ cup chopped nuts

Grease and flour a 10x15-inch pan. Blend the above ingredients and pour into the pan. Bake at 350° for 50 minutes. Cool on rack for 15 minutes and spread Glaze on top.

GLAZE:
½ cup butter
½ cup brown sugar

½ cup evaporated milk
1⅓ cups flaked coconut

Bring butter, sugar, and milk to a boil for 2 minutes. Add coconut and spread on cake. Serves 18. Enjoy!

NSHSRA High School Rodeo Cookbook

Yogurt Cake

1 cup butter
1½ cups sugar
6 eggs
1 cup plain yogurt
¼ teaspoon ground cloves
1 teaspoon cinnamon

½ cup ground walnuts
2 ounces whiskey
2 tablespoons baking powder
1 tablespoon baking soda
2 cups flour

Melt butter and let cool. Add sugar, eggs, and yogurt, and mix thoroughly. Add cloves, cinnamon, walnuts, whiskey, baking powder, baking soda, and flour; blend well. Pour into greased cake pan and bake for 45–50 minutes in 350° oven. Cool cake.

SYRUP:
2 cups water
2 cups sugar

1 cinnamon stick
Zest and juice of ½ orange

Mix water, sugar, cinnamon stick, and orange in saucepan. Boil for 10 minutes. Pour hot over cooled cake. Let stand for at least one hour before cutting.

The Great Nevada Cookbook

Italian Cream Cake

A super good cake!

5 eggs, separated
1 stick butter, softened
½ cup oil
2 cups sugar
1 cup buttermilk
1 teaspoon baking soda

2 cups flour
1 teaspoon vanilla
1 (3½-ounce) can coconut
  flakes (1⅓ cups)
1 cup chopped pecans

Beat egg whites and set aside. Cream together butter, oil, and sugar, and add egg yolks one at a time, beating in between. Mix together buttermilk and baking soda and add alternately with flour. Add vanilla, fold in egg whites, and add coconut and pecans, reserving some of the pecan halves and coconut to decorate top. Bake in 3 layers at 350° about 25–30 minutes or until done.

ICING:

1 (8-ounce) package cream
  cheese, softened
1 teaspoon vanilla

1 pound powdered sugar
½ cup butter, softened

Mix all ingredients, spread between layers and on top of cake. Decorate top with reserved pecan halves and coconut.

Historical Boulder City Cookbook

A tailor named Jacob Davis from Reno, Nevada, is credited with inventing what is known today as blue jeans. One of Davis' customers kept ripping the pockets of the pants that Davis made for him. As a way to strengthen the man's trousers, Davis put metal rivets at the points of strain, such as on the pocket corners. Since Davis regularly purchased bolts of fabric from a dry goods store in San Francisco operated by Levi Strauss, he offered Strauss a half interest in the invention if Strauss would come up with $68 for the patent. Strauss took him up on his offer, and the two men received a patent on May 20, 1873. When the patent expired 20 years later, dozens of garment manufacturers began to imitate the riveted clothing, which has become the most popular clothing product in the world.

Pumpkin Sumpthin'

1 cup milk
3 eggs
1 cup sugar
1 teaspoon cinnamon
¼ teaspoon ginger
⅛ teaspoon cloves
½ teaspoon salt

1 (31-ounce) can pumpkin
1 (18¼-ounce) yellow cake
  mix
1½ sticks margarine, melted
¾ cup chopped nuts
Whipped cream

Combine milk, eggs, sugar, spices, salt, and pumpkin, and mix well. Pour into a greased 9x13-inch baking pan. Sprinkle dry cake mix over top of mixture. Drizzle melted margarine over top. Sprinkle nuts over top. Bake at 350° for one hour or until browned. Serve with whipped cream.

Church Family Recipes

Ms. Ellen's Poundcake

6 large eggs
3 sticks butter, softened
2½ cups sugar
2½ cups flour
½ teaspoon salt

½ teaspoon baking powder
⅔ cup milk
1 teaspoon vanilla extract
2 teaspoons lemon extract

Grease and flour a 10-inch tube pan. Preheat oven to 325°. Beat eggs well in a bowl and set aside. Cream butter in separate bowl until it is light and fluffy. Add sugar and beat well. Then add beaten eggs. Beat again. Mix flour, salt, and baking powder. Add flour mixture and milk in alternating amounts to creamed mixture until it is all mixed in. Add vanilla and lemon extracts and beat another 2 minutes. (You can't beat this batter too much!) Pour into greased tube pan and bake in 325° oven for about 1 hour and 10 minutes. Cake is done when a toothpick comes out clean. Makes 10 servings.

The Best of Down-Home Cooking

Chocolate Pound Cake

½ cup buttermilk
1 tablespoon instant espresso
  or coffee powder, dissolved
  in 1½ tablespoons hot water
1 teaspoon vanilla extract
1⅓ cups sugar
1 cup all-purpose flour
6 tablespoons unsweetened
  Dutch Process cocoa,
  strained after measuring

¼ teaspoon baking powder
¼ teaspoon baking soda
½ teaspoon kosher salt
12 tablespoons sweet butter,
  room temperature
3 large eggs
Powdered sugar for dusting
  (optional)

Preheat oven to 350°. Position rack in lower third of the oven. Prepare a 6-cup decorative tube pan with spray vegetable oil. Combine buttermilk with dissolved coffee and vanilla. Set aside.

In a large mixing bowl, combine sugar, flour, cocoa, baking powder, baking soda, and salt. Mix on medium speed with an electric mixer to blend. Add butter and eggs to the bowl and mix on medium speed just until all the dry ingredients are moistened. Set a timer for 2 minutes and beat on high speed. Add buttermilk mixture and beat on high speed for 2 more minutes. Bake until cake starts to shrink away from sides of pan and toothpick inserted in center comes out clean, about 45–50 minutes. Cool cake on a rack 5–10 minutes. Invert pan to unmold. Cool on a rack. Cake can be prepared to this point, wrapped well, and kept at room temperature where it will remain moist and delicious for 4–5 days; or it may be frozen for up to 3 months. Sieve powdered sugar over cake just before serving, if desired. Yields 10 servings.

Never Trust a Skinny Chef...II

Chocolate Surprise Cupcakes

3 cups flour
2 cups sugar
½ cup cocoa
1 teaspoon salt
2 teaspoons soda

⅔ cup oil
2 cups water
2 tablespoons vinegar
2 teaspoons vanilla

Mix flour, sugar, cocoa, salt, and soda. Add oil, water, vinegar, and vanilla. Combine thoroughly and fill cup cake papers ⅔ full of mixture.

FILLING:

1 (8-ounce) package cream
 cheese, softened
1 egg
⅓ cup sugar

¼ teaspoon salt
1 (6-ounce) package chocolate
 chips

Mix cream cheese, egg, sugar, and salt until fluffy. Fold in chocolate chips. Drop one heaping teaspoon of Filling into muffin batter. Bake for 25 minutes at 350°. Frost if desired.

Virginia City Alumni Association Cookbook

Let Them Eat Cake

2 cups flour	1 cup water
2 cups sugar	1 teaspoon baking soda
1 cup (2 sticks) butter	½ cup buttermilk
¼ cup (or more) baking cocoa	2 eggs, beaten
	1 teaspoon vanilla extract

Mix flour and sugar in a large bowl. Combine butter, baking cocoa, and water in a saucepan. Bring to a boil. Pour over flour mixture and stir to mix well. Mix baking soda with buttermilk in a small bowl. Stir into cake batter. Stir in eggs and vanilla. Pour batter into a greased 10x15-inch cake pan. Bake at 350° for 30 minutes or until wooden pick inserted near center comes out clean. Cool slightly on a wire rack. Pour warm Creamy Chocolate Frosting over warm cake. Let cool before cutting. Yields 16 servings.

CREAMY CHOCOLATE FROSTING:

½ cup (1 stick) butter	1 (1-pound) package confectioners' sugar
3 tablespoons (or more) baking cocoa	1 teaspoon vanilla extract
5 tablespoons milk	½ cup chopped pecans

Heat butter, baking cocoa, and milk in a saucepan until butter melts. Remove from heat. Beat in the confectioners' sugar, vanilla, and pecans. Let cool slightly. Yields about 3 cups.

Las Vegas Glitter to Gourmet

Chocolate Buttermilk Cake

1 stick butter
4 tablespoons cocoa
1 cup water
2 cups sugar
2 cups flour
2 eggs

½ cup buttermilk with
  1 teaspoon baking soda
  dissolved in it
1 teaspoon vanilla
1 teaspoon cinnamon
  (optional)

In saucepan bring butter, cocoa, and water to a boil. Cool slightly. Combine in large bowl sugar and flour; pour cocoa mixture over and beat well. Add eggs, buttermilk mixture, vanilla, and cinnamon, if desired. Beat until smooth and pour into greased and floured cookie sheet with rim or 11½x16-inch pan. Bake in 400° oven for 20–25 minutes.

ICING:

1 stick butter
5 tablespoons cocoa
⅓ cup milk
1 (1-pound) box confectioners'
  sugar

1 teaspoon vanilla
1 cup chopped walnuts
  (optional)

Start Icing 5 minutes before cake is done. Bring butter, cocoa, and milk to a boil in large saucepan. While still hot, add confectioners' sugar and vanilla. Beat well, and add chopped walnuts, if desired. Spread warm frosting on hot cake. Cake may be cut in small squares and served like brownies.

Soup for Our Souls

Chocolate Eclair Cake

1 large package French vanilla
instant pudding
3½ cups milk
1 (8-ounce) package Cool Whip,
thawed

24 graham crackers (about 1½
packages)

Butter an 11x15-inch pan and line bottom completely with graham crackers. Make pudding with 3½ cups cold milk and fold in whipped topping. Pour pudding mixture over graham crackers and cover top of pudding completely with another layer of graham crackers. Refrigerate 5 hours or overnight.

GLAZE:
2 tablespoons unsweetened
cocoa powder
3 tablespoons soft butter
1 teaspoon vanilla

2 tablespoons white corn syrup
3 tablespoons milk
1½ cups powdered sugar

Mix all ingredients for Glaze; beat till smooth and pour over top layer of graham crackers. Keep refrigerated until ready to serve. An additional ½ teaspoon almond extract to the pudding mixture is a nice touch. Serves 10–12.

Tasteful Treasures

Old Nevada state laws:
- In Nyala, a man is forbidden from buying drinks for more than three people other than himself at any one period during the day.
- It is illegal to drive a camel on the main highway.
- In Eureka, men who wear moustaches are forbidden from kissing women.
- Everyone walking on the streets of Elko is required to wear a mask.
- In 2003, Nevada repealed a 1969 law that made it a misdemeanor for anyone other than a barber to advertise haircuts.

Fabulous Chocolate Cake

4 squares unsweetened
  chocolate, divided
½ cup plus 1 tablespoon
  butter or margarine, divided
1 cup water
2 cups sifted cake flour
1¼ teaspoons baking soda

1 teaspoon salt
2 eggs
1 cup dairy sour cream
2 cups sugar
1½ teaspoons vanilla
Fluffy White Frosting

Butter 2 (8-inch) round layer cake pans; flour lightly, tapping out any excess. Combine 3 squares of chocolate, butter, and water in the top of a double boiler; heat over simmering water until chocolate and butter melt. Remove; cool.

Sift the flour, soda, and salt into a large bowl. Beat eggs with sour cream until blended in a medium-size bowl with electric mixer; beat in sugar and vanilla. Stir in cooled chocolate mixture. Beat into flour mixture, half at a time, till smooth. (Batter will be thin.) Pour into pans. Bake in moderate 350° oven for 40 minutes, or until centers spring back when lightly pressed with fingertip. Cool in pans. Loosen around edges with a knife; turn out onto racks.

Make Fluffy White Frosting as directed below. Put cake layers together on a serving plate with about ¼ of the frosting; spread remainder on sides and top, making deep swirls with spatula. Melt remining 1 square chocolate with remining 1 tablespoon butter in a cup set in hot water; stir until smooth. Drizzle over top of cake, letting mixture drip down sides.

FLUFFY WHITE FROSTING:

2 egg whites
¾ cup sugar
½ teaspoon cream of tartar

Dash of salt
2½ teaspoons cold water
1 teaspoon vanilla

Combine egg whites, sugar, cream of tartar, salt, and water in top of double boiler; beat till blended. Place over simmering water. Cook, beating constantly with an electric or rotary beater, until mixture stands in firm peaks. Remove from water; stir in vanilla.

Traditional Treasures

Awesome Amaretto Cheesecake Loaf

The cookies make the Crust incredible. They are easy to find—they are the small cookies in the red can.

CRUST:

20 amaretti cookies, crushed
3 ounces almonds, blanched, toasted

3 tablespoons butter, chilled

Lime a 9x5-inch loaf pan with parchment paper, or use an 8-inch springform pan. Mix amaretti cookie crumbs, almonds, and butter in food processor using on/off turns till crumbly. Pat Crust into bottom and 1 inch up sides of pan.

FILLING:

24 ounces cream cheese, softened
1⅓ cups sugar
4 eggs, room temperature
3 tablespoons lemon juice
2½ tablespoons amaretto
1 teaspoon vanilla

1 teaspoon chopped candied citrus peel
½ teaspoon grated lemon peel
½ cup heavy cream, room temperature
½ cup sour cream, room temperature

Preheat oven to 325°. Beat cream cheese with mixer in large bowl on low speed till smooth, about 5 minutes. Gradually beat in sugar. Add eggs, one at a time, beating constantly on low. Add lemon juice, amaretto, vanilla, and fruit peels, and mix well. Beat in heavy cream and sour cream. Pour into prepared Crust. Set pan in larger baking pan and place in oven. Add water to larger pan to come 1 inch up sides of cheesecake pan. Bake till center is almost set, 75–90 minutes (8-inch springform pan will be closer to 75 minutes). Remove cheesecake from water bath and cool completely on rack. If using loaf pan, invert cake onto platter. Refrigerate overnight.

Note: I prefer the loaf pan. It is different and easy to work with and easy to freeze. It can be ready to defrost for unexpected company, or when you don't have time to prepare something special.

The Melting Pot

White Chocolate Cheesecake

CRUST:

1¼ cups finely ground
   shortbread cookie crumbs
¼ cup ground almonds
2 tablespoons sugar

⅛ teaspoon vanilla extract
3 tablespoons or more melted
   butter

Preheat oven to 350°. Mix first 4 ingredients in a small bowl. Blend in enough butter to bind crumbs. Press mixture firmly onto bottom of 10-inch springform pan. Bake 10 minutes. Transfer to rack. Cool completely. Reduce oven temperature to 325°.

FILLING:

6 ounces white chocolate,
   finely chopped (use good
   quality chocolate, such as
   Tobler or Narcisse)
3 (8-ounce) packages cream
   cheese, softened
1 (8-ounce) package Neufchatel
   (light cream cheese), softened

5 large eggs, room temperature
¾ cup sugar
3 tablespoons all-purpose flour
1 teaspoon vanilla
1 tablespoon crème de cassis
   (suggest Hiram Walker)

Melt chocolate in double boiler over simmering water, stirring until smooth. Cool to lukewarm. Beat cheeses in a large bowl until smooth. Blend in eggs, one at a time. Mix in sugar, flour, vanilla, and crème de cassis. Stir 1 cup of mixture into lukewarm chocolate. Now, mix white chocolate mixture into cheese mixture. Pour Filling over Crust. Bake until Filling is firm around edges but still moves slightly in the center when pan is shaken, about 40 minutes or more. Cool completely. Cover and refrigerate overnight.

WHITE CHOCOLATE MOUSSE FROSTING:

6 ounces imported white
   chocolate
3 tablespoons crème de cassis
1½ teaspoons hot water
1 cup well-chilled whipping
   cream

⅜ teaspoon vanilla
3 egg whites, room temperature
Pinch of salt
Pinch of sugar

(continued)

(White Chocolate Cheesecake continued)

Melt chocolate with liqueur in top of double boiler over hot (not simmering) water. Stir constantly. Mix in 1½ teaspoons hot water. Remove from over hot water. Beat whipping cream in a cold large bowl with vanilla until soft peaks form; refrigerate. Beat egg whites in medium bowl with salt and sugar until soft peaks form. Gently fold whites into cream. Stir 1 heaping table-spoon into chocolate; then fold chocolate into cream mixture. Smooth top and refrigerate 1½ hours. When mousse is set, pipe mousse rosettes on top of cheesecake. Refrigerate until ready to serve, at least 1½ hours.

Lake Tahoe Cooks!

Milk Chocolate Cheesecake

1 cup Oreo cookie crumbs
1 cup butter cookie crumbs
½ cup sweet butter, melted
3 pounds cream cheese, softened
2 cups sugar
6 large eggs
1 cup heavy cream
½ cup all-purpose flour
½ teaspoon kosher salt
1 teaspoon vanilla extract
1 cup melted milk chocolate

2 cups fresh raspberries
Juice of 1 lemon
¼ cup Grand Marnier
Whipped cream in a pastry bag with star tip
Chocolate curls for garnish
Fresh mint sprigs
Powdered sugar in shaker for garnish
Cocoa powder in shaker for garnish

Preheat oven to 350°. Combine crumbs and butter together. Mix well and press into a 10-inch springform pan.

In a food processor, with metal blade, mix cream cheese until smooth. Add sugar and blend. Add eggs, one at a time, to thoroughly incorporate into the cheese mixture. Add the heavy cream, flour, salt, and vanilla and blend until smooth. In a steady stream, pour in the melted chocolate. Pour into prepared pan. Bake for 1 hour and 15 minutes or until cake is set.

Remove from oven and loosen the sides from the pan with a knife. This will prevent cake from splitting down the center. Completely cool the cake before cutting.

Make raspberry sauce by combining the raspberries, lemon juice, and Grand Marnier, and allowing to sit for 2–3 hours. Place a piece of cake on a plate. Spoon raspberry sauce over the top. Garnish with whipped cream, chocolate curls, mint sprigs, powdered sugar, and cocoa powder. Yields 12 servings.

Never Trust a Skinny Chef...II

Cookies & Candies

In Las Vegas, the hotel themes are so magnificent that you feel you are in another country . . . like here in Venice! This is actually inside the Venetian Casino.

Chocolate-Covered Cherry Cookies

COOKIE DOUGH:

½ cup butter, softened
1 cup sugar
1 egg
1½ teaspoons vanilla
1½ cups flour

½ cup cocoa
¼ teaspoon salt
¼ teaspoon baking soda
Maraschino cherries, drained,
  reserve juice

Cream butter, sugar, egg, and vanilla. Add remaining ingredients, except cherries. Blend. Dough will be stiff. Shape dough into 48 (1-inch) balls. Place balls 2 inches apart on ungreased cookie sheet (or spray with nonstick spray). Push ½ cherry into each ball. When all cookies are molded, prepare Frosting and use immediately.

FROSTING:

1 cup semisweet chocolate
½ cup sweetened condensed
  milk

¼ teaspoon salt
1½ teaspoons reserved cherry
  juice

Melt chocolate with milk, stirring constantly. Remove from heat. Add remaining ingredients. Stir until smooth. Spread ½ teaspoon Frosting over each cherry. Bake at 350° for 8–10 minutes. Yields 4 dozen cookies.

Recipes from the Heart

Giant Gingersnaps

4½ cups all-purpose flour
4 teaspoons ground ginger
2 teaspoons baking soda
1½ teaspoons ground
    cinnamon
1 teaspoon ground cloves

¼ teaspoon salt
1½ cups shortening
2 cups granulated sugar
2 eggs
½ cup molasses
¾ cup coarse sugar

In a medium mixing bowl, stir together the flour, ginger, soda, cinnamon, cloves, and salt. Set aside. In a large mixing bowl, beat shortening until softened. Gradually add granulated sugar. Beat until fluffy. Add eggs and molasses and beat well. Add half of flour mixture and beat until combined. Stir remaining flour in with a wooden spoon. Using a ¼-cup ice cream scoop, shape dough into 2-inch balls. Roll in the coarse sugar. Place on an ungreased cookie sheet about 2½ inches apart. Bake in a 350° oven for 12–14 minutes, or until cookies are light brown and puffed. (Do not overbake or cookies will not be chewy.) Let stand for 2 minutes before transferring to a wire rack. Cool. Makes 25 (4-inch) cookies.

The Fruit of the Spirit

Instant Cookies

1 (18¼-ounce) dry cake mix,
  any flavor
2 cups whipped topping,
  thawed
1 egg, beaten
Powdered sugar
½ cup chopped nuts

Combine dry cake mix, whipped topping, and egg. Mix in nuts. Form into balls and roll in powdered sugar. Place on lightly sprayed cookie sheet. Press down slightly. Bake at 350° for 10 minutes.

Kitchen Chatter

Almond Shortbread

2 cups flour
1 cup sugar
1 cup butter, softened
1 egg, separated
¼ teaspoon almond extract
1 tablespoon water
½ cup chopped almonds

Heat oven to 350°. In a large mixer bowl, combine flour, sugar, butter, egg yolk, and almond extract. Beat at low speed, scraping bowl often, until particles are fine, 2–3 minutes. Press in bottom of greased 10x15x1-inch jellyroll pan.

In small bowl, beat egg white and water until frothy; brush on dough. Sprinkle almonds over top. Bake for 15 minutes or until browned. Cool completely before cutting into bars.

Twentieth Century Club Cook Book

Nestled in the shadows of the eastern Sierra Nevada range, Genoa has long been a special place in Nevada. In 1851, Mormon traders settled in the area, making it the first permanent, non-Indian settlement in what would become the state of Nevada.

Snickerdoodles

1 cup shortening
1½ cups plus 2 tablespoons
  sugar, divided
2 eggs
2⅓ cups flour

2 teaspoons cream of tartar
1 teaspoon baking soda
1 teaspoon salt
2 teaspoons cinnamon

Heat oven to 400°. Mix shortening, 1½ cups sugar, and eggs thoroughly. Measure flour by sifting. Blend flour, cream of tartar, soda, and salt. Stir well. Shape dough into 1-inch balls. Don't squeeze dough. Roll in mixture of remaining 2 tablespoons sugar and cinnamon. Place 2 inches apart on ungreased cookie sheets. Bake 8–10 minutes. Makes 6 dozen.

Family and Friends Favorites

Grandma's White Sugar Cookies

1 cup sugar
1 cup shortening
1 egg, beaten
2 cups flour

½ teaspoon baking soda
½ teaspoon cream of tartar
½ teaspoon vanilla

Cream sugar and shortening. Add egg, flour, baking soda, cream of tartar, and vanilla. Mix well. Roll into balls. Put onto ungreased cookie sheet. Press balls down with the bottom of a glass coated with sugar. Bake at 350° until light brown, about 10 minutes.

Family and Friends Favorites

Unforgettables

This is a sugar cookie you'll want to remember.

2 cups butter, softened	4 teaspoons cream of tartar
2 cups sugar	1 tablespoon vanilla extract
6 eggs	4 teaspoons almond extract
7 cups flour	
2 teaspoons baking soda	

Cream the butter and sugar in a mixing bowl until light and fluffy. Beat in eggs. Add flour, baking soda, and cream of tartar and mix well. Mix in the flavorings. Roll half the dough at a time on a floured cloth. Cut into circles and place on a cookie sheet. Bake at 350° for 10–12 minutes or until light brown. Cool on cookie sheet for several minutes. Remove to wire rack to cool completely. Frost with Cream Cheese Frosting. Decorate with sprinkles or as desired. Yields 7 dozen.

CREAM CHEESE FROSTING:

1 (8-ounce) package cream cheese, softened	1 (16-ounce) package confectioners' sugar
2 tablespoons butter, softened	2 teaspoons vanilla extract

Beat cream cheese and butter in a mixer bowl until fluffy. Add confectioners' sugar and vanilla and mix well. Add a small amount of cream or milk, if needed, to make of spreading consistency. Tint as desired with food coloring. Yields enough to frost 7 dozen cookies.

From Sunrise to Sunset

"Stately" Peanut Butter Cookies

½ cup crunchy peanut butter
1 stick butter, softened
½ cup white sugar
½ cup brown sugar
1 cup flour

1 egg
½ teaspoon vanilla
½ teaspoon salt
½ teaspoon baking soda

Mix all ingredients together. Roll into balls and place on cookie sheet. Press cookies out with a fork dipped in water so it doesn't stick. Bake at 350° for about 10 minutes or until brown. Enjoy.

Home Cooking

Chocolate Chunk Pecan Cookies

1 stick sweet butter, softened
½ cup white sugar
½ cup dark brown sugar
1 large egg
1 teaspoon vanilla extract
1 cup plus 2 tablespoons
  all-purpose flour

½ teaspoon kosher salt
½ teaspoon baking soda
½ cup chopped pecans
6 ounces good-quality
  bittersweet or semisweet
  chocolate, chopped coarsely

Preheat the oven to 375°. Place butter in bowl of electric mixer and beat until creamy. Add sugars and beat until light and fluffy. Add egg and vanilla and beat well to combine. Sift together dry ingredients and add to batter, mixing well. Remove bowl from mixer (be sure to scrape the beater) and stir in nuts and chocolate chunks by hand. Drop by teaspoons onto greased cookie sheets and bake 8–10 minutes until lightly browned. Cool 5 minutes on sheets, then remove cookies with a spatula to racks to cool.

Never Trust a Skinny Chef...II

Double-Chocolate Chip Cookies

1¾ cups flour
¼ teaspoon baking soda
1 cup (2 sticks) butter or
  margarine, softened
1 teaspoon vanilla extract
1 cup sugar
½ cup packed dark brown
  sugar

1 egg
⅓ cup baking cocoa
2 tablespoons milk
1 cup chopped pecans or
  walnuts
1 cup semisweet chocolate
  chips

Mix flour and baking soda in a bowl. Beat butter in a bowl with an electric mixer until light and fluffy. Beat in the vanilla, sugar, and brown sugar. Add egg and beat well. Beat in baking cocoa at low speed. Add milk and beat until mixed. Add dry ingredients, stirring just until blended. Stir in pecans and chocolate chips.

Drop by rounded teaspoonfuls 2 inches apart onto nonstick cookie sheets or cookie sheets lined with foil. Bake at 350° for 12–13 minutes. Cool on cookie sheets slightly. Remove to wire racks and cool completely. Yields 3 dozen.

Las Vegas Glitter to Gourmet

Chocolate Scotcheroos

Easy delicious dessert!

1 cup sugar
1 cup light Karo syrup
1 cup peanut butter

6 cups Rice Krispies
1 cup butterscotch chips
1 cup chocolate chips

Dissolve sugar and Karo syrup over low heat until hot. Add peanut butter; melt. Stir until blended. Stir Rice Krispies into melted mixture. Spread into greased 9x13-inch pan. Pat. Cool. Melt chips together over low heat. Spread over Krispies mixture. Cool. Cut into squares. Yields 24–36 bars.

Still Cookin' After 70 Years

Fudgy Brownies

1½ cups butter (3 sticks),
  softened
2⅔ cups sugar
1 tablespoon vanilla
4 eggs

2 cups flour
1 cup baking cocoa
½ teaspoon salt
1 cup chopped nuts (optional)

Grease 2 round cake pans. Heat oven to 350°. Cream butter, sugar, vanilla, and eggs in one bowl. In another bowl, combine flour, baking cocoa, salt, and nuts. Mix together. Batter may be stiff, and that's okay. Spread it out in the round cake pans. Bake until set, 30 minutes or so. Don't overbake, as they will continue to bake a little while as they are cooling.

Bless This Food

No-Bake Brownies

1 package fudge brownie mix
¾ cup butter, softened,
  divided
2 tablespoons water
2 teaspoons vanilla, divided
1 cup flaked coconut

½ cup chopped nuts
2 cups powdered sugar
1 tablespoon milk
2 or more envelopes pre-melted
  chocolate, from brownie mix
  package

In mixer bowl, beat brownie mix (reserve fudge packet), ½ cup butter, water, and 1 teaspoon vanilla on low speed until smooth and creamy. Stir in coconut and nuts. Spread evenly in a greased 9x9-inch-square pan. Refrigerate.

Meanwhile, mix remaining ¼ cup butter, powdered sugar, milk, and remaining 1 teaspoon vanilla until smooth and creamy. Spread over chilled brownie mixture. Chill one hour. Spread enough reserved pre-melted chocolate over the top to cover. Refrigerate until ready to serve. Cut in small squares (very rich). Can be frozen.

Home Cooking

Grandma Uhalde's Pawtucket
(Brownies)

½ cup butter
2 squares unsweetened
  chocolate
3 eggs, slightly beaten
1 cup sugar

¾ cup flour
½ teaspoon baking powder
1 cup chopped walnuts
1 teaspoon vanilla

Melt butter and chocolate. Add slightly beaten eggs. Add sugar, flour, baking powder, nuts, and vanilla. Spread in greased shallow 9x9-inch pan and bake at 325° for 15–20 minutes. Cut in squares and watch out—they disappear fast!

Soup for Our Souls

Date Bars

1 cup sugar
1 cup flour
2 teaspoons baking powder
2 extra large eggs
1 teaspoon vanilla

1 cup chopped pecans or
  walnuts
1 cup chopped dates
Powdered sugar

Mix sugar, flour, and baking powder together. Add lightly beaten eggs. Add vanilla, chopped nuts, and chopped dates. Bake in ungreased baking dish in 350° oven for 40 minutes, or until toothpick comes out clean. Cover generously with powdered sugar and cut into 2-inch squares.

Historical Boulder City Cookbook

Magic Cookie Bars

½ cup margarine, melted
1½ cups graham cracker
 crumbs
1 cup chopped walnuts
1 (6-ounce) package semisweet
 chocolate morsels

1⅓ cups flaked coconut
1 (15-ounce) can condensed
 milk

Pour melted butter in the bottom of a 9x13-inch Pyrex dish.
Sprinkle crumbs evenly over melted butter; sprinkle chopped
nuts over crumbs. Scatter chocolate morsels over nuts.
Sprinkle coconut over morsels, then pour sweetened condensed
milk over coconut. Bake in a moderate (350°) oven for 25 minutes. Cool in pan 15 minutes, then cut into 24 bars.

Historical Boulder City Cookbook

Lemon Bars

1 cup sifted flour
1/2 cup powdered sugar
1/4 teaspoon salt
1 cup butter, chilled
4 eggs
2 cups granulated sugar
1/3 cup fresh lemon juice

1 1/2 teaspoons grated lemon
  rind
1/4 cup flour
1 teaspoon baking powder
Confectioners' sugar for
  topping

Sift flour, powdered sugar, and salt. Cut butter into flour mixture to coarse cornmeal appearance. Press into 9x13-inch pan and bake at 350° for 20 minutes. Cool 10–15 minutes.

Beat eggs until blended. Slowly add sugar, lemon juice, and rind. Sift flour and baking powder into egg mixture. Spread evenly over baked, cooled crust. Bake for 25 minutes at 350°. Cool. Sprinkle with confectioners' sugar. Cut into squares. Keeps in tight tin 4 days; in refrigerator, 1 1/2 weeks. Makes about 16 squares.

Timbreline's Cookbook

Eggnog Logs

1 cup butter or margarine,
  softened
¾ cup sugar
1¼ teaspoons ground nutmeg
1 egg

2 teaspoons vanilla extract
½–1 teaspoon rum extract (or
  rum to taste)
3 cups all-purpose flour

In a mixing bowl, cream butter and sugar. Add nutmeg, egg, and extracts; mix thoroughly. Stir in flour. If necessary, chill dough for easier handling. On a lightly floured surface, shape dough into ½-inch diameter ropes and cut each into 3-inch long pieces. Place 2 inches apart on ungreased baking sheets. Bake at 350° for 15 minutes or until lightly browned. Cool on wire racks.

FROSTING:

¼ cup butter or margarine,
  softened
3 cups confectioners' sugar,
  divided
1 teaspoon vanilla

½–1 teaspoon rum extract (or
  rum to taste)
2 tablespoons light cream
Ground nutmeg

Cream butter until light and fluffy. Add 2 cups sugar and extracts; mix well. Beat in cream and remaining sugar. Frost cookies. With tines of a small fork, make lines down the Frosting to simulate bark. Sprinkle with nutmeg. Yields 4½ dozen.

NSHSRA High School Rodeo Cookbook

Granola Krispie Squares

¼ cup margarine
3 cups mini marshmallows
1 teaspoon vanilla
⅓ cup flaked unsweetened
  coconut

⅓ cup rolled oats
¼ cup cocoa
¼ cup raisins
¼ cup chocolate chips

Melt margarine in a large heavy saucepan. Add marshmallows and stir over low heat until marshmallows are melted. Remove from heat and stir in vanilla and remaining ingredients. Mix until evenly coated. Press into a 9x13-inch pan. Refrigerate for 30 minutes or more. Cut into 24 squares.

Exchanges: 1 square equals 1 starch and ½ fat exchange.

Sharing Our Diabetics Best Recipes

Special K Bars

1 cup white sugar
1 cup white corn syrup
2 teaspoons vanilla
1½ cups peanut butter

6 cups Special K cereal
1 cup chocolate chips
1 cup butterscotch chips

In a small saucepan, bring sugar and syrup to a boil. Remove from heat. Add vanilla and peanut butter. Stir until peanut butter is melted. Pour over cereal; mix well. Pat into a 9x13-inch pan. Frost with melted chips. Cut into bars.

Family and Friends Favorites

Forgotten Kisses

Turning the oven off is the key to success with this recipe.

4 egg whites
¼ teaspoon salt
1 teaspoon cream of tartar
1½ cups granulated sugar
1 teaspoon vanilla

Dash liquid peppermint
** flavoring**
Few drops food coloring
** (optional)**
½ cup mini-chocolate chips

Heat oven to 350°. The oven needs to be heated for at least 15 minutes before the kisses are placed in it. Grease a cookie sheet very well.

Beat egg whites, salt, and cream of tartar together until almost stiff. Gradually add sugar, alternating with vanilla, peppermint, and coloring, beating until stiff. Fold in the chocolate chips.

Using 2 teaspoons, place bite-size drops on the prepared cookie sheet. These will not change size while baking. Place sheet in center of preheated oven and turn the oven off. Forget the kisses. (Overnight is good.) These can be frozen.

God, That's Good!

Nevada is the largest gold-producing state in the nation, and is second in the world behind South Africa.

Microwave Dark Chocolate Fudge

½ cup Karo light or dark
  corn syrup
⅓ cup evaporated milk
3 cups (18 ounces) semisweet
  chocolate chips

¾ cup sifted powdered sugar
2 teaspoons vanilla
1½ cups coarsely chopped
  walnuts or your favorite nut

Line 8-inch-square pan with plastic wrap. In a 3-quart microwavable bowl, combine corn syrup and evaporated milk; heat on HIGH for 6 minutes (a rolling boil.) Add chocolate chips; stir until melted. Stir in powdered sugar, vanilla, and nuts. With a wooden spoon beat until thick and glossy; spread in prepared pan. Refrigerate 2 hours until firm. Cut into squares. Makes about 25 pieces.

Twentieth Century Club Cook Book

COOKIES & CANDIES

Genoa Candy Dance Fudge

24 ounces marshmallows
  (1½ bags)
6 cups (54 ounces) semisweet
  chocolate chips
3 cups chopped walnuts
  (optional)

3 (12-ounce) cans evaporated
  milk
6 sticks (1½ pounds)
  margarine
15 cups sugar
6 tablespoons corn syrup

Combine marshmallows, chocolate chips, and nuts in large bowl and set aside. Combine milk, margarine, sugar, and corn syrup in large saucepan and bring to a boil, stirring constantly. Cook to soft-ball stage (213°). Remove from heat. Pour over marshmallow-chocolate chip mixture and beat with spoon until it loses its gloss. Pour into tray, which has been lined with buttered butcher paper. Let set overnight.

In morning, grab butcher paper at both ends and lift carefully. Set on counter and cut into 1-inch squares. This is a creamy fudge. Makes 15 pounds.

Note: If it begins to dry out, place a piece of bread alongside and cover tightly. It will soften overnight.

The Great Nevada Food Festival Cookbook

English Toffee

1 cup butter or margarine
2 cups sugar
½ cup water

Chocolate chips
Ground walnuts or pecans

Over medium heat, bring butter, sugar, and water to 300° (hard-crack stage). You must use a candy thermometer. Pour into 10x15-inch metal jellyroll pan. Cover immediately with light sprinkling of chocolate chips; spread when glossy. Cover with finely ground nuts. When cool, chip with knife into bite-size pieces.

Traditional Treasures

237

Buckeye Balls

1½ cups peanut butter
  (plain or crunchy)
1 stick butter, softened
1 pound powdered sugar

1 teaspoon vanilla
1 (12-ounce) package chocolate
  chips
½ bar paraffin

Mix peanut butter, butter, powdered sugar, and vanilla and roll into 1-inch balls. Chill in refrigerator while melting chocolate chips with paraffin in small saucepan. Dip peanut butter balls into chocolate mixture, using toothpicks, and place on wax paper until cool. Makes approximately 50–60 buckeye balls.

Historical Boulder City Cookbook

Boston Creme Candy

3 cups sugar
1 cup half-and-half
1 stick margarine

1 cup light corn syrup
Pinch of salt
1 cup chopped nuts

Combine sugar, half-and-half, margarine, corn syrup, and salt in saucepan. Cook to soft-ball stage. Remove from heat. Cool 10 minutes. Add nuts. Beat stiff. Pour onto buttered platter to cool.

Kitchen Chatter

Pies & Other Desserts

The Nevada State Railroad Museum is located in Carson City, the state capital. The museum displays a large and important collection of vintage Virginia & Truckee Railroad equipment, including the historic steam engines, Inyo and Glenbrook.

French Chocolate Mint Pie

PIE CRUST:

38–40 vanilla wafers, crushed   ½ stick butter, softened
¼ cup sugar

Combine crumbs, sugar, and butter and press into 9-inch pie plate.

FILLING:

½ cup butter, softened   2 eggs, unbeaten
1 cup powdered sugar   ¼ teaspoon mint extract
2 squares semisweet   1 teaspoon vanilla extract
  chocolate, melted

Cream butter and add sugar gradually. Beat until fluffy. Add chocolate and beat. Add eggs, one at a time. Add mint extract and vanilla extract and beat well. Put Filling in Pie Crust and let it stand for at least 6 hours in refrigerator.

Let Freedom Ring

No Crust Pecan Pie

3 jumbo egg whites	12 unsalted soda crackers
1 cup sugar	1 teaspoon vanilla
1 cup chopped pecans	Whipped cream

Beat egg whites; beat in sugar until stiff. Add nuts. Crumble soda crackers and fold into mixture; add vanilla. Put into buttered 9-inch pie dish. Bake in 350° oven for 35 minutes or until done. When cold, top with whipped cream.

Our Daily Bread

Lite Pecan Pie

CRUST:

¼ cup crushed graham crackers	1 tablespoon cold water
1 tablespoon light margarine, softened	

Combine crushed graham cracker crumbs, margarine, and water and press into the bottom and sides of a 9-inch pie plate. Bake at 350° for 5 minutes. Remove from oven and set aside.

FILLING:

¾ cup egg substitute	½ cup light margarine, melted
Enough brown sugar substitute to replace 1 cup brown sugar	1 teaspoon vanilla
	2 cups pecan pieces

Mix egg substitute, brown sugar substitute, and melted margarine. Add vanilla and mix. Add pecan pieces and mix. Pour into prepared Crust and bake at 350° for 35 minutes. Let cool and serve at room temperature. Cut into 8 pieces.

Nutritional analysis: Calories 297; Carbohydrates 20g; Sugar 7g; Fat 4g; Sodium 179mg; Cholesterol 0; 1½ starch exchange per slice.

Sharing Our Diabetics Best Recipes

Poor Man's Pie

4 eggs (save 2 whites for
  meringue)
1 cup sugar
2 tablespoons vinegar

1 tablespoon vanilla
¼ cup butter, melted
1 (9-inch) pie shell, unbaked

Beat eggs; add sugar and stir well. Add vinegar, vanilla, and butter. Pour into pie shell. Bake at 375° for 25–30 minutes or until firm. Top with meringue.

MERINGUE:
Beat reserved 2 egg whites. When frothy, add 1 tablespoon sugar, then whip until stiff.

Partyline Cook Book

Shoo-Fly Pie

2 cups flour
5 ounces shortening
1 teaspoon salt
1 teaspoon baking powder
½ teaspoon baking soda

¾ cup boiling water
½ cup molasses
1 egg yolk, well beaten
½ teaspoon cinnamon
½ cup brown sugar

Mix together flour, shortening, salt, and baking powder. Remove 1 cup of this mixture to use as crumbs. Add enough ice water to make dough workable. Roll out dough and put into a 9-inch pie pan. Dissolve baking soda in boiling water. Add molasses and beaten egg yolk. Add cinnamon and sugar to the crumbs mixture you set aside. Alternate layers of liquid and crumbs into unbaked pie shell, starting with liquid and topping with crumbs. Bake until firm at 350°.

Church Family Recipes

Peanut Butter Pie

5 cups vanilla ice cream,
  softened
⅓ cup plus 2 tablespoons
  creamy peanut butter,
  divided
1 graham cracker crust, baked
½ cup light corn syrup,
  divided

3 packages unsweetened
  liquid chocolate
1½ cups sugar
1 cup evaporated milk
Pinch of salt
1 teaspoon vanilla
Whipped topping, thawed
Chopped nuts

Combine ice cream and ⅓ cup peanut butter. Mix until smooth and pour into graham crust. Cover with wax paper and freeze. Combine remaining peanut butter and ¼ cup corn syrup; blend well and spread on top of frozen pie. Return to freezer. Combine in a saucepan remaining ¼ cup corn syrup, unsweetened chocolate, sugar, milk, salt, and vanilla. Cook, stirring constantly about 5 minutes, or until thickened to make fudgy sauce. When ready to serve pie, defrost slightly and spoon some whipped topping, hot fudge sauce, and a sprinkle of nuts on each serving.

Kitchen Chatter

Nana's Pumpkin Chiffon Pie

1 tablespoon gelatin
  (1 envelope)
¼ cup water
¾ cup brown sugar
1 teaspoon salt
2 teaspoons cinnamon
½ teaspoon ginger
½ teaspoon allspice

1⅓ cups mashed cooked
  pumpkin
3 large eggs, separated
  (save whites for Meringue)
½ cup milk
1 (9-inch) pie crust, cooked and
  cooled

Sprinkle gelatin over cold water; set aside. In a saucepan, mix brown sugar, salt, cinnamon, ginger, allspice, mashed pumpkin, beaten egg yolks, and milk. Cook over low heat, stirring until it boils. Boil 1 minute. Remove from heat. Stir in softened gelatin. Cool. When partially set, beat until smooth.

MERINGUE:

3 large egg whites (reserved
  from above)

¼ teaspoon cream of tartar
6 tablespoons sugar

Beat egg whites until frothy, then add cream of tartar and beat until stiff. Add sugar gradually; continue beating until stiff and glossy. Carefully fold Meringue into pumpkin mixture. Pile into pie crust. Chill until set (3–4 hours).

Soup for Our Souls

 Tourism is the lifeblood of Nevada, with some 42 million visitors a year coming for vacation or conventions. On average, 28 million, or 66 percent of tourists, visit Las Vegas each year.

Delightful Strawberry Pie

3 egg whites
1½ cups white sugar, divided
¾ teaspoon cream of tartar
½ cup saltine crackers,
  crushed

½ cup flaked coconut
½ cup chopped pecans
2 cups whipped cream
½ teaspoon unflavored gelatin
4 cups sliced fresh strawberries

Preheat oven to 375°. In a large bowl, beat egg whites until soft peaks form. Gradually add 1 cup sugar and cream of tartar, continuing to beat until whites form stiff peaks. Gently fold in cracker crumbs, coconut, and pecans. Spread mixture onto the bottom and up sides of a 9-inch pie pan. Bake in preheated oven for 20–22 minutes, or until lightly browned. Cool completely. In a large bowl, beat cream, gelatin, and remaining ½ cup sugar until stiff peaks form. Fold in strawberries, then pour over egg white layer. Cover and refrigerate for 2 hours.

Traditional Treasures

Strawberry Ice Cream Pie

1 (3-ounce) package
  strawberry gelatin
1 cup hot water
½ cup cold water
1 pint vanilla ice cream

1 cup sliced fresh or frozen
  strawberries
1 (9-inch) pie shell, baked and
  cooled

Dissolve gelatin in hot water. Add cold water; stir. Cut ice cream in 6 chunks; add to gelatin mixture. Stir until ice cream melts; chill. When mixture begins to thicken, 20–30 minutes, gently fold in berries. Pour into cooled shell. Chill until firm.

Note: Lemon gelatin and peach slices may be substituted for strawberries.

A Gathering of Recipes

Soda Cracker Pie with Berries

14 soda crackers
3 egg whites
1 cup sugar
1½ teaspoons vanilla extract
2 teaspoons praline liqueur
  (optional)

½ cup chopped pecans
½ teaspoon baking powder
1 cup heavy cream
3 tablespoons sugar
1 cup fresh raspberries, washed
  and drained

Crush crackers into fine crumbs. Beat egg whites until stiff and fold in sugar. Add vanilla and liqueur. Fold in cracker crumbs, pecans, and baking powder. Bake in a buttered 9-inch glass pie plate. Bake at medium heat or 70% power in microwave oven for 5 minutes. Turn dish and bake another 2 minutes. Turn again and bake 1½ minutes. Pie shell should start to pull away from the sides of the pan. Cool completely.

Whip cream and sweeten. Stir in berries. Spoon into the cooled pie shell. Let stand in refrigerator at least 4 hours before serving. Yields 6 servings.

Note: Boysenberries or strawberries may be substituted for the raspberries.

Easy Cookin' in Nevada

Blackberry and Apple Pie

1½ pounds large cooking
   apples
2 tablespoons melted butter
4 ounces sugar, divided
2 pounds fresh blackberries
   (or frozen blackberries,
   thawed)

Pastry for 1 crust pie
1 egg yolk, mixed with
   1 tablespoon sugar
Whipped cream for garnish

Peel, core, and slice apples. In a heavy sauté pan, melt butter and cook apples over medium heat. Sprinkle with 2 tablespoons sugar and stir well. The apples should not fall apart. Combine remaining sugar with the blackberries; taste and add more sugar if necessary.

Spread blackberries in a 2-inch-deep pie dish. Spoon apples over top. Cover whole surface of pie with crust, sealing the edges (to edge of pie dish). Brush top with egg yolk-sugar mixture. Bake for 20–25 minutes in a 400° oven or until the crust is golden brown. Cool pie at room temperature and serve with whipped cream.

A Gathering of Recipes

Pioche is known as having been the roughest mining town in Nevada. Local legend suggests 75 men were buried in the cemetery before anyone actually died of natural causes.

Peach Cobbler

3 cups sliced peaches	1 teaspoon cinnamon
⅛ teaspoon salt	1 tablespoon water
¼ teaspoon sugar	1 tablespoon flour

Heat oven to 350°. In a large bowl, mix peaches, salt, sugar, cinnamon, water, and flour until peaches are coated. Place in greased 8x8-inch baking dish.

TOPPING:

6 tablespoons flour	½ cup brown sugar
½ cup rolled oats	6 tablespoons butter

Combine flour, oats, and brown sugar; cut in butter until crumbly. Place over peaches. Bake 40–45 minutes.

Family and Friends Favorites

Apricot Kugen

½ cup butter, softened	1 teaspoon ground cinnamon
2 cups sugar, divided	2 tablespoons lemon juice
8 large eggs, divided	¼ cup cornstarch
1½ cups flour	1¼ cups sour cream
9 cups halved, pitted firm ripe apricots	1 teaspoon vanilla

With a mixer, beat butter and ½ cup sugar until fluffy. Add 4 eggs, one at a time, beating well after each addition. Stir in flour. Spread batter in greased 9x13-inch pan.

Mix apricots with ½ cup sugar, cinnamon, and lemon juice. Arrange fruit, cut-side-up, in batter. Mix remaining ½ cup sugar with cornstarch. Add sour cream, remaining 4 eggs, and vanilla; beat until blended. Pour over apricots. Bake at 350° until cake surrounding apricots in center is firm when gently pressed, about 1 hour and 20 minutes. Let cool for at least 30 minutes. Serve warm or cool.

Note: You can substitute small apple halves for apricots.

Lake Tahoe Cooks!

Taffy Apple Pizza

1 (18-ounce) package
   refrigerated sugar cookie
   dough
¼ cup creamy peanut butter
1 (8-ounce) package cream
   cheese, softened
½ cup packed brown sugar
½ teaspoon vanilla

3–4 medium Granny Smith
   apples
1 cup lemon-lime soda
Ground cinnamon
¼ cup caramel ice cream
   topping
½ cup chopped peanuts

Preheat oven to 350°. Remove ½ of cookie dough and reserve for another use. Roll remaining dough into a 14-inch circle on a greased 15-inch baking pan, using a lightly floured rolling pin. Bake 11–14 minutes or until light golden brown. Cool 10 minutes. Carefully loosen cookie from pan with serrated bread knife; cool immediately.

Combine peanut butter, cream cheese, sugar, and vanilla in large bowl, mixing until smooth; spread over top of cookie. Peel, core and slice apples. Dip apples into lemon-lime soda to prevent browning; arrange over cream cheese mixture. Sprinkle lightly with cinnamon.

To heat caramel topping, microwave on HIGH 30–45 seconds or until warm. Drizzle over apples. Sprinkle with peanuts. Cut with large knife or pizza cutter. Yields 16 servings.

CASA Cooks

It is believed that the Ruby Mountain range emerged 20 million years ago and was shaped by the melting Alpine glaciers of the Ice Age.

Pike's Peak Spiked Apple Crisp

5 cups peeled and sliced
  apples (Pippin, Jonathan,
  or Winesap)
½ teaspoon cinnamon-sugar
1 teaspoon grated lemon rind
1 teaspoon grated orange rind
1 jigger Grand Marnier
1 jigger amaretto

¾ cup granulated sugar
¼ cup packed light brown
  sugar
¾ cup sifted flour
¼ teaspoon salt
½ cup butter or margarine
Cream, whipped cream, or
  ice cream for topping

Arrange apple slices in greased 2-quart-round casserole. Sprinkle cinnamon-sugar, lemon and orange rinds, and both liqueurs on top of apples. In a separate bowl, mix sugars, flour, salt, and butter with a pastry blender until crumbly. Spread mixture over top of apples. Bake, uncovered, at 350° until apples are tender and top is lightly browned, approximately 1 hour. Serve warm with cream, whipped cream, or with vanilla or cinnamon ice cream.

Twentieth Century Club Cook Book

Apple Strudel

1¼ teaspoons salt	3 tablespoons plus ¼ cup
1 egg	melted Crisco, divided
1 cup warm water	Chopped apples
1¼ tablespoons salad oil	1 cup sugar
2 cups flour (generous)	Pinch of nutmeg or cinnamon

Mix salt, egg, water, and oil well. My mother used to beat this for some time. Add flour and knead in slowly until dough is not sticky, but spongy and soft. (Let dough set for about ½ hour.) While you wait, mix Crumb Mixture.

Spread large tablecloth over surface (fairly large table). Pull dough outward from center with back of hand under the dough. Keep hands floured to keep dough from sticking. Pull dough until very thin. Should be able to read through dough (no broken places). Wipe surface with 3 tablespoons melted Crisco to help stretching. Next lay over surface chopped apples, covering about ½ the surface. Mix Crumb Mixture with 1 cup sugar and a pinch of nutmeg. Pour this over apples. Pour remaining melted Crisco over. Tear off thick edges of dough. Roll jellyroll fashion by picking up edge nearest apples and start to roll (will roll itself). Put on well-greased cookie sheet in tight ring. Glaze. Bake in a 375° oven for 45 minutes.

CRUMB MIXTURE:

1½ cups bread crumbs	⅓ cup sugar

Combine well.

Virginia City Alumni Association Cookbook

Caramel Dumplings

SAUCE:

½ cup brown sugar
1 cup white sugar
2 cups hot water

2 tablespoons butter
½ teaspoon salt

Bring to a boil in saucepan. Allow to simmer for 10 minutes.

DUMPLINGS:

2 tablespoons butter, softened
½ cup sugar
1½ cups flour
½ teaspoon salt

2 teaspoons baking powder
½ cup milk
½ teaspoon vanilla

Cream butter and sugar. In a separate bowl, sift flour, salt, and baking powder. Add flour mixture, milk, and vanilla to butter mixture. Drop into gently boiling Sauce. Cook slowly for 20 minutes. Serve with cream.

The Ruby Valley Friendship Club Cookbook I

Food for the Gods

6 eggs, separated
1 cup sugar
½ teaspoon salt
1 cup graham cracker crumbs

2 teaspoons baking powder
1 cup chopped dates
1 cup chopped nuts

Beat egg yolks in a mixer bowl until thick and pale yellow. Add sugar and salt and beat until smooth. Mix cracker crumbs, baking powder, dates, and nuts in a bowl. Add to the egg yolk mixture and mix well. Fold in stiffly beaten egg whites. Spoon into a greased and floured 10x14-inch baking pan. Bake at 350° for 30 minutes. Cool on a wire rack. Cut into squares and serve with whipped cream. Yields 3 dozen squares.

From Sunrise to Sunset

Raspberry Swirl

¾ cup graham cracker crumbs
3 tablespoons butter, melted
2 tablespoons sugar
3 eggs, separated
1 (8-ounce) package cream
 cheese, softened

1 cup sugar
⅛ teaspoon salt
1 cup heavy cream
1 (10-ounce) package frozen
 raspberries, partially thawed

Combine graham cracker crumbs, butter, and sugar well. Lightly press mixture into a well-greased 7x11x1-inch pan. Bake in moderate oven at 375° for about 8 minutes. Cool thoroughly.

Beat egg yolks until thick. Add cream cheese, sugar, and salt; beat until smooth and light. Beat egg whites until stiff peaks form. Whip cream until stiff and thoroughly fold with egg whites into cheese mixture. In a mixer or blender, crush raspberries to a pulp. Gently swirl ½ of fruit pulp through cheese filling and spread mixture into crust. Spoon remaining purée over top and swirl with a knife. Freeze, then cover and return to freezer. Makes 6–8 servings.

NSHSRA High School Rodeo Cookbook

Boiled Rice and Milk

12 cups milk
1½ cups uncooked white rice
1 cup raisins (optional)

1½ cups sugar
2 cinnamon sticks

Mix all ingredients in a heavy saucepan and simmer for 30–45 minutes or until rice is well done. Be sure to use low heat, as this burns easily. Serve warm.

Partyline Cook Book

Rice Pudding

8 cups milk
1 cinnamon stick
¼ teaspoon salt
¾ cup long-grain rice
3 eggs

¾ cup sugar
1½ teaspoons vanilla
½ pint (8 ounces) whipping
cream
Ground cinnamon

Bring milk with cinnamon stick and salt to boil. Add rice. Cook for 35 minutes. In a bowl, beat eggs. Add sugar and vanilla. To this mixture add whipping cream. When rice is done, turn it off. To the egg mixture, put about ½ cup of the rice, and stir so the eggs will not curdle. Add this mixture gradually to the rest of the rice. Bring to a boil again, then turn off. Cool and serve with ground cinnamon.

Elko Ariñak Dancers Cookbook

Our Grandma Adelaide's Old-Fashioned Plum Pudding

2 cups soft bread crumbs
1 cup flour
1 teaspoon baking soda
½ teaspoon salt
2 teaspoons ground cinnamon
½ teaspoon ground cloves
4 ounces chopped suet
1 cup sugar

2 eggs
⅓ cup orange juice
1 cup milk
1 cup dark seedless raisins
1 cup currants
1 cup chopped nuts
1 cup candied fruit

Mix all ingredients thoroughly. Put in well-greased plum pudding pan or mold and steam for 5–6 hours.

SAUCE:

1 cup sugar
2 tablespoons cornstarch
¼ teaspoon salt

2 cups boiling water
¼ cup butter
½ cup dark rum

Mix sugar, cornstarch, and salt. Add boiling water. Then slowly add butter to mixture. Stir well. Add rum; serve hot over plum pudding.

Historical Boulder City Cookbook

The TV Western *Bonanza*, was set in Virginia City, Nevada, after the Civil War and discovery of the famous Comstock Silver Lode. Film crews shot a good deal of the series on location just outside Lake Tahoe at the "Ponderosa Ranch," now preserved as a historic film site and Old West town. *Bonanza* enjoyed a successful fourteen-year run, from 1959 to 1973. It was also the first western in television history to be broadcast in color.

Flan
(Basque Custard)

5 cups milk
Pinch of salt
1 cinnamon stick

8 eggs
¾ cup sugar
3 teaspoons vanilla

In a saucepan, bring milk, salt, and cinnamon stick to a boil. Set aside for an hour or so, so that the cinnamon stick will flavor the milk. When ready to make custard, beat eggs, then add sugar and vanilla. Reheat milk and gradually add to egg mixture. Pour into a 2-quart caramelized pudding pan or mold (see instructions below). Set in a pan of warm water and bake in oven at 350°–375° for 1½ hours. Set aside to cool, then refrigerate until ready to serve.

TO PREPARE CARAMELIZED PUDDING PAN:
Put 6 tablespoons of sugar in a 2-quart pudding pan or mold on the stove. Melt sugar until golden brown. Turn pan so the sugar will cover the bottom and sides. This helps to turn the custard onto serving dish when it is cold.

Note: The water in the pan should not boil, as that makes the custard boil, too. Too hot of an oven will make the custard watery and coarse.

Elko Ariñak Dancers Cookbook

Cold Grand Marnier Soufflé

2 envelopes unflavored gelatin	2 cups sugar, divided
¾ cup orange juice, divided	¼ cup Grand Marnier
6 eggs, separated	¼ cup lemon juice
Grated rind of 2 oranges	Salt to taste
and 1 lemon	2½ cups whipping cream

Cut a piece of wax paper long enough to serve as collar of soufflé dish. Fold paper into halves, oil inside, and tie around dish. Soften gelatin in ½ cup orange juice in small bowl. Place in hot water; stir until gelatin dissolves. Combine remaining orange juice with egg yolks, orange rind, lemon rind, 1¼ cups sugar, liqueur, lemon juice, and salt in heavy saucepan; mix well. Cook until sugar dissolves and mixture coats spoon; remove from heat. Beat in gelatin mixture. Cool over ice or in refrigerator just until mixture is syrupy.

Beat egg whites in mixer bowl until soft peaks form. Add remaining ¾ cup sugar gradually, beating until stiff peaks form. Reserve a small amount of whipped cream for topping. Fold remaining whipped cream and beaten egg whites into gelatin mixture. Spoon into prepared dish. Chill overnight or until firm.

Remove collar carefully. Pipe reserved whipped cream into rosettes on top; garnish with candied violets. Yields 12 servings.

Approximately per serving: Cal 365; Prot 5g; Carbo 39g; Fiber <1g; Total Fat 21g; 52% Calories from Fat; Chol 174mg; Sod 50mg.

Best Bets

Rose Petal Sorbet

1 cup fructose
1¼ cups water
Petals of 3 large roses

Juice of 2 lemons
1¼ cups nonalcoholic white
   wine

Dissolve fructose in water; bring to boil for 5 minutes. Place remaining ingredients in processor and liquefy. Pour in ice trays until mushy; beat well and freeze until hard. Decorate with crystallized rose petals.

The Food You Always Wanted to Eat Cookbook

Raspberry Ring

1 (6-ounce) package raspberry
   Jell-O
2 cups boiling water
2 (10-ounce) packages frozen
   raspberries
1 (8-ounce) package cream
   cheese, softened

½ cup powdered sugar
1 small carton Cool Whip
1½ cups crushed pretzels
½ cup sugar
¾ cup butter, melted

Dissolve Jell-O in boiling water. Add frozen raspberries; stir until thawed. Let set in mold (pan). In small bowl, cream together cream cheese and powdered sugar. Fold in Cool Whip. Spread mixture on top of Jell-O mixture. Mix pretzels, sugar, and melted butter, and bake at 350° for 15 minutes; stir. Add to top of mold and pat lightly. When set, invert onto plate and serve.

Family and Friends Favorites

Angel Feathers

GRAHAM CRACKER CRUST:

16 graham crackers, rolled fine

4 tablespoons brown sugar
Melted butter

Mix crushed crackers with brown sugar and enough butter to make it hold together. Line an 8-inch-square pan with this mixture. Pour in custard. May reserve a small amount of the graham cracker mixture to garnish the top of this dessert.

⅓ cup sugar
½ cup milk
2 eggs, separated
1 teaspoon vanilla

1 tablespoon (1 envelope) gelatin, soaked in ½ cup cold water
½ pint cream, whipped

Make a custard of sugar, milk, and 2 egg yolks in a double boiler. When smooth, remove from heat and add vanilla and soaked gelatin. Cool; add whipped cream and 2 egg whites, beaten stiff. Place this mixture in a Graham Cracker Crust. Sets in an hour. Cut in squares to serve.

The Ruby Valley Friendship Club Cookbook I

Peras al Vino
(Pears in Wine)

2 quarts plus 4 cups water,
  divided
2 tablespoons Fruit Fresh,
  Ever Fresh, or similar
  product

6 pears
½ cup sugar
1 cup red wine

Place 2 quarts water and Fruit Fresh in a large bowl. Select pears that are ripe and firm. Peel pears carefully, leaving on stems. Place immediately into Fruit Fresh solution to keep pears from turning brown.

In 3-quart saucepan, mix sugar, wine, and remaining 4 cups water. Bring to a boil. Gently place whole pears into boiling liquid. Adjust heat to maintain a gentle simmer. Simmer, uncovered, for about one hour, turning pears occasionally with a large slotted spoon. Remove pears from liquid and place in a casserole. (The pears should have turned a nice purple color.)

Boil liquid remaining in saucepan over moderate heat, without the lid, until liquid is at least ¼ reduced. This can take about ½ hour. Pour liquid over pears. Allow to cool. Cover casserole and refrigerate. May be served at room temperature or chilled.

To serve, place each pear upright in a wine glass, filling each glass ⅔ full of the pear-wine nectar. Yields 6 servings.

Chorizos in an Iron Skillet

 A mummy excavated in 1940 and stored at the Nevada State Museum in Carson City was recently dated to ca. 7420 B.C., making it the oldest mummy ever discovered in North America.

Bananas Foster

1½ sticks butter
4 bananas, sliced lengthwise
½ cup brown sugar
Orange peel, grated (optional)

⅓ cup brandy
Cinnamon (optional)
Vanilla ice cream

Melt butter in saucepan. Add sliced bananas. Add brown sugar, and orange peel, if desired. Caramelize. Add brandy and flame the dessert (if you don't, the alcohol will not be weakened). If you like, sprinkle cinnamon into flame to add sparkle. Pour over ice cream and serve immediately. Serves 4.

Feeding the Flock

Rhubarb Crunch

CRUMB CRUST/TOPPING:
1 cup sifted flour
¾ cup uncooked rolled oats
1 cup brown sugar

½ cup butter, melted
1 teaspoon cinnamon

Combine ingredients until crumbly. Press half of crumbs into 9-inch greased pan, reserving half for top.

FRUIT MIXTURE:
4 cups sliced rhubarb
1 cup sugar
2 tablespoons cornstarch

1 cup water
1 teaspoon vanilla

Place sliced rhubarb in crust. In a small saucepan, combine sugar, cornstarch, water, and vanilla. Cook, stirring until thick and clear. Pour over rhubarb. Cover with reserved crumbs. Bake at 350° for 1 hour.

The Ruby Valley Friendship Club Cookbook II

Sopapillas

A favorite fried bread served with Mexican food.

1½ cups flour
2 teaspoons baking powder
¾ teaspoon salt
2 tablespoons vegetable
  shortening

½ cup lukewarm water
Vegetable oil for frying

Combine dry ingredients. Add shortening and cut in with pastry blender until mealy. Add water and form a ball. Knead on a lightly floured board about 5 minutes. Allow dough to rest 15 minutes. Divide dough in half and roll out until ⅛ inch thick. Cut into wedge-shape pieces and deep-fat fry in oil at 360°–375° until they are very puffy and light brown. Turn often. Fry one at a time. Drain on paper towels. Serve with butter and honey while very hot. Yields 6 servings.

Easy Cookin' in Nevada

Catalog of
Contributing Cookbooks

Elko is home to the annual Cowboy Poetry Gathering where folks come from everywhere to try their skills at storytelling, dancing, singing, rhyming, and showing off their western wear.

Catalog of Contributing Cookbooks

All recipes in this book have been selected from the cookbooks shown on the following pages. Individuals who wish to obtain a copy of any particular book may do so by sending a check or money order to the address listed by each cookbook. Please note the postage and handling charges that are required. State residents add tax only when requested. Prices and addresses are subject to change, and the books may sell out and become unavailable. Retailers are invited to call or write to same address for discount information.

ALL AMERICAN MEALS COOKBOOK

The JB Ranch Staff
JB Publications   Phone 775-629-0554
8025 Cheyenne Trail   www.jbpenterprises.com
Stagecoach, NV 89429

All American Meals Cookbook features delicious recipes and menus celebrating America and American cuisine. Menus include an all-American brunch, picnic, barbecue, Sunday dinner, game day party, cocktail party, and classic dinner party. Partial proceeds support the USO.

$10.00   Retail price
 $2.00   Postage and handling

Make check payable to JB Publications

AUTHENTIC COWBOY COOKERY THEN & NOW

by Carol Bardelli & F. E. "Lizzie" Hill
JB Publications   Phone 775-629-0554
8025 Cheyenne Trail   www.jbpenterprises.com
Stagecoach, NV 89429

Authentic Cowboy Cookery features historic recipes from the notebook of Lizzie Hill and her granddaughter, Carol Bardelli, both ranch women, one from the 20th century and the other from the 21st century. Enjoy cowboy chuck served in the style of the Old West and the new West.

$10.00   Retail price
 $2.00   Postage and handling

Make check payable to JB Publications

BEST BETS

Nathan Adelson Hospice   Phone 702-796-3133
4141 Swenson Street   Fax 702-796-3195
Las Vegas, NV 89119   www.nah.org

This wonderful 224-page cookbook contains recipes from some of the world's most innovative and exciting Las Vegas hotel/restaurant chefs as well as a complete range of recipes for every occasion. Each recipe also contains useful nutritional information.

$14.95   Retail price   Visa/MC/Disc/Amex accepted
 $1.12   Tax for NV residents   ISBN 0-87197-383-9
 $2.40   Postage and handling

Make check payable to Nathan Adelson Hospice Foundation

THE BEST OF DOWN-HOME COOKING

The Holy Trinity AME Church Courtesy Club
Rita Langford
1205 Stoneypeak Avenue
North Las Vegas, NV 89031-3240

Phone 702-642-6127
Fax 702-642-5982

The Best of Down-Home Cooking contains some recipes passed down from our slave ancestors. Others are modern, quick, and easy recipes. All are savored by our families and friends. We urge you to cook, eat, and enjoy!

$15.00 Retail price
  $5.00 Postage and handling

Make check payable to Holy Trinity AME Church

BLESS THIS FOOD

First Baptist Church
P. O. Box 505
Indian Springs, NV 89018

Phone 702-879-3203

Compiled by members, family, and friends of First Baptist Church in Indian Springs, this cookbook brings you potluck favorites along with many sought-after recipes. Enjoy the wonderful dishes that always bring the folks back for second helpings.

$10.00 Retail price
  $2.50 Postage and handling

Make check payable to First Baptist Church

CASA COOKS

CASA Foundation
601 N. Pecos Road
Las Vegas, NV 89101

Phone 702-455-4306
Fax 702-455-5297
www.casaclark.org

CASA Cooks is a collection of terrific recipes compiled by members of the CASA Foundation of Clark County. Proceeds supplement the program's budget, and help ensure the safety and security of abused and neglected children.

$12.00 Retail price
  $4.50 Postage and handling

Make check payable to CASA Foundation

CHORIZOS IN AN IRON SKILLET

by Mary Ancho Davis
University of Nevada Press
Mail Stop 166
Reno, NV 89557-0076

Phone 1-877-NV-BOOKS (877-682-6657)
Fax 775-784-6200

With recipes for everything from Dominga's Basque Chorizos to Dried Apricot Pie, these Basque ranch dishes offer a multitude of delicious ideas for down-home cooking. Illustrated with photographs from the Ancho family plus helpful advice on ingredients and cooking techniques. 224 pages. 36 photos.

$21.95 Retail price
  $4.50 Postage and handling (UPS)

Visa/MC/Disc/Amex accepted
ISBN 0-87417-445-7

Make check payable to Board of Regents

CHURCH FAMILY RECIPES

Carson Valley United Methodist Church   Phone 775-782-4600
1375 Centerville Lane   Fax 775-782-1230
Gardnerville, NV 89410   cvumc@ableweb.net

Church Family Recipes is a compilation of tried-and-true favorite recipes by members and friends of Carson Valley United Methodist Church. Pure feasting delight from cooks past and present—recipes are easy to understand and ingredients are easy to find. Nothing fancy, just plain old delicious!

   $5.00   Retail price
   $3.00   Postage and handling

Make check payable to Carson Valley U.M.C.

A COWBOY COOKIN' EVERY NIGHT

by Clancy Hawkins and Carol Bardelli
JB Publications   Phone 775-629-0554
8025 Cheyenne Trail   www.jbpenterprises.com
Stagecoach, NV 89429

A Cowboy Cookin' Every Night features real cowboy cuisine from real cowboy cooks. Taste the diverse flavors of the American West and eat like a cowboy or cowgirl every night. Experience great grub from mild to wild!

   $10.00   Retail price
    $2.00   Postage and handling

Make check payable to JB Publications

EASY COOKIN' IN NEVADA
& TALES OF THE SAGEBRUSH STATE

by June Broili
Anthony Press
P. O. Box 836
Reno, NV 89504

This truly remarkable book delivers something for everyone, from old favorites to exciting new ethnic varieties. June Broili has not only brought you a magnificent recipe collection, but she also shares with you some of the historical highlights of Nevada. Readers will be intrigued and enlightened. Enjoy!

   $19.95   Retail price   ISBN 0-961557-8-5

Make check payable to Anthony Press

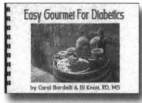

EASY GOURMET FOR DIABETICS

by Carol Bardelli and BJ Knott, RD, MS
JB Publications   Phone 775-629-0554
8025 Cheyenne Trail   www.jbpenterprises.com
Stagecoach, NV 89429

Diabetics can eat gourmet cuisine, too! *Easy Gourmet for Diabetics* features international cuisine and elegant meals you'll be proud to serve to your family and guests. And they'll never know they're eating meals geared for the needs of the diabetic. Nutritional analysis of every recipe is included.

   $10.00   Retail price
    $2.00   Postage and handling

Make check payable to JB Publications

ELKO ARIÑAK DANCERS COOKBOOK

Elko Basque Club   Phone 775-738-7103
789 Railroad Street   Fax 775-738-4563
Elko, NV 89801

This cookbook was compiled using family recipes from the Elko Basque Dancers' families and friends so the recipes can be passed down to future generations. All proceeds go to the dancers to buy uniforms and pay for travel expenses.

 $10.00 Retail price
  $3.00 Postage and handling

Make check payable to Elko Basque Club

FAMILY AND FRIENDS FAVORITES

by B. Knight
10140 Black Duck Court
Las Vegas, NV 89117

Enjoy a collection of family and friends' favorite recipes. You will look forward to making these recipes for a special occasion or just sharing them with people you love. The dessert section will cure your sweet tooth. Happy eating!

  $9.00 Retail price
  $3.00 Postage and handling

Make check payable to B. Knight

FEEDING THE FLOCK

Meadow Fellowship Foursquare Church   Phone 702-254-1725
7801 W. Alexander Road   Fax 702-656-3398
Las Vegas, NV 89129

This cookbook was compiled by the congregation of Meadow Fellowship Foursquare Church. All proceeds will go toward our building fund. Within the cookbook are delicious recipes submitted by members of our church body.

 $10.00 Retail price
  $3.00 Postage and handling

Make check payable to Meadows Fellowship

THE FOOD YOU ALWAYS WANTED TO EAT

THE FOOD YOU ALWAYS
WANTED TO EAT
COOKBOOK

by
LINDA GOODMAN

by Linda Goodman
Nevada Spine Institute
Boulder City, NV

These extremely easy recipes can be combined into complete meals including everything from soup to nuts, all in a vegetarian format. This book is currently out of print.

FROM SUNRISE TO SUNSET

Sunrise Children's Foundation   Phone 702-731-8373
3196 S. Maryland Parkway #307   Fax 702-731-8372
Las Vegas, NV 89109   www.sunrisechildren.org

From Sunrise to Sunset is a collection of recipes to share throughout the day. The 180 recipes found on 168 pages are the "tried-and-true" family favorites of the volunteers, staff, and friends of Sunrise Children's Foundation. Artist Louise H. Crosby beautifully illustrated the hardcover book with pictures of children.

$19.95 Retail price   Visa/MC accepted
  $1.75 Postage and handling   ISBN 9653731-0-X

Make check payable to Sunrise Children's Foundation

THE FRUIT OF THE SPIRIT

First Baptist Church of Reno   Phone 775-323-7141
1330 Foster Drive   Fax 775-323-7142
Reno, NV 89509

Our cookbook was compiled by our congregation, family, and friends to share their best recipes. The cookbook contains 250 recipes in eight categories. A labor of love.

$9.00 Retail price
$2.00 Postage and handling

Make check payable to First Baptist Church of Reno

A GATHERING OF RECIPES

Western Folklife Center   Phone 775-738-7508
501 Railroad Street   www.westernfolklife.org
Elko, NV 89801

Hot off the press—*A Gathering of Recipes* is a cookbook compiled of favorite recipes and poems of past National Cowboy Poetry participants and cooking workshops.

$12.50 Retail price
  $5.00 Postage and handling

Make check payable to Western Folklife Center

GOD, THAT'S GOOD!
RECIPES AND REMINISCENCES FROM ST. PETER'S PARISH

St. Peter's Episcopal Church   Phone 775-882-1534
305 N. Minnesota Street   Fax 775-882-6459
Carson City, NV 89703

God, That's Good! contains 249 pages of terrific indexed recipes seasoned with personal stories and graces. Recipes originate everywhere, like friends in our community. The cookbook reflects our love of God, food, friends, and family in our reverently irreverent style.

$15.00 Retail price
  $2.00 Postage and handling

Make check payable to St. Peter's

THE GREAT NEVADA COOKBOOK ★

A *Nevada Magazine* Cookbook

Nevada Magazine   Phone 775-687-5416
601 N. Carson Street   Fax 775-687-6159
Carson City, NV 89701   www.nevadamagazine.com

The Great Nevada Cookbook is a sampling of some of the prominent ethnic and regional foods found in Nevada. Recipes are from restaurants, as well as those passed down from generation to generation.

$4.95   Retail price   ISBN 1-890136-02-6
$2.50   Postage and handling

Make check payable to *Nevada Magazine*

THE GREAT NEVADA FOOD FESTIVAL COOKBOOK

A *Nevada Magazine* Cookbook

Nevada Magazine   Phone 775-687-5416
601 N. Carson Street   Fax 775-687-6159
Carson City, NV 89701   www.nevadamagazine.com

The Great Nevada Food Festival Cookbook is a celebration of the state's food-related special events. With such a cornucopia of culinary affairs, it was natural that the editors of *Nevada Magazine* collect some of the unique recipes associated with the state's various food festivals.

$4.95   Retail price   ISBN 1-890136-04-2
$2.50   Postage and handling

Make check payable to *Nevada Magazine*

HISTORICAL BOULDER CITY COOKBOOK

Boulder City Museum and Historical Assn.   Phone 702-294-1988
P. O. Box 60516   Fax 702-294-4380
Boulder City, NV 89006

Historical Boulder City Cookbook is a book of favorite recipes, compiled by members, family, and friends of the Boulder City Museum and Historical Association. From appetizers to desserts, you'll find something for every appetite, and for every occasion. Proceeds from the sales of this cookbook go toward support of the museum.

$11.95   Retail price
 $4.00   Postage and handling

Make check payable to Boulder City Museum and Historical Association

HOME COOKING

Truckee Meadows Habitat for Humanity   Phone 775-323-5511
160 Hubbard Way #D
Reno, NV 89502

A wonderful blend of family and entertaining recipes, *Home Cooking* serves up over 100 enticing dishes from Nevada politicians, celebrities, chefs, and Habitat for Humanity homeowners in this useful collection. Favorite culinary creations and personal anecdotes make this an original and practical cookbook.

$12.00   Retail price
 $5.00   Postage and handling

Make check payable to Truckee Meadows Habitat for Humanity

A JB Ranch Limited Edition Cookbook
By Carol Bardelli & John Cuneo Sr.

THE HOOKED COOK

by Carol Bardelli and John Cuneo, Sr.
JB Publications   Phone 775-629-0554
8025 Cheyenne Trail   www.jbpenterprises.com
Stagecoach, NV 89429

If you or someone close to you is a fisherman, you're always wondering what to do with all that catch. *The Hooked Cook* features a wide variety of fish recipes to suit everyone's tastes. Next time, fix up a dish that'll make them wish that fish had been even bigger.

$10.00   Retail price
 $2.00   Postage and handling

Make check payable to JB Publications

HOOVER DAM COOKS ★ 1933

HOOVER DAM COOKS, 1933

Cynthia R. Oakley
Toothpick Productions   Phone 702-354-4268
P. O. Box 60132   www.hooverdamcooks.com
Boulder City, NV 89006-0132

This classic cookbook includes 300+ recipes from the women who cooked for the men that built (Boulder) Hoover Dam. Ladies from all over the United States brought treasured recipes with them as they followed their husbands to the Nevada desert to build the dam.

$9.95   Retail price   ISBN 0-9727694-0-4
 $.75   Tax for NV residents
$1.80   Postage and handling

Make check payable to Toothpick Productions

KITCHEN CHATTER
by Pat Duran

KITCHEN CHATTER

by Pat Duran   Phone 702-436-3208
2050 W. Warm Springs Road, #1323
Henderson, NV 89014

Best collected recipes from Pat Duran and family compiled into an attractive keepsake cookbook. This one-of-a-kind limited edition cookbook contains over 325 well-loved recipes, including appetizers, main dishes, desserts, microwave hints, calorie counter, and much more.

$10.00   Retail price
 $2.00   Postage and handling

Make check payable to Pat Duran

LAKE TAHOE COOKS!

LAKE TAHOE COOKS!

Parents' Clubs of Zephyr Cove Elementary School, Kingsbury Middle School, and George Whittell High School
Mrs. Carolyn Nunnaly   Phone 775-588-7856
P. O. Box 860   Fax 775-588-5544
Zephyr Cove, NV 89448

Lake Tahoe Cooks! is a cookbook of 600 treasured recipes. Some are family keepsakes and some are new; however, they all reflect the love of good cooking. All funds raised equally benefit our Lake Tahoe, Nevada schools.

$15.00   Retail price
 $3.00   Postage and handling

Make check payable to Zephyr Cove Elementary School Parents' Club

LAS VEGAS GLITTER TO GOURMET

Junior League of Las Vegas   Phone 702-822-6536
6126 West Charleston Boulevard   Fax 702-822-6538
Las Vegas, NV 89146   www.jllv.org

From appetizers to entrées, you'll find your just desserts in this exciting compilation of recipes contributed by JLLV members. Named as the "Official Cookbook of Las Vegas," it's the perfect gift for Las Vegans—and those who like to eat as if they are!

$24.95   Retail price   ISBN 0-961-4100-4-3
  $4.50   Postage and handling

Make check payable to JLLV

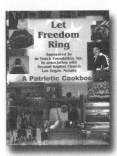

LET FREEDOM RING
A PATRIOTIC COOKBOOK

In Touch Foundation
7200 Forest Court
Windsor Heights, IA 50311

Let Freedom Ring is a patriotic cookbook with special Nevada recipe contributions, cookie recipes, special kid recipes with jokes, heart-healthy recipes, and trivia about the state.

$25.00   Retail price   Visa/MC accepted
  $4.95   Postage and handling

Make check payable to In Touch Foundation, Inc.

THE MELTING POT

Moms In Business Network
Henderson, NV 89016

Working mothers are so busy, and let's face it, we can't always be a gourmet chef. That's why it's great to have easy, delicious recipes from women just like you! These are Mom-tested-and-approved recipes that are successful at satisfying even the pickiest of eaters. Currently out of print.

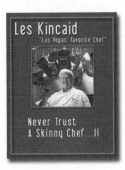

NEVER TRUST A SKINNY CHEF...II

by Les Kincaid
Les Kincaid Books   Phone 702-871-5145
P. O. Box 81407   www.leskincaid.com
Las Vegas, NV 89180-1407

Cooking is said to be therapeutic. So just get into the kitchen and be creative using your imagination. It need not be a gourmet meal or anything grand, just something simple and satisfying. I've included many personal, user-friendly recipes and some common sense advice throughout these many pages.

$17.95   Retail price
  $1.30   Tax for NV residents
  $3.00   Postage and handling

Make check payable to Les Kincaid Enterprises

NSHSRA HIGH SCHOOL RODEO COOKBOOK

Nevada State High School Rodeo Association
Battle Mountain, NV

The Nevada State High School Rodeo Association Crisis Fund was established in 2001 to promote high school rodeo on a state level and to assist members and their families when need arises. This cookbook was developed to help fund the program. Compiled by members and their families, recipes are tried-and-true favorites, handed down for generations. This book is currently out of print.

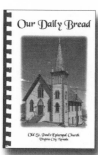

OUR DAILY BREAD

Old St. Paul's Episcopal Church
Jody Lediard, Priest; Sandra Hudgens, Sr. Warden
P. O. Box 1004   Phone 775-246-0878
Virginia City, NV 89440

Our Daily Bread is compiled by members, old and new, of Old St. Paul's Episcopal Church, established 1863. Some of these recipes were taken from a 100-year-old cookbook. Others were gathered by current members. All are tried-and-true treasures. Enjoy!

  $10.00   Retail price
   $3.00   Postage and handling

Make check payable to Old St. Paul's Episcopal Church

PARTYLINE COOK BOOK

Jackson Mountain Homemakers
Dale De Long   Phone 775-623-2854
P. O. Box 1058
Winnemucca, NV 89446

In its third printing, this Jackson Mountain Homemakers Club cookbook contains between 800 and 900 recipes. Proceeds from the sales of this book go to help with community needs.

  $10.00   Retail price
    $.70   Tax for NV residents
   $2.00   Postage and handling

Make check payable to Jackson Mountain Homemakers

THE PROTEIN EDGE

Compiled by the Iron Mountain Gym Staff
Edited by Carol Bardelli
JB Publications   Phone 775-629-0554
8025 Cheyenne Trail   www.jbpenterprises.com
Stagecoach, NV 89429

The Protein Edge cookbook features gourmet high-protein, low-carb, low-fat recipes designed for bodybuilders and dieters on low-carbohydrate diets. Eating right to achieve your health and fitness goals can be delicious. Nutritional analysis of every recipe is included.

  $10.00   Retail price
   $2.00   Postage and handling

Make check payable to JB Publications

RECIPES FROM SUNSET GARDEN CLUB

by Diane McIntyre
Henderson, NV 89015

Tasty dishes compiled by the good cooks of the Sunset Garden Club. This book is currently out of print.

RECIPES FROM THE HEART

St. Mark Lutheran Church and Preschool
277 Willow Street
Elko, NV 89801

Phone 775-738-4750
Fax 775-738-5456

Compiled by parents and children involved in our preschool, as well as teachers, board, council, and congregational members, this book is dedicated to children everywhere! We acknowledge our preschool and cookbook success is only through God's grace and love. 196 recipes.

  $6.25 Retail price
  $2.00 Postage and handling

Make check payable to St. Mark Lutheran Preschool

THE RUBY VALLEY FRIENDSHIP CLUB COOKBOOK I

Ruby Valley Friendship Club
HC 60 Box 860
Ruby Valley, NV 89833

Ruby Valley is a beautiful, remote ranching community with the best cooks anywhere. "Can I have that recipe," developed into two best-selling cookbooks, which have been reprinted many times over the past 26 years. No exotic ingredients, just delicious food fit for weddings, the holidays, or a local potluck.

  $10.00 Retail price
   $3.25 Postage and handling

Make check payable to Ruby Valley Friendship Club

THE RUBY VALLEY FRIENDSHIP CLUB COOKBOOK II

Ruby Valley Friendship Club
HC 60 Box 860
Ruby Valley, NV 89833

The success of the first Ruby Valley cookbook prompted contributors to submit more of their favorite recipes to be included in this second edition. We hope you will enjoy it as much as the first edition.

  $10.00 Retail price
   $3.25 Postage and handling

Make check payable to Ruby Valley Friendship Club

SHARING OUR DIABETICS BEST RECIPES

St. Rose D.A.T.E. (Diabetes Awareness Teaching and Education)
102 E. Lake Mead Drive   Phone 702-616-4327
Henderson, NV 89015   Fax 702-616-4696

Sharing our Diabetics Best Recipes is 58 pages packed with 72 healthy-body, diabetic-friendly recipes. All the recipes were contributed by participants in our D.A.T.E. (Diabetes Awareness Teaching and Education) program. We hope you enjoy them as much as we do.

   $8.00   Retail price
   $2.00   Postage and handling

Make check payable to St. Rose D.A.T.E.

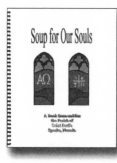

SOUP FOR OUR SOULS

St. Paul's Episcopal Church   Phone 775-358-4474
P. O. Box 737   Fax 775-358-5939
Sparks, NV 89432-0737   www.stpaulssparks.org

Soup for Our Souls reflects the diversity and communion of our congregation. You will find recipes that fill soul and tummy—almost 200 pages of hearty potluck recipes, desserts, amusing anecdotes, and prayers that will make you smile!

   $12.00   Retail price
    $5.00   Postage and handling

Make check payable to St. Paul's Church

STILL COOKIN' AFTER 70 YEARS

Grace Community Church
Boulder City, NV

Dedicated to the 70th anniversary and life of Grace Community Church—its members—past, present, and future. This book is no longer in print.

TASTEFUL TREASURES

Reno First United Methodist Church
209 West First Street
Reno, NV 89501

There is a special bond among those who break bread together, a custom established by our Lord Jesus Christ. We hope this collection of recipes by members and friends of Reno First United Methodist Church will bless all those who use them.

   $10.00   Retail price
    $2.00   Postage and handling

Make check payable to Reno First United Methodist Church

TIMBRELINE'S COOKBOOK

Ammon Ra Temple #56 Timbreline Group, Daughters of Nile
Reno, NV

This book is currently out of print.

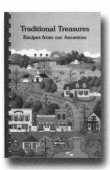

TRADITIONAL TREASURES
RECIPES FROM OUR ANCESTORS

Sun City Aquacize Club   Phone 702-233-5763
10308 Bent Brook Place   Fax 702-233-5764
Las Vegas, NV 89134

Being able to pass on these family treasures to others is especially rewarding
to us, but you'll be rewarded, too, when you see the look of satisfaction these
recipes will bring to your families. All tried-and-true favorites, passed down
through the generations, you'll have trouble deciding what to make first!

$7.00   Retail price
$2.50   Postage and handling

Make check payable to Sun City Aquacize Club

TWENTIETH CENTURY CLUB COOK BOOK

Twentieth Century Club   Phone 775-786-6304
3240 Dutch Creek Court
Reno, NV 89509

Published in 1994, this book celebrates the 100th birthday of the Twentieth
Century Club. It contains 316 pages of recipes plus a 12-page index.
Handsomely bound, each section is separated by a tabbed photo page of peo-
ple and places in Reno, Nevada.

$20.00   Retail price
$1.46   Tax for NV residents
$4.50   Postage and handling

Make check payable to 20th Century Club

USE YOUR NOODLE!
THREE ITALIANS COOK

by Carol Bardelli, Nikki Diavolo, and Dante "Blue" Azzurro
JB Publications
8025 Cheyenne Trail   Phone 775-629-0554
Stagecoach, NV 89429   www.jbpenterprises.com

What happens when you combine three Italian cooks and a noodles cook-off?
You get a cookbook filled with Old World recipes from Alfredo to stroganoff
and a mini-course on the art of the sauce. An insider's peek at old family
recipes enjoyed for generations in Italian-American kitchens.

$10.00   Retail price
$2.00   Postage and handling

Make check payable to JB Publications

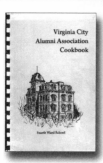

VIRGINIA CITY ALUMNI ASSOCIATION COOKBOOK

Historic Fourth Ward School Museum   Phone 775-847-0975
P. O. Box 4   Fax 775-847-1011
Virginia City, NV 89440   www.fourthwardschool.com

For over a century, the home kitchens of Virginia City Alumni have built an enviable reputation for succulent and legendary food unequaled anywhere. The alumni agreed to share their guarded recipes to benefit the Historic Fourth Ward School. 113 pages.

  $8.50   Retail price
  $3.00   Postage and handling

Make check payable to Historic Fourth Ward School

WILD MAN GOURMET

by Carol Bardelli and The JB Ranch Staff
JB Publications   Phone 775-629-0554
8025 Cheyenne Trail   www.jbpenterprises.com
Stagecoach, NV 89429

An eclectic collection of wild game recipes from a Nevada ranch kitchen. From simple to elegant, recipes range from alligator to wild boar. Includes a brief history of the hunt from ancient times to today. A must for any hunter's kitchen. Eat like a wild man every day.

 $10.00   Retail price
  $2.00   Postage and handling

Make check payable to JB Publications

Index

PHOTO © NEVADA COMMISSION ON TOURISM

One of Nevada's most prominent ghost towns, Rhyolite was once a bustling metropolis. Gold was discovered in the area in 1904, and Rhyolite was born. By 1911, the gold had played out and Rhyolite was abandoned. Today you can still see the three-story stone frame of the $90,000 Cook Bank Building, among others.

INDEX

INDEX

INDEX

INDEX

INDEX

INDEX

INDEX

INDEX

Best of the Best State Cookbook Series

Best of the Best from
ALABAMA
288 pages, $16.95

Best of the Best from
ALASKA
288 pages, $16.95

Best of the Best from
ARIZONA
288 pages, $16.95

Best of the Best from
ARKANSAS
288 pages, $16.95

Best of the Best from
BIG SKY
Montana and Wyoming
288 pages, $16.95

Best of the Best from
CALIFORNIA
384 pages, $16.95

Best of the Best from
COLORADO
288 pages, $16.95

Best of the Best from
FLORIDA
288 pages, $16.95

Best of the Best from
GEORGIA
336 pages, $16.95

Best of the Best from the
GREAT PLAINS
*North and South Dakota,
Nebraska, and Kansas*
288 pages, $16.95

Best of the Best from
HAWAI'I
288 pages, $16.95

Best of the Best from
IDAHO
288 pages, $16.95

Best of the Best from
ILLINOIS
288 pages, $16.95

Best of the Best from
INDIANA
288 pages, $16.95

Best of the Best from
IOWA
288 pages, $16.95

Best of the Best from
KENTUCKY
288 pages, $16.95

Best of the Best from
LOUISIANA
288 pages, $16.95

Best of the Best from
LOUISIANA II
288 pages, $16.95

Best of the Best from
MICHIGAN
288 pages, $16.95

Best of the Best from the
MID-ATLANTIC
*Maryland, Delaware, New
Jersey, and Washington, D.C.*
288 pages, $16.95

Best of the Best from
MINNESOTA
288 pages, $16.95

Best of the Best from
MISSISSIPPI
288 pages, $16.95

Best of the Best from
MISSOURI
304 pages, $16.95

Best of the Best from
NEVADA
288 pages, $16.95

Best of the Best from
NEW ENGLAND
*Rhode Island, Connecticut,
Massachusetts, Vermont,
New Hampshire, and Maine*
368 pages, $16.95

Best of the Best from
NEW MEXICO
288 pages, $16.95

Best of the Best from
NEW YORK
288 pages, $16.95

Best of the Best from
NO. CAROLINA
288 pages, $16.95

Best of the Best from
OHIO
352 pages, $16.95

Best of the Best from
OKLAHOMA
288 pages, $16.95

Best of the Best from
OREGON
288 pages, $16.95

Best of the Best from
PENNSYLVANIA
320 pages, $16.95

Best of the Best from
SO. CAROLINA
288 pages, $16.95

Best of the Best from
TENNESSEE
288 pages, $16.95

Best of the Best from
TEXAS
352 pages, $16.95

Best of the Best from
TEXAS II
352 pages, $16.95

Best of the Best from
UTAH
288 pages, $16.95

Best of the Best from
VIRGINIA
320 pages, $16.95

Best of the Best from
WASHINGTON
288 pages, $16.95

Best of the Best from
WEST VIRGINIA
288 pages, $16.95

Best of the Best from
WISCONSIN
288 pages, $16.95

All cookbooks are 6x9 inches, ringbound, contain photographs, illustrations and index.

Special discount offers available! *(See previous page for details.)*

To order by credit card, call toll-free **1-800-343-1583** or visit our website at **www.quailridge.com.**
Use the form below to send check or money order.

Call 1-800-343-1583 or email <u>info@quailridge.com</u> *to request a free catalog of all of our publications.*

- -

 **Order form**

Use this form for sending check or money order to:
QUAIL RIDGE PRESS • P. O. Box 123 • Brandon, MS 39043

❏ Check enclosed

Charge to: ❏ Visa ❏ MC ❏ AmEx ❏ Disc

Card # _____

Expiration Date _____

Signature _____

Name _____

Address _____

City/State/Zip _____

Phone # _____

Email Address _____

Qty.	Title of Book (State) or Set	Total

Subtotal _____

7% Tax for MS residents _____

Postage ($4.00 any number of books) + 4.00

Total _____